Aging Parents and Adult Children

Aging Parents and Adult Children

Edited by

Jay A. Mancini
Virginia Polytechnic Institute
and State University

Lexington Books
D.C. Heath and Company/Lexington, Massachusetts/Toronto

Library of Congress Cataloging-in-Publication Data

Aging parents and adult children.

  Bibliography: p.
  Includes index.
  1. Parents, Aged—United States.   2. Adult
children—United States.   3. Intergenerational
relations—United States.   I. Mancini, Jay A.
HQ1063.6.A45 1989   306.8'74   85-50706
ISBN 0-669-18015-9 (alk. paper)

Published simultaneously in Canada
Printed in the United States of America
International Standard Book Number: 0-669-18014-9
Library of Congress Catalog Card Number: 85-50706

The paper used in this publication meets the minimum requirements of
American National Standard for Information Sciences—Permanence of
Paper for Printed Library Materials, ANSI Z39.48-1984. ∞™

  90 91 92 8 7 6 5 4 3 2

To the generations in my family:
Geary and Lavinia Gray
Vincent and Concetta Mancini; Lillian Reynolds
Jay Albert Mancini and Vetra Mancini Bishop
Sharon, Nathan, David, and Suzanne Mancini

Contents

Part 3: Caregiving and Care-Receiving   197

Part 4: Current and Future Perspectives on Theory and Research 283

Tables and Figure

Tables

Figure

Preface and Acknowledgments

Aging Parents and Adult Children is intended as a partial response to the need for a more grounded understanding of how parents and their mature children interrelate. It is also intended to provide those who study such relationships with a roadmap for future research. Reflected in this book are a number of conceptual approaches to the parent-child relationship that are drawn from the social and behavioral sciences. Within the book are empirical studies, descriptions of theory, and state-of-the-art analyses. The authors are associated with the fields of family studies, sociology, marriage and family therapy, psychology, social gerontology, and anthropology, and they have approached the parent-child relationship with regard to the context in which it exists, its internal dynamics, and special problems the relationship faces.

I am indebted to the individual contributors to *Aging Parents and Adult Children*. In addition, I owe thanks to Wynn Washle and Nadean Jarels for assistance in editorial matters, and to Margaret Zusky, my editor at Lexington Books, for her expertise, encouragement, and patience. I appreciate the support of Joseph Maxwell and the Department of Family and Child Development at Virginia Polytechnic Institute and State University. Vira Kivett and Erdman Palmore engendered my interest in family gerontology, and Dennis K. Orthner and Hyman Rodman guided my development as a social scientist. I appreciate their influence.

Introduction

1
Family Gerontology and the Study of Parent-Child Relationships

Jay A. Mancini

Perhaps the most enduring human relationship is that between parents and their children. Unlike involvement in work and in marriage, the link of parent and of child has no end. Once a person becomes a parent there is no mechanism by which one can leave that status; the same is true of being a child; at no time can one cease to be someone's offspring. Over time the roles of parent and of child change, but they are never divorced from the history of the relationship. In addition, they experience current events, normal changes, and unanticipated circumstances for which there is little preparation. Older persons and their offspring continually struggle with issues of dependence, independence, and interdependence. In many respects older adults and their families, especially their children, ". . . are the new pioneers of our era. They have ventured into uncharted areas of human relationships . . ." (Shanas 1980 p. 14). This book seeks to illuminate the characteristics of these pioneers and to describe how they are experiencing age in the context of family life. For the social and behavioral scientist the examination of parents and their children in later life may have significance for the understanding of socialization processes, the nature of change in relationships, and for conceptualizing the family system and its environment.

The Family Context of Adult Relationships

Early Socialization

The bond that develops between parents and children is complex and intriguing. Consider that the newborn child is entirely dependent on others, typically the parents. A great deal of what we expect young children to do and how we expect them to develop represents achieving independence. We also have considerable expectations for the learning of cooperation. The parent is presumed to be a teacher, the primary figure responsible for showing the child how to get along successfully. Language and social skills are imparted by the parent, as are methods of persuasion and communication. Even as independence, autonomy, self-sufficiency, and cooperation are encouraged, and perhaps demanded, the parent retains authority and the right to have the final say. The parent is responsible for how well the child is socialized and how effectively the environment is mastered. Parents tend not to expect support from the child, and the child's agenda for adolescence and young adulthood rarely includes supporting one's parents. These respective expectations are generally what parents and children desire, for all have been socialized to value independence and autonomy.

Throughout the child's developmental years, critical, linchpin events occur that demand the attention of parents. For the younger child the entrance into formal education is one such transition point. Or a mother's employment outside of the home may also reflect a transition point. The experience of adolescence, especially as it involves the child's sexual development and being accorded greater freedoms by parents, are also "events" that seem to require or to generate more intensity in the relationship. In all these instances parents are the keepers of authority, are allowed to possess and use power in making decisions, and are still largely responsible for the consequences of the child's development.

Continued Relationship Development

Throughout the years parents and children continually define and negotiate their relationship. Particular events usually assist in defining that relationship. At some point parents and children are considered adults, and therefore can exercise more choice in how their relationship is experienced. The opinions of parents may be solicited but there is less obligation to behave accordingly, such as when children decide to marry, choose a field of study, or pursue an occupation. Somewhat concurrently, parental responsibility declines and may cease altogether. The middle years of the parent-child relationship are marked by fewer pivotal events in the child's life (though the bearing of the next generation is one family event that ought to be considered) and by events in the parents' lives to which the adult child is not privy. While some years earlier the child's development was noticed and marked at its every turn, how one's parents change receives little notice. During these middle years successful parent-child relationships are found among those who see themselves as equals and who behave as friends. Their respective independencies are valued, and by and large they operate in their own developmental tracks. But the parent generation is experiencing subtle change that leads to several transition points that potentially will rewrite the rules governing their relationships as aging parents and adult children. For some parents employment runs its course and active work is changed by virtue of choice or mandate. Health may change significantly, and the death of one parent will change a family's composition. Because of these events the parent-child relationship becomes more complex, especially if its history is considered. Dependence, independence, and interdependence are issues that again come into play. However, the guidelines for how these relationships are maintained are not clear. Families and individuals in families are subject to a far-ranging variety of contingencies that will shape how their relationships are experienced. The issues they face may take myriad forms.

Research on Parents and Children

Parents and children have received a great deal of attention from social and behavioral scientists. Sociologists have analyzed the parent role—that is, the normative expectations of those who occupy the position called "parent"—and psychologists have endeavored to discover the short and long-term effects parents have on their children. Family therapists seek to identify ways to intervene when these relationships decay. Historically these inquiries have had as their focus relationships in which children were younger, usually pre-adults, and the parents were in early middle age. But what do we know of enduring relationships? What of those parents and children who, in fact, are all adults? In the minds of many, socialization begins and ends by the time a child is eighteen or so years old, and yet we recognize that learning about the world, both impersonal and interpersonal, is practically ongoing. Even as some would assume that a person's socialization as an individual ends early in life, there are those who presume there is little to learn about relationships between parents and their children much beyond those early years. But here again I believe we really know that the interpersonal aspects of life are fluid and everchanging. These relationships do not exist in a vacuum and are not insulated from outside contingencies. Over the years numerous scholars of the family and of aging have examined the many dimensions of the aging parent-adult child relationship. So that this book can be better placed in context, I will briefly review the shape of the family gerontology field as it involves parents and their children.

The Study of Family Gerontology

In many respects this book has its origins in several published reviews of the literature in family gerontology (Bengtson & DeTerre 1980; Blieszner 1988; Hagestad 1987; Mancini 1980, 1984; Mancini & Blieszner, in press; Streib & Beck 1980; Troll 1971; Troll, Miller & Atchley 1979). Most of these reviews have treated the broadest conception of family gerontology, including marital relations, sibling relations, the grandparent role, and widowhood. All of them include some focus on parent-child relationships, and, in addition, each discusses issues and problems that cut across the various family gerontology content domains. I will discuss these critiques chronologically.

Research during the 1960s. The first such review that received wide attention from scientists in family studies and in gerontology was written by Lillian Troll (1971). She reviewed the period of 1960 to 1969 with respect to the research and theory on later life families. It was noted that before the 1960s much of the research on the family life cycle focused on its earlier stages. Troll said much more was known about the parenting of young children than about parent-child relations when the child is an adult. Until that time the later phases of the family life cycle received little attention, and it appeared that gerontologists were more interested in the topic than family social scientists. In her discussion of kinship structure Troll said there were four types of measurement: residential nearness, assessed by asking how close relatives lived to each other; frequency of interaction, including questions on how often face-to-face, telephone, and letter-writing contact occurred; mutual aid, particularly with respect to economic exchanges; and, relationship quality, including assessments of affection and family togetherness. Research on interaction and on mutual aid seemed to capture the attention of many investigators but relatively fewer studies were conducted on family life quality. These "qualitative measures" were introduced during the 1960s but it was not until the following decade that the area received relatively more attention. In Troll's opinion the major achievement of the 1960s research was the documentation that extended kin relations were important and that contact and interaction among the generations was continuous, especially when it involved parents and their children. She also felt that one task of the 1970s would be to fully investigate the qualitative dimensions of kinship. The following are among her suggestions for future research: delineation of family developmental processes, qualitative differences in relationships in and out of the family, value similarity and family interaction, parent-child relationships after the launching stage and before old age, and the transmission of values across multiple generations. Troll also felt strongly about the need for integrating theory with empirical work.

Research in the 1970s. Nearly ten years after this review, Troll, along with Sheila Miller and Robert Atchley, wrote the first text devoted to family gerontology (Troll, Miller & Atchley 1979). While their primary goal was not to criticize the literature but rather to describe what was known about the area, it becomes clear from reading the volume that little progress had been made in the decade of the 1970s. These authors were still making note of the need to understand the "ebb and flow" in family life. The process of relationship development and maintenance is at the core of understanding relationship quality. In concluding their chapter on parents and children they summarize: most older people in America have living children and are in regular contact with them; the generations do not live in the same household unless there are financial and health constraints; parents and their children prefer autonomy; parents and children are important sources of mutual assistance; and, the generations prefer to live near each other. What is interesting is that after listing those facts from the literature they then conclude that the reasons why these relationships endure are mostly unknown. That is, the roles that obligation, shame, enjoyment, and meaningfulness play in the nature of these parent-child relationships had yet to be assessed. Among their suggestions for future research were: the family dynamics of conflict, negotiation, and cooperation; complex nature of older-parent–adult-child relations; return migration to be closer to family; adult-child–older-parent relationships over the life course; and, greater focus on qualitative studies. The lack of theoretical approaches remained a problem.

In 1980 a number of family gerontology reviews appeared (Bengtson & DeTerre; Mancini; Streib & Beck). That by Vern Bengtson and Edythe DeTerre substantiated what Troll (1971) and Troll, Miller and Atchley (1979) had contended. Bengtson and DeTerre (1980) were interested in documenting aspects of social change in the United States, analyzing current research on family relations in later life, and then suggesting the meaning for those who work with elders and their families. They discuss seven changes: improvements in life expectancy; increase in the sex mortality differential (women living longer than men); increase in the number of very old people who are women; increases in the number of the youngest generation who will have grandparents; decreases in the number of younger relatives that old people will have; expansion of womens' roles beyond family responsiblity; and, the emergence of new institutions to care for the aged. Toward the end of their article they discuss the relationship between family life and the well-being of older people. While one research perspective—that assessing perceived psychological well-being—suggests that the family has minimal impact, the other—that pointing to the nature of instrumental family support—argues that the family has a substantial effect. Among the areas of needed research suggested by Bengtson and DeTerre are: ways in which older family members spend time with, assist, feel about, and agree with other family members; specific financial information regarding intergenerational financial assistance; parent-child relationships over the whole life cycle; mediating role of family on behalf of older members; positive dynamics of family life; characteristics of healthy families; and the relationship between personal well-being in old age and one's history as a child, a spouse, and a parent.

My initial review of research needs in family gerontology addressed three questions (Mancini 1980): What do we know about the importance of family life for older adults? Are the research findings "translatable" into programs designed to build family strengths? What more do we need to know about family life and life quality among older adults? Much of my discussion dealt directly or indirectly with the parent-child relationship. The context of my discussion noted two major research themes, one concerning the alienation hypothesis (Shanas 1979), and the other concerning the enrichment hypothesis (Mancini, Quinn, Gavigan & Franklin, 1980). The former suggests that older people are isolated from kin and neglected, while the latter suggests that the lives of older adults are necessarily improved by interaction with kin. In the course of suggesting areas of needed research I cited the extant literature on kin contact, on physical proximity, and on psychological well-being. That chapter concluded with areas in which further research was needed: the use of time in a family context; the family's role in the dependence and independence of its older members; the dynamics of family size; determinants of contact between parents and their children; instrumental and affective intergenerational exchange; the effects of a relationship's history on present interaction; communication styles in relationships; the importance of family rituals; and, the nature of the parent role as one ages.

The third review to appear in 1980 was written by Gordon Streib and Rubye Beck. Their review was organized around four family functions: nurturance, economic, residential, and legal and cultural. Within these four domains they presented and discussed the highlights of the literature published from 1970 to 1979. It should be noted that Streib and Beck reviewed some areas of study that were purposely excluded by Troll in her review of the 1960s, principally economics, law, and public policy. One of their conclusions is that the interface between the microenvironment (feelings and emotions that occur in relationships) and the macroenvironment (social programs and the like) is a rich area of future research. They are less convinced that the microenvironment alone is a fruitful research domain, and in this respect their review differs from those already cited. However, much of what they suggest to be needed information pertains to the parent-child relationship. They call for research on intergenerational relations between launching of the last child and entrance into old age and the manner in which health and economic factors shape the structure and function of older families—especially how the old relate to their children.

Research in the 1980s. In 1984 I analyzed a number of previously published reviews of family gerontology (Mancini 1984). While my review dealt with a broad array of family gerontology areas, a number of the suggestions for future research involved the aging-parent–adult-child relationship: conditions under which contact with family promotes well-being; effects of discretionary and obligatory activity on quality of life; the confidant role of family members; influence of family structure on family relationship quality; the nature of exchange and intimacy at a distance; generational differences in viewpoints on exchange; and the meaning behind exchange. I also noted deficits in the application of theory to research on older persons and their families.

Rosemary Blieszner's (1988) review of the literature examined older marriages, parent-child relations, grandparent-grandchild relations, and the interface between aging families and community services. Throughout her article she notes that family gerontologists have tended to research the same content areas again and again, while ignoring other areas with equal consistency. This conclusion complements earlier critiques of this literature. Among her suggestions for future research is a greater interest in the multiple roles that adults participate in, the role health plays in how parents and their children relate, the role gender plays in parent-child interaction and support, and the family's role in mediating between social agencies and elders.

Very recently Gunhild Hagestad (1987) examined trends and gaps in research specifically on aging parents and adult children. She notes the changing demography of parent-child relationships, such as changes in life expectancy. She also reviews trends dealing with family structure, patterns of contact, consensus, similarity and socialization, norms and expectations, patterns of support, and the affective quality of ties. She suggests that the research on older parents and their children would benefit from accessing theories developed on earlier life cycle phases, and feels that researchers ought to focus on more than a single parent-child dyad (noting that people are both parents and children and that this dual linkage ought to be recognized by investigators). Other needs for research include: focus on four- and five-generation families; relationships in which there is little to no contact; mutual influence between adults in the family; the complexity of exchange and of support; how parents and children influence each other's feelings of competence; closeness in parent-child relationships; attachment over time; the influence that cultural change has had on expectations of intimacy and closeness; and research that truly is life-span oriented. Throughout Hagestad's discussion is the call for theory development.

The final examination of the literature in family gerontology discussed at present, and one that focuses on parents and their children, is written by Rosemary Blieszner and me (in press). It revolves around issues of roles and responsibilities, parent-child interaction (contact patterns, exchange, assistance, and support), individual well-being, relationship quality, and caregiving by adult children. The article endeavors to cite the dominant themes in the current literature, indicates where new research ought to be directed, and examines the role theory plays in current research.

Among our conclusions regarding scientific work on aging parents and their adult children are: there are few longitudinal approaches and therefore our understanding of the developmental aspects of the relationship is lacking; research tends not to be guided by *a priori* theorizing; qualitative research is underrepresented in the literature; relatively few studies examine relationship conflict; the "myth of abandonment" has been over-researched; psychological well-being ought to be reconceptualized so that studies of parent-child relationships that incorporate it would have a more logical base; work should be expanded on families where multiple generations are chronologically old; investigations ought to consider a family rather than a dyad focus; theories from child development could be readily adapted in research on older family relationships; there is a need for a greater emphasis on the use of discretionary time within a family context; studies of the affective aspects of the parent-child relationship are rudimentary; and, research should continue to examine relationships where there are no special needs for caregiving.

Summary of Critiques of the Literature. All things considered, the study of family gerontology, generally, and the study of aging parents and their adult children, specifically, need to take a different form. All the reviews just listed lament deficits in theory and in research. With regard to the former, social scientists tend to underuse extant theory and tend not to connect their empirical work with theoretical ideas; in the case of the latter, research interests have not changed despite repeated calls for the need for change.

Issues of the Aging Family

We ought to consider aging parents and their adult children with regard to the physical and interpersonal environment in which they live, the dynamics of their relationship, and the special needs that may be involved in their family. Among the many questions that we might ask are: What kind of family support is desired by both parents and children? Are there optimal levels of interaction between parents and children? Where are the points of conflict? What role does socialization play, especially as it involves normative adult transitions? Which aspects of the parent-child relationship seem to be conducive to the morale of both of the generations? What role do in-laws play in the support of older family members? In what measure does marital separation and divorce change intergenerational relationships? Of what importance is the broader family context for how parent-child relationships function? What kind of feelings of attachment and connectedness do parents and children have, and how are their respective self-concepts interrelated? How are aging parents and their adult children interdependent? What psychological and practical benefits does interacting with an adult child provide to the parent? How do equity and obligation enter into the give and take between parents and their children? Which social change events are influencing the parent-child relationship? What does the middle generation believe it owes to the younger and older generations? How do obligatory and discretionary motives for caregiving compare? What are the support behaviors of sons and of daughters when a parent is in need? In cases of parental frail health, how is commitment, communication, and affection changed? And with regard to many of the above issues, what are considerations of morality? This volume addresses these questions via empirical studies, theoretical discussions, and state-of-the-art analyses.

Over the course of a parent-child relationship there are individual and family events. Some have minimal effect on those not directly experiencing the event, while others remake the entire family system. Throughout the life of this relationship there is a process of giving and getting and of ebb and flow. In each phase of the relationship developmental tasks must be grappled with, and a number of these are relationship tasks. Affection, communication, antagonism, decision-making, and closeness are relationship activities that are developed and maintained. Twenty-five or more years of interaction with specific others provides the time framework in which complex and intriguing relationships develop. The bonding and attachment may be considerable and the significance of the relationship for successful aging may be substantial. This is the context in which social scientists have examined these family relationships.

Focus of the Book: Theory and Research

The chapters in this book are designed to address the need for considering the theoretical aspects of examining parent-child relationships in adulthood. They are also concerned with how future research ought to be conducted. The questions previously listed are addressed by the various chapters.

The chapters are organized into four parts: Family Structure and Kin Context; Parent-Child Dynamics and Interaction; Caregiving and Care-Receiving; and Current and Future Perspectives on Theory and Research. When the contributors were preparing their chapters they were asked to attend to theoretical considerations and to research needs; they were encouraged to be creative and speculative. The result is a book that incorporates, in varying degrees, theory from the social and behavioral sciences. These contributions also provide a considerable number of guidelines for future research.

References

Bengtson, V. L., & DeTerre, E. 1980. Aging and family relations. *Marriage and Family Review*, 3, 51–76.

Blieszner, R. 1986. Trends in family gerontology research. *Family Relations, 35*, 555–562.

Hagestad, G. O. 1987. Parent-child relations in later life: Trends and gaps in past research. In J. B. Lancaster, J. Altmann, A. S. Rossi, & L. R. Sherrod (eds.), *Parenting across the life span: Biosocial dimensions* (405–433). New York: Aldine de Gruyter.

Mancini, J. A. 1980. Strengthening the family life of older adults: Myth-conceptions and investigative needs. In N. Stinnett, B. Chesser, J. DeFrain & P. Knaub (eds.), *Family strengths: Positive models for family life* (333–343). Lincoln, Neb: University of Nebraska Press.

Mancini, J. A. 1984. Research on family life in old age: Exploring the frontiers. In W. H. Quinn & G. A. Hughston (eds.), *Independent aging: Family and social systems perspectives* (265–284). Rockville, Md.: Aspen.

Mancini, J. A.; Quinn, W. H.; Gavigan, M. A.; & Franklin, H. 1980. Social network interaction among older adults: Implications for life satisfaction. *Human Relations, 33*, 543–554.

Mancini, J. A., & Blieszner, R. In press. Aging parents and adult children: Current and prospective social science research themes. *Journal of Marriage and the Family*.

Shanas, E. 1979. Social myth as hypothesis: The case of the family relations of old people. *The Geronologist, 19*, 3–9.

Shanas, E. 1980. Older people and their families: The new pioneers. *Journal of Marriage and the Family, 42*, 9–15.

Streib, G. F., & Beck, R. W. 1980. Older families: A decade review. *Journal of Marriage and the Family, 42*, 937–956.

Troll, L. E. 1971. The family of later life: A decade review. *Journal of Marriage and the Family, 33*, 187–241.

Troll, L. E.; Miller, S. J.; & Atchley, R. C. 1979. *Families in later life*. Belmont, Calif.: Wadsworth.

Part 1
Family Structure and Kin Context

2
Mother-in-Law and Daughter-in-Law Relations

Vira R. Kivett

S trong bonds between mothers- and daughters-in-law in later life may serve to reinforce the support networks of many older women. The more positive aspects of the mother-in-law–daughter-in-law relationship have received little attention in studies of the American family (Fischer 1983). Most available conclusions have been inferred from cross-cultural studies that generally speak to the mother-in-law–daughter-in-law crisis or to the negative aspects of the relationship (Troll 1971). These findings have important implications for the support structure of older women.

Relationships with mothers-in-law for both men and women appear to be principal points of stress in most Western marriages (Fischer 1983). The mother-in-law–daughter-in-law predicament is sometimes referred to as the "avoidance tendency" or the disposition of women to avoid interaction with or attachment to wives of sons because of the threatening nature of the latter's successor role. Fischer (1983) observed that although mother-daughter and mother-in-law–daughter-in-law relationships are strikingly similar in a number of ways—they are both female-female bonds, they are intergenerational and asymmetrical relationships, and they are bounded and defined by kinship networks—they diverge sharply in their orientations toward primary loyalties.

Troll (1971) made daughter–daughter-in-law comparisons by pointing out that, although daughters fall into the same successor role category, mothers tend to focus hostility mainly on the daughter-in-law, which, in turn, serves to actually strengthen the mother-daughter bond. Nydegger (1986), in a study of father–son-in-law problems from a parent's perspective, found that although the father–son-in-law relationship was the modal source of tension among her middle-class families, the most serious intrusions to family unity were caused by wives (daughters-in-law alienating their husbands from their families).

Characteristics of the American kinship system may provide, in part, some explanation for mother-in-law–daughter-in-law tensions, when they do exist. For, although the American kinship system is primarily bilateral in type (similar levels of interaction and association with both the husband and wife's kin), considerable asymmetry may be observed in "kin tending" on the part of female members (Fischer 1983). Nydegger (1986), explaining the relationship between asymmetry and in-law tension among American families, pointed out that because each member of a new marital unit is relatively unknown to his or her in-laws, and kin groups are often dispersed, affiliation with affinal kin (daughters-in-law) usually takes place only during visits and is often slow and problematic. At the same time, given the wide dispersion of kin, time spent with one group of parents is usually at the expense of the other. The resulting pattern is most likely to be matrifocal asymmetry of contact, or bias toward affiliation with the wife's family. This occurrence is pivotal for in-law relations, often resulting in a downward spiral of decreasing contact and increased tension. As a consequence, family bonds may be permanently disrupted, distancing parents and sons.

Others, too, have addressed the asymmetry principle and its contribution to family tension. Lee (1980) made the point that although women in American society tend to maintain more contact with kin than do men, they do not necessarily take responsibility for interaction with the husband's kin. Similarly, Troll (1971) asserted that the mother–daughter-in-law bond is weakened because sons tend to transfer their affection, allegiance, and obligation to their wives' parents, consequently contributing to less contact with their family of orientation.

Children, too, have been found to have a negative impact on the mother–daughter-in-law relationship. Fischer (1983), in a study of in-law relationships from the perspective of the child, found that orientation around a child increased the ambiguity of the relationship between mothers-in-law and young adult daughters-in-law, increased strain among them, and contributed to less interaction (compared to that of mothers and daughters).

Life span attachment theory, sometimes used to explain protective and attachment behaviors between parents and children, may also have implications for affinal relationships (Cicirelli 1983, 1985). For example, if protective behaviors toward older parents in later life stem from the child's basic attachment bond, what are the implications for helping and other interactive patterns with children acquired through marriage relationships?

Despite generally negative generalizations of the mother-in-law–daughter-in-law relationship, recent research suggests that mother-in-law status may provide a viable role for many older women, especially the widowed. Heinemann (1983) found in a study of widows age twenty to ninety-six that mother-in-law was one of the three most salient roles among her sample. Approximately three-fourths of the women age sixty to seventy-four viewed the mother-in-law role as a specific role. This attitude was also reflected by the very old in her sample, those older than seventy-four. Similarly, Lopata (1979) found that, among widows, the mother-in-law role offered a stable role extending over long periods of time, especially when grandchildren were involved. Lopata (1979) also observed that the in-law relationship appeared to take on more salience at the onset of widowhood. The mother-in-law role, too, contributes additional individuals to the older woman's primary family circle to whom she might turn for physical, emotional, and economic support.

Mother–Daughter-in-Law Solidarity

The in-law relationship, although categorically affinal in type, that is, connected by a marital link, by nature of its relationship to consanguineous kin (blood kin or kin of common ancestry) is sometimes classified as consanguine (Shanas, Townsend, Wedderburn, Friss, Milhoj & Stehouwer 1968). This conceptualization has important implications for relationships especially as they relate to solidarity or to family cohesion. For example, this implies that, in a marriage relationship, the spouse relates to the mother/father-in-law in ways similar to that of the biological child.

The Concept of Solidarity

The concept of family solidarity has been a dominant theme in studies of the older parent-child bond (Bengtson, Olander, & Haddad 1976; Atkinson, Kivett & Campbell 1986; Mangen, Bengtson & Landry 1988). More recently, the conceptualization of solidarity has come under some scrutiny because of its narrow focus and its theoretical conceptualization. Although some of this concern is rightly justified, the concept of solidarity, particularly as it relates to the extent of association between generations, would seem to remain a viable measure of intergenerational relationships (McChesney & Bengtson 1988). Much work remains to be done, however, on the etiology of older parent-child bonds and on alternate ways of determining their strength.

Bengtson et al. (1976) identified three dimensions of family cohesion as indices to intergenerational solidarity: association, affection, and consensus. Recent empirical testing of their model showed some serious limitations with regard to the correlation between these three constructs and their use as a multidimensional measure (Atkinson et al. 1986). Association appears to be the strongest of the three components of the solidarity construct in terms of its predictability. Although primarily addressing consanguine relationships, Bengtson and his colleagues' conceptualization of intergenerational solidarity, especially as it relates to association, has potential application for the mother-in-law–daughter-in-law relationship.

Predictors of Associational Solidarity

Many factors have been found to be important predictors of intergenerational solidarity. Proximity of residence, or residential propinquity, contributes to cohesion (Adams 1968; Bengtson et al. 1976; Kivett 1985; Marshall & Rosenthal 1985; Shanas et al. 1968). Most research shows the nearer the older parents and adult children live to one another the greater their association and feelings of positive affect. The dependency needs of older adults, such as health, also influence solidarity between generations (Bengtson et al. 1976; Cicirelli 1983; Kivett 1985; Schlesinger, Tobin & Kulys 1980). The mutual exchange of services between generations (which requires some form of association) also serves to heighten family solidarity (Bengtson, et al. 1976). Types of services exchanged may vary greatly depending upon the stage of family cycle for each generation, ethnic subculture, socioeconomic level, and formal supports available (Brubaker 1985).

The extent of indirect contact, too, has been found to contribute to solidarity between generations. Telephoning and writing increase intergenerational cohesion (Bengtson et al. 1976). Demonstrations of intent to stay in touch or to monitor the health or other needs of older parents may result from either feelings of obligation or affection. At any rate, they have a generally positive effect upon the relationship. Family cohesion, too, may be a function of associated ties through marriage (Kivett 1985). In this case, intergenerational solidarity might be expected to be stronger when affinal kin (daughters-in-law) are married to consanguine kin (sons) of frequent contact (Bengtson et al. 1976).

Hypothesis

The purposes of the present study were to observe patterns of association and helping between older mothers and daughters-in-law and to determine if mothers-in-law could be categorized according to level of family solidarity with daughters-in-law as observed through association. The hypothesis for the study was that older mothers-in-law could be categorized as having high, medium, or low levels of associational solidarity with their daughters-in-law of most contact based upon one or more of six physical and social variables. While the present research descriptively analyzed affectional and consensual solidarity as defined by Bengtson et al. (1976), the major focus

was on associational solidarity. Parallel data on mother-daughter association and helping were used for comparative purposes.

Methods

Participants

This research was part of a larger study of the kin support network of 321
adults sixty-five to ninety-six years of age living in a rural-transitional area
(Atkinson et al. 1986; Kivett 1985; Kivett & Atkinson 1984). The study
employed a compact cluster sampling strategy in a nonmetropolitan county
in the Southeast. The county is characterized as having changed from a
chiefly agricultural economy to an industrialized one over the past three
decades. Subjects were interviewed in their homes and responded in detail
to questions about their patterns of interaction with a relative of most
contact in each of seven levels of consanguine and affinal kin. Older adults
were asked about the son-in-law or daughter-in-law with whom they had
the most contact. Consequently, for purposes of the present study, only
women whose frequent child-in-law association was with a daughter-in-law
(N = 86) were included in the analysis.

The majority of the respondents, 98 percent, were white, with a mean
age of 74.6 (SD = 6.76) and a mean educational level of 10.1 (SD = 3.57)
years. Similar percentages were either married, 47 percent, or widowed, 48
percent, with the remainder being either divorced, separated, or single. The
older women had a mean of 1.7 daughters-in-law with a range of one to
five. Daughters-in-law ranged in age from 27-74 years with a mean of 44.4
years (SD = 8.69). Daughters-in-law had a mean educational level of 13.1
years (SD = 2.77). Approximately 60 percent of the daughters-in-law were
employed, usually in clerical (17 percent), operative (10 percent), or professional (11 percent) occupations. Approximately one-half of the daughters-
in-law of most contact lived within ten minutes of mothers-in-law and
generally were married to the son of most contact (68 percent).

Measurement and Analysis

A multiple discriminant analysis using six social and physical variables was
performed to determine if mothers-in-law and daughters-in-law could be
distinguished according to level of solidarity, such as high, medium, or low.
The discriminant analysis procedure allows for the statistical differentiation
between two or more groups, in this case, three groups of older women:
those with high, medium, and low daughter-in-law solidarity. This distinction is made based upon a number of discriminating variables having previ-

ously been either empirically or theoretically observed to be related to the group variable. The dependent or group variable used in the discriminant analysis, *solidarity*, was operationally defined as associational solidarity and was a measure of the frequency with which older mothers had engaged in eleven activities with the daughter-in-law of most contact during the past year (Bengtson et al. 1976). Cronbach's alpha for the reliability of the association scale was .72. A frequency distribution with scores ranging from 10 to 45 was used to form three classifications (groups) of solidarity: low = < 18 (n = 21); medium = 18 to 21 (n = 23); and high = > 21 (n = 33) (Note: nine subjects were dropped from the discriminant analysis because of missing data).

Discriminating variables included: proximity to daughter-in-law, health and marital status of the mother-in-law, frequency of telephoning and writing, amount of help exchanged, and whether the daughter-in-law was married to the son of most contact. *Proximity to daughter-in-law* was a six-point functional measure of the time required to get to the daughter-in-law's house. *Health (dependency) of the respondent* was a self-rated measure ranging from zero to nine. *Frequency of telephoning and writing* was a nine-point frequency measure ranging from "never" to "daily." *Mutual help* was the amount of help given and received during the past year. Help received was measured by asking the respondents the frequency with which they had received assistance in eleven areas from daughters-in-law and daughters of most contact during the past year. Help given was determined by asking the respondents the extent to which they had given help to daughters-in-law and daughters during the past year. The same nine-point scale was used as with the association measure. Both help received and given were summed to form the discriminator *mutual help*. Whether the daughter-in-law was married to the son of most contact and marital status of the older adults were treated as dummy variables. *Marital status* was dichotomized to single or married status and the married status category served as the referent. A "yes" response to *being married to the son of most contact* served as the referent for that discriminator.

Six variables, linked to associational, affectional, and consensual solidarity, were analyzed descriptively. In addition to association and help given and received, the others were consensus, feelings of closeness, and the extent to which mothers and daughters-in-law "got along." Consensus was obtained by asking the respondent to rank on a scale of zero to nine the extent to which she generally shared the same life views with the daughter in-law. The last two measures were based upon five-point Likert scales and were obtained by asking the respondents the extent to which they felt "close to" and "got along" with the daughter-in-law. These last two measures represented measures of affection while the consensus scale was an index of consensus or accord.

Table 2–1
Association with Daughters-in-Law
and Daughters

Type of Association	Daughters-in-Law (%)	Daughters (%)
Commercial recreation	9.4	27.7
Home recreation	38.8	50.5
Outdoor recreation	8.8	21.5
Visits	78.8	82.3
Vacation	20.0	32.3
Family reunions	49.4	54.8
Emergencies	34.1	47.3
Working together	3.6	5.4
Babysitting	8.3	18.3
Happy occasions	83.5	93.5
Church	47.1	61.3
Shopping	40.0	75.0
Other	1.2	3.3

Note: $N = 86$ for daughters-in-law
$N = 94$ for daughters
Percentages are for association one or more times a year.

Results

The majority of older mothers-in-law, 91 percent, reported that they got along very well with daughters-in-law (96 percent indicated getting along very well with daughters of most contact) and 85 percent reported feeling very close to their son's wife (92 percent reported feeling very close to their daughter of most contact). Mothers also generally indicated a high degree of consensus with daughters-in-law of focus (8.19 on the consensus scale 0-9, $SD = 0.14$) (Daughters $= 8.46$ with a SD of .97 and a range of 3-9).

Table 2–1 shows that older women were more likely to report getting together with daughters-in-law for visits and happy occasions than for other events. Associations with daughters attained higher levels than with daughters-in-law on all dimensions and especially in nonobligatory areas such as recreation, church, and shopping. Daughters were also more likely to have been associated with emergency situations.

Table 2–2 indicates that more than one-half of the respondents had received help in a least one area from the daughter-in-law of most contact during the past year. Transportation was the most commonly received type of help, followed by shopping and help when ill. Daughters had provided considerably more help in all areas but the order of type of assistance was somewhat similar to that provided by daughters-in-law. Daughters were one and one-half times more likely to have helped with transportation; four times more likely to have helped with household repairs and yard work; and twice more likely to have helped with housekeeping, shopping, and during an illness. They also were considerably more likely to have provided financial aid. Ten percent of older women reported having helped the daughter-in-law of focus in the past year in at least one area. Mothers had provided less help to both daughters and daughters-in-law in most areas than they received. Assistance was most likely to have been given to daughters-in-law with transportation and in illness and decision-making. Mothers usually reported providing more help in all areas to daughters than to daughters-in-law. There were relatively high levels of indirect contact between mothers and daughters-in-law via the telephone. Approximately 54 percent of mothers-in-law reported talking on the telephone one or more times a week with their daughter-in-law. Writing was considerably less frequent, a probable consequence of close proximity.

The results of the discriminant analysis showed that, overall, 54 percent of the respondents could be correctly classified according to level of associational solidarity by the six discriminating variables [$F = 3.15$ $(2,74)$, $p <$ .001]. As a result, the overall hypothesis was supported. Older mothers could be distinguished according to the level of associational solidarity that they had with their daughters-in-law of most contact. Mothers reporting high levels of solidarity had the highest percentage of grouped cases correctly classified, 82 percent; followed by mothers with low solidarity, 52 percent; and mothers reporting medium solidarity, 19 percent. Prior probabilities or the proportion that might have been correctly classified by chance alone according to group were: high, 43 percent; medium, 30 percent, and low, 27 percent.

Results showed that the six discriminating variables combined to form two linear combinations with the ability to separate older women according to level of daughter-in-law solidarity. The first and most important function served to distinguish between respondents who had high or medium versus low solidarity with daughters-in-law. This function explained 82 percent of the variance in the model and was a measure of direct and indirect accessibility as observed through the importance of geographical proximity, telephoning, and writing. Mothers and daughters-in-law with high or medium solidarity lived in closer geographical proximity and showed higher rates of telephoning and writing than mothers and daughters of low solidarity. The second function explained 18 percent of the variance in the model and was a measure of contact or interaction as observed through mutual help and telephoning and writing. The function served to distinguish mothers and

Table 2–2
Help Given to and Received from Daughters-in-Law and Daughters

	Help Received		Help Given	
Type of Assistance	Daughters-in-Law (%)	Daughters (%)	Daughters-in-Law (%)	Daughters (%)
Transportation	52.3	79.6	8.3	24.3
Household repairs	11.6	40.2	2.4	4.3
Housekeeping	25.6	52.7	7.1	20.4
Shopping	32.6	71.0	7.1	30.4
Yardwork	10.5	40.1	3.6	4.3
Car care	1.2	11.0	2.4	2.2
Help in illness	32.6	61.3	9.5	33.3
Decision making	24.4	64.5	9.5	29.0
Legal aid	3.5	18.3	2.4	4.3
Financial aid	3.5	16.1	3.5	15.1
Other aid	—	1.1	1.2	2.2

Note: $N = 86$ for daughters-in-law
 $N = 94$ for daughters
 Percentages are for association one or more times a year.

daughters-in-law of medium solidarity from those of high and low solidarity. A medium level of associational solidarity was characterized by higher frequencies of telephoning and writing but a larger discrepancy between indirect (telephoning and writing) and direct contact (helping) than for the other two groups, that is, low solidarity (low helping, low telephoning and writing); high solidarity (high helping, high telephoning and writing); and medium solidarity (moderate helping and high telephoning and writing). Health and marital status of the mother-in-law and whether the daughter-in-law was married to the son of most contact were not important to mother–daughter-in-law solidarity.

Discussion

The results of this research show that most older mothers had at least two daughters-in-law, one of which usually lived within a ten-minute distance from their home. Association was most likely to occur as a result of obligatory occasions such as birthdays, special holidays, and other "happy occasions" than nonobligatory occasions. Considerable positive affect and perceived consensus were reported by older women for daughters-in-law but there was relatively infrequent exchange of services. Older mothers were more likely to receive assistance from their daughters-in-law than to give help. Distinctions could be seen in the patterns of association with daughters and daughters-in-law with association being higher with daughters. Proximity of residence was an important factor in the strength of the mother-in-law—daughter-in-law bond, with close proximity distinguishing between high, medium, and low solidarity. More accessibility as seen through geographical proximity and telephoning and writing enhanced solidarity. Others, too, have pointed out the important relationship between residential proximity and indirect contact and family cohesion (Bengtson et al. 1976; Marshall & Rosenthal 1985).

The norms regulating the mother-daughter relationship appeared to be somewhat obscure. Observations of the importance of proximity of residence and types of association between mothers-in-law and daughters-in-law suggested the importance of convenience and obligation to the relationship, while the lack of importance of the marital status and health of older women suggested low "protective" behaviors on the parts of daughters-in-law. These variations in types of commitment are supported by literature. The American kinship system, for example, has been characterized as having relatively flexible norms of obligation and option for consanguineal kin (Johnson 1988). Data from the present research suggest that norms for affinal kin may be even more pliant, that is, more blurred with regard to generational priorities and societal expectations than for consanguine kin.

Mother—Daughter-in-Law Affect

The results of this research in general do not support the usual negative generalizations regarding the mother—daughter-in-law relationship, especially as they relate to expressions of affection. At least among daughters-in-law of most contact, mothers-in-law expressed strong feelings of closeness and agreement and similar consensus regarding life views. Furthermore, there appears to be a moderate degree of contact, both direct (physical presence) and indirect association (telephoning) between the two generations. Some potential negativism in the relationships between these mothers and daughters-in-law may have been relaxed through the fact that, given the rural-transitional nature of the area and the blue-collar status of the sample, many mothers-in-law knew daughters-in-law before their marriage to their sons. This factor has been found to be important to affinal relationships in early marriage. Given these socioeconomic characteristics and low geographical mobility, patterns of interaction and positive affect could have been well-established over the years.

Support of Attachment Theory

In terms of attachment theory, mothers' verbal expressions of affection toward daughters-in-law suggest considerable attachment. Fischer (1983), however, observed that mothers were less likely than daughters-in-law to recognize conflict, which could have explained, in part, high levels of expressed affection (along with social desirability). In this study contrasts in attachment behavior (as indicated through mutual help) between mothers and daughters and daughters-in-law indicated only moderate levels of affection between mothers and daughters-in-law. This observation can be related to findings by Cicirelli (1985) who found that, among elderly mothers and children, helping behavior was a function of attachment behavior. In the present study, strong attachment behavior appeared to be absent through observations of protective motivators. Neither mothers in poor health nor those who were widowed had more association with daughters-in-law than other mothers. As a result of these observations, the data are equivocal in their support of attachment theory, that is, the lack of an early common history would contribute to low attachment behavior. Although not explicit, the marital role probably carries with it some expectation of attachment behaviors (helping, protective behaviors, association) between affinal kin, especially parents and children. Also, a relatively long common history between mothers and daughters-in-law, albeit as recent as twenty years or less, no doubt has some bonding effects. Some attachment, too, may be transferred to spouses of children through continuing parental imperatives to promote and/or support the son's family of procreation.

The data do not appear to strongly support the notion of an avoidance tendency among mothers and daughters-in-law, although association was modest and generally of the obligatory type. They do show that the mother–daughter-in-law relationship is less salient than the mother-daughter relationship as seen though patterns of association and mutual help. The fact that most daughters-in-law worked outside the home and, in many cases, were caught up in the launching of their own children, may have been related to the relatively low levels of association and helping. Other data in this study suggested that mother–daughter-in-law association was based largely upon convenience or easy accessibility.

Importance of the Mother-in-Law Role

This research suggests the mother-in-law role in later life to be of relatively high psychological significance in terms of feelings of closeness, getting along with, and sharing world views with daughters-in-law of most contact—all elements contributing to compatibility and friendship. Affectional solidarity as demonstrated through mutual helping can be best described as moderate. In other words, the mother-in-law role was relatively unimportant in terms of the amount of functional help given to daughters-in-law. This observation becomes even more important when taking into consideration that relationships reported here represented maximum mother–daughter-in-law contact; that is, the study did not reflect interaction and affect between older mothers and daughters-in-law of occasional or no contact and when the child of most contact was a son-in-law. Despite this potential limit to generalizations and daughters'-in-law peripheral role as contrasted to the daughters' role, it appears that daughters-in-law are geographically accessible (at least in some nonmetropolitan areas) and figure importantly into the support system of many older women, especially in the fulfillment of primary needs as transportation, help with shopping, and help during illness.

Directions for Future Research

The increasing need for expanded support networks for the elderly and the accumulating numbers of affinal kin brought about through rapid social changes necessitate more research in the area of affinal kin. Research needs appear in four areas: theoretical or conceptual frameworks, measurement and analysis, clarification of norms of affinal roles, and intergenerational affinal relations.

Theoretical or Conceptual Frameworks

There has been an increased interest in the construction and development of theory in the area of the family during the past two decades. Because of the relatively uncharted area of affinal relationships in old age, there is the need to examine these relationships under numerous lenses, that is, various theoretical perspectives and in joint analyses. The use of a multiple theoretical approach in the study of older parent–child-in-law relationships would provide a fuller understanding of affinal behaviors. Three broad theories showing complementary features and frequently used in studies of the family would seem to serve as conceptual frameworks for affinal relationships as we understand them at this stage: social exchange theory, symbolic interactionism, and conflict theory. Research based on a multiperspective model such as that suggested here would have relevance to both practitioners and academicians. For the most part, key constructs for each of these theories can be easily implemented and measured. Future studies of affinal relations based upon a well-defined multiperspective model would yield results that can be more easily compared to the numerous data currently available on consanguineal relationships.

Measurement and Analysis

New strategies, too, are needed for studying families in the later years and, in particular, affinal relationships. The first of these strategies deals with observational techniques. More direct naturalistic observations are needed to capture the richness of interactions. Strategies long used in observational studies of children can serve as models. The use of these observational types may call for the development of new variables by which to measure simultaneous behaviors. A second area of measurement to be considered is unit of analysis with more of a moving away from dyad observations. More methods, for example, should be incorporated that allow for the studying of family units such as multigenerational units. In the case of in-law relationships, other members possibly mediating the mother–daughter-in-law relationship should be studied, that is, grandchildren and adult children (spouses of the in-law of focus).

Multitheoretical models of investigation call for analytical models to measure important interrelationships. There must be continued movement away from more simplistic models and procedures such as descriptive and bivariate analyses.

Clarification of Norms of Affinal Roles

Norms of behaviors or commitment between affinal kin, especially as they relate to intergenerational relationships, are unclear. To adequately determine theoretical frameworks and measurement procedures, information is needed on factors predisposing relationships between older adults and children-in-law. Little is known about the extent to which a husband or wife supports the parent of a spouse. Most research has dealt with child-to-parent relationships and exchanges. More information is needed on the "principle of substitution" as it relates to assistance to a parent by marriage in the absence of the biological child, that is, because of death or divorce. Also important is information on norms of behaviors and commitment among newer emerging family types. Data also are lacking on the relative importance of obligatory and optional norms in affinal relationships. Basic information on role expectations provides a necessary "backdrop" for research on affinal relationships.

Intergenerational Affinal Relationships

Future research should examine the effects of factors such as role load, age, and health of the daughter-in-law upon the mother-in-law relationship. Information is needed on the mediating effect of daughters (sisters-in-law) upon the mother–daughter-in-law relationship. Other factors possibly impinging upon relationships include the quality and length of the marriage of the daughter-in-law and family life cycle stage, that is, working status and the presence of children in the home. Other than factors facilitating relationships, information is needed on the value of the roles as measured by economic, emotional, and instrumental exchanges. Questions of the importance of equity of exchanges to the relationship and psychological well-being of mothers and daughters-in-law is an important area of focus. Underscoring future research on intergenerational affinal relationships is the need for more multicultural studies, or research on the extent to which ethnicity influences the mother–daughter-in-law relationship. Future research should also examine the changing structure of the mother–daughter-in-law dyad (as well as the intergenerational unit) and of society economical cycles, public policy, and societal values.

Although little is known about the status and dynamics of the mother–daughter-in-law relationship, there is considerable evidence that the daughter-in-law plays a pivotal role in the care of many older women. Future research that clarifies the expectations and characteristics of that role and the accompanying implications for the family will fill an important void in intergenerational studies.

References

Adams, B. N. 1968. *Kinship in an urban setting.* Chicago: Markham.

Atkinson M.; Kivett, V. R.; & Campbell, R. T. 1986. Intergenerational solidarity: An examination of a theoretical model. *Journal of Gerontology, 41,* 408–416.

Bengtson, V. L.; Olander, E. B.; & Haddad, A. A. 1976. The 'generation gap' and aging family members: Toward a conceptual model. In J. F. Gubrium (ed.), *Time, roles, and self in old age* (237–263). New York: Human Sciences.

Brubaker, T. H. 1985. *Later life families.* Beverly Hills, Calif.: Sage Publications.

Cicirelli, V. G. 1983. Adult children and their elderly parents. In T. H. Brubaker (ed.), *Family relationships in later life* (31–46). Beverly Hills, Calif.: Sage Publications.

———. 1985. Adult children's attachment and helping behavior to elderly parents: A path model. In B. C. Miller & D. H. Olson (eds.), *Family studies review yearbook* (Vol. 3) (413–423). Beverly Hills, Calif.: Sage Publications.

Fischer, L. R. 1983. Mothers and mothers-in-law. *Journal of Marriage and the Family, 45,* 187–192.

Heinemann, G. D. 1983. Family involvement and support for widowed persons. In T. H. Brubaker (ed.), *Family relationships in later life* (127–148). Beverly Hills, Calif.: Sage Publications.

Johnson, C. L. 1988. Relationships among family members and friends in later life. In R. M. Milardo (ed.), *Families and Social Networks* (168–189). Beverly Hills, Calif.: Sage Publications.

Kivett, V. R. 1985. Consanguinity and kin level: Their relative importance to the network of older adults. *Journal of Gerontology, 40,* 228–234.

Kivett, V. R. & Atkinson, M. P. 1984. Filial expectations, association, and helping as a function of number of children and older rural-transitional parents. *Journal of Gerontology, 39,* 499–503.

Lee, G. R. 1980. Kinship in the seventies: A decade review of research and theory. *Journal of Marriage and the Family, 42,* 923–934.

Lopata, H. Z. 1979. *Women as widows.* New York: Elsevier.

Mangen, D. J.; Bengtson, V. L.; & Landrey, D. H., Jr. (eds.). 1988. *Measurement of intergenerational relations.* Newbury Park, Calif.: Sage Publications.

McChesney, K. Y., & Bengtson, V. L. 1988. Solidarity, integration, and cohesion in families. In D. J. Mangen, V. L. Bengtson, & D. H. Landrey, Jr. (eds.), *Mea-*

surement of intergenerational relations (15–30). Newbury Park, Calif.: Sage Publications.

Marshall, V. W. & Rosenthal, C. J. 1985. The relevance of geographical proximity in intergenerational relations. *The Gerontologist, 25* [Special Issue], 15.

Nydegger, C. N. 1986. Asymmetrical kin and the problematic son-in-law. In N. Datan, A. L. Greene, & H. W. Reese (eds.), *Life-span developmental psychology: Intergenerational relations* (99–123). Hillsdale, N.J.: Lawrence Erlbaum Associates, Inc.

Schlesinger, M.; Tobin, S.; & Kulys, R. 1980. The responsible child and parental well-being. *Journal of Gerontological Social Work, 3,* 3–16.

Select Committee on Aging. 1983. *Status of the rural elderly* (Vol. 2) (Comm. Pub. No. 98–398). Washington, D.C.: U.S. Government Printing Office.

Shanas, E.; Townsend, P.; Wedderburn, D.; Friis, H.; Milhoj, P.; & Stehouwer, J. 1968. *Old people in three industrial societies.* New York: Atherton Press.

Troll, L. E. 1971. The family of later life: A decade review. *Journal of Marriage and the Family, 33,* 263–290.

U.S. Bureau of the Census. 1973. *1970 Census of the population (Vol. 1): Characteristics of the population* (Part 35, North Carolina). Washington, D.C.: U.S. Government Printing Office.

3

Divorce-related Changes in Relationships: Parents, Their Adult Children, and Children-in-Law

Colleen Leahy Johnson

T he relationship between parents and adult children understandably changes over the life course because of both normative and unanticipated life events. One important influence on this relationship throughout adult development comes when the adult child's marital status changes. With marriage, for example, a child transfers loyalties to a new spouse, thus establishing more distance from parents. With divorce, this distance is often reduced when the child as a single parent turns to parents for help. With a child's remarriage, further changes occur which usually again increase the distance from parents.

This chapter consists of findings from a longitudinal study of divorcing families in which members of three generations were interviewed. Originally the purpose was to examine how divorce affected the grandparents' role. Upon initial study, however, we concluded that the grandparents' role was derived from two factors: the grandparents' relationships with their child and child-in-law and their position and roles in the child's family during the processes of family reorganization following divorce.

This chapter will analyze the changing family structures accompanying marital changes as households reform and loyalties are transferred to new social units. I propose that structural changes in the household with marital changes initiate three types of changes in the parent-child relationships. First, with divorce the level of privacy in a nuclear household decreases and more actions of its members become public and observable to parents and others. Second, divorce and remarriage entail processes of social reorganization. If young children are involved, relationships are redefined among in-laws and kin as well as those within the nuclear family. Third, with marital

This chapter is based upon research projects funded by the National Institute of Mental Health and the National Institute on Aging. I wish to thank Barbara Barer for her assistance in the preparation of this chapter.

changes, estrangement occurs in some relationships and new solidarities develop in others. These changes in turn shape and redefine the relationship between parents and their adult children.

The empirical findings of this research are reported elsewhere (Johnson 1983, 1985, 1988a, 1988b, 1988c; Johnson & Barer 1987; Johnson, Schmidt & Klee 1988). This chapter is confined to an analysis and generalizations on the parent-child relationship as it is mediated by the child-in-law during the processes of marital changes. Because divorce and remarriage initiate dynamic changes in the family and consequently in intergenerational relationships, the processes are interesting conceptually, for the fast-paced events illuminate dimensions of adult-child relationship that are not as apparent in more stable times.

American Family Structure and Functioning

It is conventional today among researchers on family change to reject the structural-functional theories as too mechanistic and remote from the more dynamic processes of family life. This stance, in fact, has become so popular that a recent handbook on the current state of the art in family research no longer considers this theoretical framework applicable to family research (Burr, Hill, Nye & Reiss 1979). With less concern for family structure, the implications of divorce-related changes in the family are considered only to the extent that a nuclear family is viewed as an abbreviated and usually problematic unit isolated from other social units (Wallerstein & Kelly 1979; Wallerstein 1987). This deficit approach ignores the possibility that grandparents and other members of the extended family may be important resources during divorce. Another approach using different assumptions may be in order, for an examination of structural changes accompanying marital changes reveals complex processes of restructuring and reorganization (Ahrons & Rodgers 1987). Presumably these changes in households and nuclear families also has an impact on relationships among parents, their adult child and their child-in-law.

It is useful first to review the dominant structural characteristics of the American family system. First, marriage initially entails a rearrangement of units of social structure (Cohen 1971). In our culture, individuals make a sharp break with their family of origin and transfer their loyalties to a new spouse (Parsons 1949). The extent to which loyalties change depends upon cultural norms. In our society, our norms strongly endorse the belief that the solidarity of the marital pair should take precedence over loyalties to either partner's family of origin. With the strong norm of noninterference in the life of a nuclear household, parents usually become relatively uninvolved in the daily life of their married children.

Second, interactions between parents and children change with marriage. With separate households, there is less opportunity for interactions. The intimate marital dyad remains quite private from others, usually to the exclusion of parents (Berger & Kellner 1964; Laslett 1978). Although there are class variations, couples in companionate marriages are likely to deal with their parents jointly rather than independently. The importance of the marital dyad in our culture is reflected in how frequently family specialists concentrate on this research interest, often to the exclusion of the relationships between a parent and adult children. In fact, one is impressed with the extent the study of the contemporary family is essentially a study of marriage.

Third, from a cross-cultural perspective, relationships within the American family and kinship systems are noted for being relatively unstructured, with only vague norms of obligation and reciprocity (Furstenberg 1981; Schneider 1968). Consequently, individuals are able to develop strategies to mold relationships to meet their personal preferences. In fact, if they choose, they can forego kinship relationships altogether; or they can have higher commitments to friends or relatives by marriage than to their blood relatives. Because divorce and remarriage also are processes particularly noted for being incompletely institutionalized, a period of "social limbo" is created. We can assume that these periods permit even more flexibility to individuals to relate to whom one chooses (Cherlin 1978).

Fourth, there are major gender differences in family involvement, with women being the key persons who manage and orchestrate family and kin affairs (Troll & Bengtson 1979). They are also the primary socializers of children in both intact and divorced families. There are more continuities in the mother-daughter relationship throughout the family cycle than is usually found among fathers and sons. Finally, in old age, women are more likely than men to survive and more likely to be integrated into a family system. The caregivers of the elderly also are likely to be women.

In-law Relationships in American Kinship Systems

Studies of kinship in small-scale societies indicate there is a fundamental opposition between relatives by blood and relatives by marriage (Radcliffe-Brown 1952). Unilineal kinship systems that trace their descent through either the paternal or maternal lineages require that one partner transfer his or her loyalties from the family of origin and establish permanent membership in the spouse's lineage. In the process of transferring the loyalties to a new family system, feelings of ambivalence about in-laws are likely to arise. Most societies recognize a dual basis of relatedness with in-laws. To a grandmother, for example, a daughter-in-law is not only a relative by a son's marriage, but also is related to her as the mother of her grandchild.

Where this twofold tie is recognized and the in-law relationship cannot be severed, there are usually structural mechanisms to reduce these tensions.

In the American kinship system tensions are usually controlled through the geographical distance created by establishing a separate residence upon marriage. Given the privatization of the nuclear family, and the normative priorities granted to the marriage over the parent–adult-child bond, social and emotional distance as well as geographical distance are likely to occur. As a result, in-law relationships may be problematic but only on an intermittent basis. Not surprisingly, conflict among in-laws is commonly reported. The most conflict reported in the rather sparse literature on this subject is found between women, and women are found to be the most common instigators of conflict (Marotz-Baden & Cowan 1987).

Because women are the key persons in organizing kin interactions, they have to interact with each other more than men. Lucy Fischer (1983) found that, with the birth of a child, strains occur between mother-in-law and daughter-in-law centering on child care. Since there is a propensity for new mothers to seek out their own mothers, their mothers-in-laws are excluded. Although mothers of sons are as likely to take as strong an interest in how their grandchildren are raised, the norm of noninterference often prevents them from influencing child-rearing practices. They either must passively wait for their daughter-in-law's initiative or risk being sanctioned for being interfering (Johnson 1983, 1985). This situation provides more opportunity for conflicts between mothers-in-law and their daughters than mothers-in-law and sons-in-law. Duvall (1954) suggests that a new nuclear family must establish its own autonomy to transcend the tensions among in-laws. Although there are some subcultures where the mother–adult-child relationship remains strong after the child's marriage, this pattern of solidarity is a variant rather than a normative one.

Family Changes With Divorce

Because marriage is the basis of the household in our society, divorce results in greater dislocations than are found in societies where households are based upon intergenerational ties. Three major relocations occur that affect relations between parents and their adult child (Johnson 1988c). First, the high level of privatization of the nuclear family changes with martial changes. Divorce, for example, entails the intrusion of the public domain into family life as the legal system oversees the division of property and the allocation of responsibility for dependent children (Burgoyne & Clark 1984). At the micro level, the day-to-day privacy of the nuclear unit also diminishes if custodial parents need help from parents, friends, and community agencies. More of the actions of family members are observable by others so, for example, parents become more familiar with the intimate aspects of a child's life. In the process, the boundary around the nuclear family becomes looser and more open to the influence of those outside the nuclear household.

Secondly, women's status is particularly problematic after divorce. Custody is granted to women in 90 percent of the cases. In fact, males' participation in their children's lives drops off sharply after divorce so that within a year, one-half of the divorced men in one national survey had no contact with their children (Furstenberg & Spanier 1984). Women are more likely than men to experience stressors as single parents and to suffer economic hardships. Because they also are less likely to remarry, they are in greater need of assistance over time. They more commonly turn to their own mothers for help in child care than sons, which further strengthens the female-linked bond. These female-linked kinship relationships between mothers and daughters can pose problems for mothers of sons if their sons cannot provide them access to their grandchildren. In such cases, they may have to develop strategies that continue a female-linked kinship tie with former daughters-in-law.

The research on which this article is based found that most individuals turned to their parents for help immediately following their divorce (Johnson 1983, 1985, 1988a). Such a pattern was particularly prominent among mothers and daughters, families in which the grandparents significantly eased the strains of divorce. This renewed closeness did result in some ambivalence on the part of both the parents and their adult children. This solution appeared to be temporary, however, for after forty months, most of those who had been dependent on their parents assumed a more independent status and attempted to reestablish the privacy of their nuclear household. Mothers of sons were significantly more likely to retain relationships with their former daughters-in-law and in this capacity have easy access to their grandchildren (Johnson & Barer 1987).

From my study and others, we can conclude that the relationship between parent and adult child varies according to the child's marital status. To trace relationships between the parent, adult child, and child-in-law through the processes of marital changes, it is useful first to consider the types of dyads, triads, and more complex relationships that occur. Here I have confined the analysis to the mother not only for greater clarity, but also to demonstrate the key role women play in our family system. Where a mother is married, she and her husband frequently interact as a coalition in their relationships to their children and children-in-law. Nevertheless women as the key personnel who orchestrate kin affairs play a more important role following a child's divorce than do men. The model, however, can also be applied to the father in some instances.

Marriage

Our norms make it quite clear that parents should not interfere in a married child's household; their relationship with an adult child can appropriately be redefined to be "intimate at a distance." A strong coalition between husband and wife develops upon marriage, an event likely to weaken the ties between a mother and her married child. Couples usually form a coalition and deal with their parents jointly. Much of the lives of the younger generation is private from the parents, who have only as much access as their child and child-in-law will permit. In some ethnic group families, of course, ties between mothers and married children continue to be strong after their marriage and can compete with the solidarity between husband and wife.

Divorce

During divorce, a series of changes takes place that affects intergenerational relationships. Initially, structural changes result in the departure of one spouse leaving an abbreviated household. In the process, relationships between parents, their divorcing child, and child-in-law change markedly. That between parent-in-law and child-in-law ends legally, laying the groundwork for a possible strengthened bond between parent and adult child. A child-in-law is no longer present to compete with the relationship. Also, when divorced individuals turn to their own parents for help, they become more dependent upon them. This change in status potentially gives parents more power over their adult child.

Often a coalition forms between mother and daughter in the course of the mother's extending help. This arrangement is far more common between mother and daughter because of the pressing needs of the daughter as a single custodial parent. In any case, because it is difficult to retain relationships of equal solidarity with one's daughter and her former husband, the mother's relationship with her former son-in-law either dissolves or becomes more distant at the same time her relationship with her daughter is strengthened.

The divorce-related changes in the relationship between adults and their parents also vary if there are grandchildren. Grandparents continue to have a strong interest in their grandchildren's welfare. Sometimes, however, they do not have ready access to their grandchildren if their former child-in-law is the custodial parent. That individual is no longer legally related to them, although they continue to share a biological link to the grandchildren. For this reason also, any study of parents and adult children should include an examination of the role of the child-in-law not only during the marriage but also during and after the divorce.

Paternal grandmothers have more difficulty in maintaining access to their grandchildren, for their own sons are not always able to provide it. In numerous cases, paternal grandparents retain and often strengthen their relationship with their daughter-in-law to preserve their access to their grandchildren. Female-linked networks thus become particularly prominent after divorce, a factor important in understanding the post-divorce reorganization of the kinship system. Given the dual basis of relatedness among in-laws, they are no longer related by law, yet they retain a shared biological linkage to the children of the marriage.

Mothers of sons often face problems in two situations. First, their sons do not usually have custody of their grandchildren, so they may be confined to occasional visitation rights. If, for example, a son only sees his children every other weekend, his mother is hesitant to monopolize any of his time. Second, in other situations, parents may feel the need to compensate for a son's deficiencies as a parent. In both situations, parents form coalitions with their former daughter-in-law. Because of the difficulty of maintaining equal loyalties to both their child and child-in-law, however, such coalitions usually weaken their relationship to their son. These restructurings of relationships with divorce result in stronger bonds of solidarity between women—that between mother and daughter or between mother and daughter-in-law.

Remarriage

Remarriage of an adult child creates an even more complex kinship system and correspondingly an ever-more changing relationship between parents and adult children. With remarriage, the sheer number of relationships increases by the addition of in-laws and step-relatives. Moreover, because of the shared biological link to the children of the dissolved marriage, relationships with former in-laws do not usually completely break down. With remarriage, the relationship between parents and their adult child must compete with the increasing numbers of new in-laws and step relatives. Any divisions created by divorce are paralleled by the formation of new units of solidarity, any of which can potentially affect the parent-adult child relationship. Further divisions are paralleled by the formation of new units of solidarity, for example, between relatives of multiple marriages.

A series of permutations occurs in relationships between parents, their children, and children-in-law when the divorcing child remarries. It is difficult for remarried individuals to maintain relationships of equal quality and importance with relatives from multiple marriages. It is also difficult to dissolve relationships with former in-laws if one recognizes the importance of the blood tie with the children of the marriage. Thus, grandparents may have divided loyalties between their son and the mother of their grandchildren.

When a daughter remarries, maternal grandmothers generally have little difficulty with a transfer of loyalties from a former son-in-law to a new son-in-law. Because her grandchildren are likely to live with her daughter before and after her remarriage, there are fewer dislocations for her than for the paternal grandmother. However, greater distance is created in the relationship between the parents and their daughter with her remarriage. Once again the daughter has formed a unit of solidarity that takes priority over her relationship with her parents. Her household becomes more private to the exclusion of parents, so the intergenerational relationship usually becomes more distant than when she was divorced.

The relationship between parents and sons is more complicated with his remarriage, because he is even less likely than when he was divorced to be a connecting link between his parents and his children by his first marriage. Thus this problem of access becomes magnified for paternal grandparents. A son usually expects his parents to transfer their loyalties to his new wife. Many women, however, have a friendly relationship with their son's former wife and through her have retained access to their grandchildren. Such a coalition with a former daughter-in-law usually places a strain on her relationship with her son and his new wife. If parents do not transfer their commitments to a new child-in-law, their child often perceives them as disloyal. If parents do transfer their loyalties to the new in-law they not only may dissolve a friendly relationship with the former child-in-law, but they also may lose their access to their grandchildren.

Summary

To review this analysis of the relationship between parents and their adult child throughout the processes of the child's marital changes, the analysis has stressed the need to consider the child-in-law. If young children are present in divorcing families, parents and their former child-in-law share a biological linkage to the children of the marriage. Consequently, the in-law relationship is not always dissolved and may continue to have some effect on the relationship parents have with their child.

The processes themselves have been depicted in terms of oppositional forces where conflict and estrangement develop in some relationships at the same time new solidarities form in other relationships. Such assumptions are based upon the fact that it is difficult for individuals whose families are affected by marital changes to retain loyalties and commitments of equal intensity to present and former in-laws. Because the divorce process is usually conflictual, some means are found to reduce the tensions occurring when loyalties are transferred and families are reorganized. When examined at an abstract level, one can identify how the parent and adult child relationship fluctuates according to these modifications in the family and kinship system.

When an individual remarries, he or she transfers loyalties from the parental unit to a new spouse, a move that establishes more distance from parents. As solidarity develops in the marriage, a husband and wife deal jointly rather than individually with each one's parents. With divorce, an individual again deals with a parent singly. Usually the solidarity between parents and the adult child increases when divisions form in the child's marriage. With remarriage in turn, the commitment to a spouse usually supercedes commitment to parents. Because in-law relationships are not always dissolved and stepchildren are often involved, however, a remarriage never reaches the level of privacy of the first marriage, because each one retains some relationships from the divorce. Nevertheless, the changing levels of distance and intimacy between parents and their adult children are responses to the child's marital status.

We have attempted to go beyond the view of divorce and remarriage as social problems to place the events of family breakdown and reorganization into the context of a kinship analysis. With such a perspective, it is possible to glean useful insights on the contemporary family. At the structural level of analysis, one can see that the fluctuations in relationships between parents and adult children with any marital change are colored by structural changes in households and the position and role of the child-in-law. In the particular population we studied, how these relationships are redefined are consistent with common conceptions of the American family and kinship systems. These systems are flexible and constantly changing in response to the needs and wishes of individual members, and its members are not compelled to conform to institutional norms. When viewed objectively as social scientists, these processes of reorganization are reasoned and logical.

At another level however, two critical issues arise. Just what impact do these social processes have on individuals in these families? And how do individuals adapt to the marked changes in family structure and organization accompany marital changes? In an era when divorce is more often a normative life event rather than an unanticipated one, there have also been marked changes in values and ideology on the family itself. With greater permissiveness in values, divorce is less likely to be viewed as a threatening life event, at least by the younger generations. The widely held view among the formerly married—that divorce is less harmful than previously thought—is not widely endorsed by the grandparent generation, which was much more likely to view its effects on children and grandchildren with concern and even alarm. Thus, in many families, conflicts are likely to occur because of their markedly discrepant values.

Another issue arising from this data concerns the differential structures that develop according to gender. The female-linked kinship bond so often noted in the American kinship system is most prominent during the processes of family reorganization. With divorce, in fact, the bond between mothers and daughters-in-law can compete with the mothers' relationships with their sons. Such a solidary bond between women may in part account for the father's peripheral status and lack of involvement with his children after a divorce. Other research has suggested that women have stronger biological anchorages in the family (Johnson et al. 1988), a factor most prominent following divorce. Women usually have custody; the father's participation markedly declines over time. Men, on the other hand, are more likely to remarry and appear to be better able to transfer their allegiances to stepchildren of their remarriage. One must then question what effects the solidarity of women and the female-linked kinship bonds have on the status and role of fathers in the contemporary family and how these bonds among women affect biological relationships between generations.

References

Ahrons, C., & Rogers, R. 1987. *Divorced Families*. New York: Norton.

Berger, P., & Kellner, H. 1964. Marriage and the construction of reality. *Diogenes*, 46, 1–25.

Burgoyne, J., & Clark D. 1984. *Making a go of it: A study of step-families in Sheffield*. London: Routledge & Kegan Paul.

Burr, W. R.; Hill, R.; Nye, F. I; & Reiss, I. (eds.). 1979. *Contemporary theories about the family*. New York: Free Press.

Cherlin, A. 1978. Remarriage as an incomplete institution. *American Journal of Sociology*, 84, 634–650.

Cohen, R. 1971. *Dominance and defiance: A study of marital instability in an Islam African society*. Washington, D.C.: American Anthropological Association.

Duvall, E. 1954. *In-laws: Pro and con*, New York: Associated Press.

Fischer, L. 1983. Mothers and mothers-in-law. *Journal of Marriage and The Family*, 45, 187–192.

Furstenberg, F. 1981. Remarriage and intergenerational relations. In R. Fogel, E. Hatfield, S. Keesler, & E. Shanas (eds.), *Aging: Stability and change in the family* (115–142). New York: Academic Press.

Furstenberg, F., & Spanier, G. 1984. *Recycling the family: Remarriage after divorce*. Beverly Hills, Calif.: Sage Publications.

Johnson, C. 1983. A cultural analysis of the grandmother. *Research on Aging, 5,* 547–567.

———. 1985. Grandparenting options in divorcing families. In V. Bengtson & J. Robertson (eds.), *Grandparenthood* (81–96). Beverly Hills, Calif.: Sage Publications.

———. 1988a. Active and latent functions of grandparenting during the divorce process. *The Gerontologist, 28,* 185–191.

———. 1988b. Postdivorce reorganization between divorcing children and their parents. *Journal of Marriage and the Family, 50,* 221–231.

———. 1988c. *Ex familia: Grandparents, parents, and children adapt to divorce*. New Brunswick: Rutgers University Press.

Johnson, C., & Barer, B. 1987. American kinship relationships with divorce and remarriage. *The Gerontologist, 23,* 612–618.

Johnson, C.; Schmidt, C.; & Klee, L. 1988. Conceptions of parentage among children of divorce. *American Anthropologist, 90,* 24–32.

Laslett, B. 1978. Family membership, past and present. *Social Problems, 25,* 476–490.

Marotz-Baden, R., & Cowan, D. 1987. Mothers-in-law and daughters-in-law: The effects of proximity on conflict and stress. *Family Relations, 36,* 385–390.

Parsons, T. 1949. The social structure of the family. In R. Anshen (ed.) *The family: Its function and destiny* (241–274). New York: Harper & Row.

Radcliffe-Brown, A. 1952. *Structure and function in primitive society.* New York: Free Press.

Schneider, D. 1968. *American kinship: A cultural account.* Englewood Cliffs, N.J.: Prentice Hall.

Troll, L., & Bengtson, V. 1979. Generations in families. In W. Burr, R. Hill, F.I. Nye, & I. Reiss (eds.), *Contemporary theories about the family* (127–161). New York: Free Press.

Wallerstein, J. 1987. Children of divorce: Report of a ten-year follow-up of older children and adolescents. *American Journal of Orthopsychiatry, 57,* 444–458.

Wallerstein, J., & Kelly, J. 1979. Children of divorce: A review. *Social Work, 24,* 468–475.

4

Scripts, Transaction, and Transition in Family Relations over the Life Course

William H. Quinn

There is a story of a man who encountered another man late at night in the parking lot. The second man was stooped over looking for something under a lamppost. The first man asked, "What have you lost?", and the other replied, "my car key." The first man noticed that no car was in sight and asked, "Why are you looking for it here?" The car owner replied, "Because the light is better here".

This chapter examines an underemphasized conceptual domain pertaining to family relations over the life course. Presented is a conceptualization of parent and child relationships that examines the context and process of transaction. First, a call is made for the need to understand these dyadic relations as part of a larger family and ecological base. Second, it is suggested that parent and child relationships are organized by mental processes, role images, and scripts. And third, it is suggested that these cognitive processes are intertwined with ongoing behavioral patterns and are central to transitional imperatives present in intergenerational family relationships.

Parent-Child Relationships in a Family Context

Over the years there have been reminders in the literature that mobility in society has not prompted the decomposition of the extended family (Demos 1979; Shanas 1984). Urbanization and increased geographic mobility have not fragmented the extended family. As Hagestad (1981) points out, there is an interweaving of individual lives within a family that affects the lives of all others. This phenomenon remains apparent whether interpersonal influence and change are developmental and normative, or nonnormative and problematic.

It is, then, a matter of life course that all behaviors are part of a larger context. These behaviors are connected in ways that are observable, such as verbal interaction, play, or task completion, or symbolic, such as value transmission, decision-making, obligation, or coordinated cognitive process.

The pattern or modus operandi that exists across the generations in organizing relationships is likely a negotiated process continually open to challenge and subject to change in responses to underlying conflicts of interest (Sprey 1969).

Choosing to study older parents, the old-old, middle age family caregivers, and the like has generated a better understanding of family factors related to patterns of contact (Jarrett 1985; Mancini, Quinn, Franklin, & Gavigan 1980), management (Butler & Lewis 1982), or affection (Quinn & Keller 1983; Spark & Brody 1970). One's choice of central character provides a definition of the study and a link to hypothesis formation; however, such an approach limits the frame necessary to form a more complete comprehension of the context (interpersonal and circumstantial influences) in which a 'central character' realistically shares the stage with other 'central characters'.

Many questions remain unanswered. Some of these include: (1) How are middle-aged family caregiver patterns influenced by spousal relationships, demands of child-rearing, or work demands? (2) How are interaction patterns of middle-aged children and their parents influenced by transactional process over the course of time, or by critical life events such as a divorce, parental abuse, or marital problems of the older parents during child-rearing? (3) What kind of individual developmental demands or issues influence the ebb and flow of transactional process related to emotional closeness or caregiving (that is, the need for autonomous functioning in decision-making)? These issues are obscured because "the light to find the key" in the minds of many is presumed to be represented by a particular generation.

Rather than examine the family mosaic that is comprised of a network of family members of several generations, the temptation is to study a smaller part, such as the 'old-old' or the 'sandwich' generation, as if by removing a piece of the mosaic, the pattern will become more vivid or clear. An increased understanding of the characteristics of these relationships has been accomplished by examining such dyadic relations. Yet by removing a corner or a part from the middle of the tapestry, the visual image is no longer the same and the identity of the fragment is changed. Firth, Hubert, and Forge (1969) drew such a conclusion: "One of the most significant factors of kinship is that it consists of social relationships, the ultimate basis of which is independent of the choice of the central individual involved."

The following case in family treatment illustrates the interweaving of individual lives, which removes from focus or shrinks the image of any central character. Any case material presented in this chapter is for illustration only. All names have been changed and identifying information has been deleted.

Jonathan is a nine-year-old boy who is doing poorly in his school work. The last three weeks of the school year he refused to attend school. Jonathan is polite and respectful of adults. He has a six year old brother, Brian. Sandra, their mother, has been divorced twice but has a cooperative and friendly relationship with her second husband, the father of Jonathan and Brian. He lives nearby and has regular interaction with the children. Sandra lives in a home on land that her mother and father allotted her on their property. Sandra has expressed serious concerns about Jonathan, who rarely sleeps in his own bed through the night. Within the last two years he has become very preoccupied with "Pops," his grandfather, who has heart trouble and an artificial hip. Because Jonathan and Brian live near their grandparents, they have grown up spending a great deal of time with them. Because Pops has physical limitations, he is home a great deal and spends a lot of time with his grandchildren. The boys' grandmother is employed, but devotes most of her nonworking time in caring for her husband (Pops) and Jonathan and Brian. Grandmother admits to spoiling them, an irritant to Sandra, who must see to it that the children learn to be responsible for picking up toys and must limit their opportunities to buy treats and toys. Sandra tries to make certain the boys do not seek solace in their grandparents to complain about her discipline. The boys spend one or two nights a week with Grandma and Pops, and go in and out as if it was their own home. In effect, the boys have two homes. The entire family is worried about Jonathan. They all worry most about school, that he won't go because of his preoccupation with Pops' condition. Jonathan demands to go to Pops' house and kiss him every night, and when Jonathan sees Pops drive out at night to do an errand, he becomes emotionally upset. Just recently, Sandra found out about a book Jonathan's teacher read to the class three weeks before the end of the school year, entitled *Annie and the Old One.* The "old one" in the story is Annie's grandmother, who weaves rugs. While the "old one" is teaching Annie how to weave, she says that when she finishes the rug she will die. Annie is upset about this and sneaks in at night to unravel the rug. When "the old one" discovers this she and Annie discuss death. Sandra's discovery of this event led her to realize that Jonathan's reluctance to go to school was because of the emotional struggle he had with this story, placing his own grandfather in the story as the "old one." Jonathan's mother made it clear to him that she is grateful he loves Pops so much, but worries about Jonathan's fear of losing him. As Sandra puts it, "My dad is like that, people who are around him just love him." She said, "Growing up I was like that too, and he is special to me, too." While Sandra believes she has matured enough to be prepared for her father's death whenever it may come, she is worried that, if Pops' heart fails, Jonathan in particular will not recover from the loss and that this could prompt chronic emotional disturbance.

It is clear that Jonathan's life experiences are embedded in a larger family context of three generations. Jonathan is only a central character if the goal structure in the therapeutic system is to resolve Jonathan's difficulties. However, to understand the family's context, including Jonathan's difficulties, requires the inclusion, physically and conceptually, of the family members who are also actors on the stage.

The interconnections among family generations, as this case so richly documents, organize particular behaviors and perceptions that resonate throughout the family network over time. Often these ties are even greater between older parents and their divorced children who have children of their own (Aldous 1987).

Jonathan has the opportunity to grasp onto a warm, secure, and trusted partner, Pops. Jonathan, at the same time, is also limited because he loves Pops so much that the mere strength of it burdens him, and the lives of other family members. In particular, Sandra is responsible for seeing to it that Jonathan progresses in school without age-inappropriate impediments, like the fear of losing his physically vulnerable grandfather. At the same time, she admires her father for what he symbolizes, and can be sympathetic of Jonathan's fear of losing such a special friend. Yet, Pops and Jonathan have established such a covenant that Sandra fears Jonathan will be unable to separate himself from Pops in time to become autonomous. Will Jonathan be able to establish friendships, achieve school success, or an intimacy with another person and, in general, make an appropriate adjustment into adulthood?

Sandra has obligations to prepare Jonathan for adulthood by promoting more responsible and autonomous behavior. Pops, as well, possesses a desire or need for serving as 'counsel' for his grand-children. Grandma holds an ambiguous role. She can indulge Jonathan and Brian, yet because of their constancy in her household, she must also provide discipline. She also may be a valuable link in teaching family history and tradition to her grandchildren (Gladstone 1988). In a way, each member in this family is a central character, but can only be one if others posture themselves to make it so (such as Sandra's expressing concern about Jonathan). Yet, the configuration in this family shifts like a Rubik's Cube with no central character over time. Instead, an organizing pattern emerges.

Mental Process and Transaction

"What game is reality? First, there must be at least two players who want to play it. They create a large board with lots of objects on it which they agree to call 'The World'. Then they put themselves on the board and invent a set of rules for the objects. These rules they agree to call 'The Laws of Nature'. . . . Now they can play. The goal of the games is for both to agree on how they themselves shall move on the board, even under disagreement. It is clear that A can win only when B wins and vice versa. For if B loses, A is lost, too. The reality disappears and the nightmares begin"— von Foerster (Segal 1986, 148).

It may be productive to consider this family as an illustration of a three-generational structure with complex role configurations. They are complex because their definitions and enactments vary by time. Sandra is a parent to Jonathan and Brian, yet a child to Pops and Grandma, particularly as she is careful to instruct her own parents in discipline of Jonathan and Brian. Pops is a wise counsel and playmate, especially for Jonathan, but an ill older man as well who organizes Jonathan and Grandma to be preoccupied with caregiving. Jonathan is a young boy full of the spirit of adventure, yet possessed with a fear of isolation and loneliness with the potential loss of his grandfather. Grandma must help parent Jonathan and Brian, yet is unwilling to deprive herself of the opportunity to pamper the young boys.

For these family members, the life cycle is a series of steps taken in which they perceive and enact roles that are corroborated by other family members and the environment. Whether it is similar to their peers and befitting of their chronological age is less important. For them it is a realization that the lifetime consists of unfolding. The definition of development, contrary to some who connote it with increased competence, is "to evolve the possibilities of," or "to cause to unfold gradually" (Webster's New Collegiate Dictionary 1981). This family, like all social systems, is in constant motion as each part postures itself in relation to other parts.

Role Images

Parents and children over the life course have constructed and reconstructed mental processes that evolve into particular role images. In any interaction, these role images play a part in the interactional pattern. Put metaphorically, interaction can be viewed as a dance in which two persons establish a rhythm and in a series of steps calibrate each other's language. The role image is the music, in which the steps and the rhythm are organized by this music. A role image, then, influences the interactional dance. In turn, the interactional dance, influences and/or modifies the role image.

This is particularly true for parents and children over the life course as past events, the content of memories, and previous interactions have been translated into a role image. Ferreira (1963) describes these as family myths, blueprints for actions that are necessary in every interaction. Family scripts (Byng-Hall 1988) are similar to blueprints and dictate the pattern of family interaction in particular contexts. Each family member holds a mental representation of each character. Scripts are typically learned through repetition over many years, as parents and children play prescribed parts. Sequences of interaction over time become anticipated as each action is cued in by a preceding one and serves to cue in the next one.

Scripts

Scripts define rules of relationships as they specify who does what with whom and when. As role images are portrayed via these scripts, family interaction evolves with some degree of efficiency as tasks get completed and relevant information is exchanged. Normally each mental representation has a comparator function in which a family member's beliefs are compared to observable behavior. For example, any differential that appears in such analysis leads to an emerging synthesis. An adult child who has always viewed a parent as robust and immortal will likely feel shaken when that parent becomes seriously ill or dies. The comparator function disturbs and subsequently adjusts the role image. The former script can not be adhered to, as the child is now compelled to interact differently as a revision in the family mythology is required. Byng-Hall (1988) refers to this change as moving from a "replicative" to a "corrective" script to recreate a more relevant and useful interaction pattern.

While this moment-to-moment mental processing of relationships is natural and undoubtedly based on a personal desire for bondedness, it can be, nonetheless, problematic at times in the life course. Treatment for Jonathan and his family was conceptualized as an attempt to resolve the presenting problem of Jonathan's fear of Pops' death and his reluctance to leave him for school, by redefining loyalty and relationship role images, and by creating new possibilities. Debts and legacies remain salient issues over the life course (Boszormenyi-Nagy & Spark 1973), such as Sandra's dilemma of allowing her father satisfaction in bonding with Jonathan, yet seeing that Jonathan become independent and not overprotected. These psychological formulations require reformulation to provide a context for a separation-individuation. These evolving parent and child relations are dependent on such reformulations not only in early stages, but across the life cycle (Mahler 1972).

Perception, Context, and Behavior

Some illustrations of these psychological formulations and corresponding scripts are offered. One can visit parents and then leave to have experienced this contraction and expansion. When one visits parents, archaic roles can become alive again. One can be assertive and dogmatic in living with the chosen environment, but visiting parents can turn one into a meek and patronized young child. One can be a competent and rational citizen, and return to a parent's nest to become ignorant and inexperienced. One can live in a peaceful family atmosphere only to return to visit parents and reexperience the interactive tensions of an alcoholic family. Or, one can struggle in a marriage with an inattentive spouse but be softened after a visit with parents who are compassionate and affirming.

For persons in relationships that have endured time, the particulars that calibrate cognition and behavior become more symbolic. Behavior is always noted and used to punctuate subsequent behavior (such as, if you prepare a nice meal I will give you a kiss). However, over time such behavior is based not only on the antecedent behavior, but all of the behaviors before that. Not only will you get a kiss for preparing a wonderful meal, but for preparing all the wonderful meals before that. Mental process representing all prior experiences becomes the organizing force of a relationship.

This conceptual lens, in my view, is a useful one in which to examine parent-child relationships over the life course. This is so for two reasons: 1. Mental process, or cognition, is a vital part of relationship functioning with its focus on perception, attribution, and communication; 2. Relationships over time have a history full of varied experiences that play a part in moment-to-moment interactions. Metcoff and Whitaker (1982) describe these threads in the family's fabric as 'microevents,' sequences of observable interpersonal behaviors—both verbal and nonverbal—that "define, sustain, or provide a springboard for modification of interpersonal relationships" (p. 251). These microevents are "embedded in a broader context. . . and have historical roots in some hypothetical 'macroevent'—the microevent is the visible legacy of the macroevent" (p. 253).

This legacy for Jonathan and his family might be the mandated affectional dependence (Bowlby 1979) for Pops. While Sandra can no longer appropriately adhere emotionally to Pops and achieve separation-individuation, Jonathan can be a stand-in, an invisible loyalty (Boszormenyi-Nagy & Spark 1973). The present interactions serve as microevents in this family's destiny.

This set of experiences is how one comes to "know" someone else. This knowing is not an objective or empirical knowledge, but a synthesis of fragments of shared experiences over time that culminates in an image or series of images about someone else and one's relationship with someone else. von Glasersfeld (1984) proposes that "knowledge does not reflect an 'objective' ontological reality, but exclusively an ordering and organization of the world constituted by our experience." For both parent and child, the relationship of the two is both a consequence of their shared experiences over time, which each constructs an organization of, and an entity that makes a contribution to further relationship development or unfolding. von Glasersfeld goes on to suggest that "experience as well as all objects of experience are under all circumstances the result of *our* ways and means of experiencing and are necessarily structured and determined by space and time and other categories derived from these."

For parents and children over the life course, this principle becomes quite useful. The relationship of an older parent and an adult child is experienced as the synthesis of all previous experiences. The way a parent and child relate is determined by perceptions of previous events, how these events define(d) the relationship, and what significance such a relationship holds. This is not to suggest that a relationship is a product, but instead shared experience which is directed by a reforming of a reforming of mental process which will again be reformed in the future. For example, the story of *Annie and the Old One* penetrated Jonathan's mental process as it pertained to Pops and reformed his relationship despite Pops' unwitting participation in this reforming.

Case Illustration. The following is an example of a family struggling with loyalty issues, yet compelled to reformulate role images. The script includes both replicative and corrective parts. A family referral from a psychiatric hospital came in for family therapy. Lucy is a twelve-year-old girl admitted to the hospital because she refused to leave the house, demanded that curtains and doors remained shut, and believed there were big holes outside with poisonous insects in them. Lucy was given psychotropic drugs in the hospital, and she still takes the medication. Lucy lives with her parents, Mike and Sheila, and her ten-year-old sister, Louise. Louise, her younger sister, is much bigger than Lucy. Lucy and Louise fight a lot, usually about keeping the curtains, windows, and doors closed. Both Mike and Sheila work, so Sheila's mother, who the family calls Little Nanny, comes to supervise when the parents expect to get home late. When Little Nanny is not present and Lucy and Louise have a fight, Lucy calls Little Nanny to help her. Little Nanny tries to intervene over the telephone. Mike's parents, Big Nanny and Papa live in the community also, and visit less frequently but remain involved. Sheila complains that her mother, Little Nanny, over the years has told bizarre things to Lucy. Little Nanny is a small person with a quiet, polite demeanor. Little Nanny has told Lucy that she should watch out for poisonous insects, and that she could fall in a hole outside and never be seen again. Mike and Sheila accuse her of undermining their efforts at helping Lucy be more like a twelve-year-old, to go out to play, eat dinner with the family, and do her household chores. In the third session of treatment, which included the entire three-generational family, Mike, Sheila, Lucy, Louise, Little Nanny, Big Nanny, and Papa, the following transaction occurred.

Sheila: A lot of time Lucy doesn't act like a twelve-year-old. Louise at ten is more grown-up than Lucy. I have told her that if she acts like twelve she'll be treated like a twelve-year-old. A lot of times Lucy calls Little Nanny and discusses things with her as if she was a baby. . .and it isn't fair to her or us as parents.

Therapist: I would like you to talk to Little Nanny.

Sheila: (very cautiously disburbing a family script) When I discipline Lucy I think it is between her and me.

Little Nanny: Go ahead, but you act ugly toward her and cuss her.

Sheila: I do not cuss my child! Wait a minute, Momma (visibly angry at the accusation, now leaning forward and pointing directly at her mother). Every time I spank Lucy you have always interfered, and yes, when I discipline her, she tries to hide behind you. It is my right to do it. (initiation of corrective script)

Little Nanny: Lucy complained her leg was swollen, and was crying . . .

Sheila: Stop! What was I spanked with as a child, Momma?

Little Nanny: A switch.

Sheila: And what else, Momma? What did Daddy spank me with?

Little Nanny: I don't know what your daddy did. (Sheila's deceased father remains a participant in the family's configuration).

Sheila: You were in the house, Momma. If you step between me and my child, why didn't you step in between me and my daddy? (reflecting the mental process of a past event which influences their present relationship) What's the difference? If you want to get into it, we will! (even more angry)

Little Nanny: It wasn't right to spank Lucy the way you did (Lucy begins to cry and shake as she listens to this argument).

Sheila: But she had no right to call Louise the names she does.

Little Nanny: She called you a fool!

Sheila: (courageously, realizing she is revising the script) But the ones she calls Louise are worse, and she needs to grow up. I'm not trying to hurt you, but you know you interfere. Lucy has to grow up and you're not helping.

Little Nanny: You want it that way, it'll be that way.

Sheila: Until Lucy grows up.

Little Nanny: (trying to defuse the tension between the replicative and corrective scripts) I'll just stay away.

Therapist: (recognizing a premature desire to reduce the tension in the conflict) The anger got in the way and Little Nanny got defensive. Can you tell Little Nanny what you want?

Sheila: I would just like, when she's around Lucy, to make her act her age.

Little Nanny: I just try to love her.

Mike: (forming a team with his wife as his own frustration surfaces) Yeah, but let her grow up.

Sheila: Lucy, you think that if you stay a baby, Little Nanny will always love you, and you need to break out of that.

Lucy: You're trying to keep me from seeing her. (crying)

Sheila: No, I'm not trying to.

Little Nanny: I'll just stay away, you're putting the blame on me.

Therapist: I think what you're (mother) asking is, can we redefine your role (to Little Nanny) . . . I don't think they're asking you to remove yourself, but can you be involved in a different way?

Sheila: Yes, when you're with Lucy, treat her as a twelve-year-old.

Therapist: (Asks mother to sit next to Lucy and comfort her, blocking the temptation for Little Nanny to do it and promoting a corrective script).

Sheila: We just want you, darlin', to grow up. Do you want to stay a little girl?

Lucy: Yes. (holding on to a replicated script)

Mike: We're not going to live forever, sugar, and we just want you to grow up.

Sheila: And Little Nanny has to want you to grow up, too.

In this interaction, extreme hostility and resentment is expressed by Sheila toward Little Nanny, her own mother. Little Nanny appeared to remain calm, though her comment that she would just stay away if she wasn't needed was her way of expressing her own hurt feelings. Members of the family do not wish Little Nanny, Big Nanny, or Papa to stay away. However, Mike and Sheila both desire more room to function as parents and to have their parenting decisions respected by Little Nanny. Sheila describes her relationship with her own mother when growing up as not close, but civilized. One could speculate that Little Nanny may feel guilty about her parenting of Sheila or her lack of warmth and now wants to make up for it by warmly parenting Lucy. Nonetheless, what is evident is that Sheila and Little Nanny have a need to resolve longstanding issues by revising a script in order to free Lucy from her mother and grandmother's conflict. Only then will Lucy be permitted to be released as Little Nanny's protector and begin to participate more in her social world. Furthermore, this correction will prompt further corrections in the script between Little Nanny and Lucy, which will promote a reforming of mental process leading to a different role image.

Families have 'role images' (Byng-Hall 1988) that are accepted by the family group as representing each member. Each family member is then provided with an assigned role, in particular interactions with others who reflect a role, an identity—who they are and are not, and in their personal expectations. Over time, role images can remain steadfast or they can be softened or converted via life experience, social influences, or renegotiation. Even if they appear steadfast, or consistent, such consistency is still an outcome of a reforming of experience.

In the case of parent-child relations, this notion is useful in understanding how each person determines meaning. Furthermore, it is a useful way of beginning to comprehend the complexity of parent-child relations over the life course. This constructivist view "to social interaction . . . stresses the interplay of shared and individual interpretive processes by which individuals define situations and construe the perspectives of others within them in making the anticipations necessary to joint conduct and the coordinated conduct of shared meanings" (Delia 1977, 70).

Transitions

"Shared beliefs are tenacious—nowhere more so than in families" (Byng-Hall 1988, 167).

Any study of relationship development, or unfolding, impresses upon the observer the assumption that there are requirements for change over time. These properties of change are frequently conceptualized as transitional markers. Much of the literature on lifespan development places this notion in a central position, such as "anticipated and centrifugal separation" (Stierlin 1974), differentiation, mature dependence, and psychological interdependence (Cohler & Geyer 1982).

What seems to be to social scientists as a cornerstone to understanding psychosocial changes in family relationships, that of successful negotiation within chronological or developmental time frames, has not been accompanied with a similar emphasis on the transactional or contextual domain in which it is embedded. There appears to be more familiarity with the *idea* that this occurs than with the *process* by which it occurs.

Families, like other social groups, are parts of a larger whole and are influenced by whatever is associated with it. As Bridges (1980) points out: "It is characteristic that although their members may consciously try to change the parts that they or others play in the system, the members also often unwittingly perpetuate the system in its current form by undermining attempts to change it" (p. 69). In this latter case, while Sheila attempts to renegotiate with her own mother to lay claim to the 'parent' title, Little Nanny permits Lucy to continue to call her and rescue her when Lucy and Louise fight. While some members work toward change, others work to restrain change. In the next case, Lydia and Tricia persevere for change, while Ken remains adamant about stability and irresponsibility.

In transition the relevance of what is ending is based primarily on a change in self-image or an idea of the world. For Little Nanny, Sheila's request symbolically implies a relinquishing of her significant place in Lucy's life, a request that Little Nanny cannot easily consider. Why has Sheila's request not come sooner, given that Lucy's close bond with Little Nanny has stirred Lucy's anxiety about her environment (poisonous insects in the yard, big holes to fall into) for several years?

Parents and children are bonded and burdened by demands for restructuring roles. Sometimes they feel compelled to execute behaviors reflecting family loyalty (Quinn 1984) while at times they relish the opportunity. These desires can be about supporting a family role (such as Little Nanny's wanting to be Lucy's confidant) or a formidable and possibly extreme set of filial expectations of caregiving. This compelling drive for either the child, adult child, or older parent can be executed to the exclusion of self-identity. The consequences of such an outcome are the restrictions that exist on that adult child's independence, and the role ambiguity perceived by the adult child's own child. In the Jameson case to follow, the father, Ken, could not establish a declaration of 'personal authority' (Williamson 1981) with his own parents, and Tricia was confused about how to relate to Ken, her biological father, who concurrently was the dependent son of her grandparents.

Family transition among the generations is not achieved by forsaking family loyalty. Instead, family loyalty is incorporated into the context of negotiation. This is done when adult children and parents exercise their individuality and reexamine their differing responsibilities which converge.

The following is a recent case seen in family treatment:

Tricia came in for family therapy with her father and grandparents. Tricia is a thirteen-year-old girl who lives with her grandparents, Jack and Lydia, who are both in their late seventies. Tricia is the only child of Carol and Ken. Ken is Jack and Lydia's son. Carol died from childbirth complications with Tricia. Ken, having severe asthma himself, and having physical problems from being one hundred pounds overweight, perceived himself to be incapable of rearing Tricia. Jack and Lydia, who lived in the same town, offered to take care of Tricia. The family came to therapy because of the grandparents' concern with Tricia's acting-out behavior and refusal to follow their household rules. Tricia is presently dating a seventeen-year-old boy with whom she is suspected of having sex. She is also staying out half the night on weekends, ignoring curfew rules, and being secretive about her whereabouts. Tricia's schoolwork has suffered. Lydia is very upset with Tricia and accuses her of being hateful and uncooperative. Jack agrees with Lydia, but is not as vociferous in his expressions of anger toward Tricia. Jack runs a business that Ken has worked in for many years. Ken, who has lived by himself near his parents' house, is quiet and expresses only modest concern. He is presently suffering some heart problems and continues to be a heavy smoker. Ken misses a lot of work because of his health problems.

Jack is in anguish about this because the business is suffering and he considers his son to be incompetent to take over the company. Yet, Jack is sensitive to Ken's health problems; thus, he faces the dilemma of allowing him leeway in his work schedule while coaxing him to get better and be more responsible (a loyalty issue). Lydia, on the other hand, believes Ken to be too ill to manage the business, or for that matter, Tricia. In essence, Lydia is convinced that Ken is unable to be a parent to Tricia, yet proclaims her own futility in moving Tricia toward more age-appropriate and functional behavior. When discussing history in the family, Ken became visibly upset and moved to tears when discussing Carol's death, an event that occurred more than twelve years ago. Yet, Ken does not regret that he didn't take more responsibility in rearing Tricia. Over the years, Ken's role with Tricia has been one of an uncle who visits the house but takes no role in discipline or affection with Tricia. In effect, Jack and Lydia continue to raise persons in two generations, Ken and Tricia. While they are generally quite healthy, they doubt their physical abilities in the future to carry out all the tasks of parenting. And they wonder, "Should we have to do this at our age?" However, their commitment to Tricia and Ken compel them to execute their parental responsibilities.

Family treatment will not be discussed here since this is not the thrust of this chapter. However, some observations might be appropriate to make. It is unlikely that Tricia's rebellious behavior is not connected to life events in this family's history. Carol's death, Ken's health problems and belief that he was, and is, incapable of rearing Tricia, and Jack and Lydia's disappointment in their expectations and hopes for their son, are likely linked to Tricia's acting-out, which is a form of expressing sadness around the family's dilemmas and misfortune. These life events may also propel Tricia into action, as the rebellious behavior provides for a glimpse of breaking away from this tragic social group or providing corrective role images. The role images appear discrepant and dissatisfying. Lydia can not participate with Tricia in a way she thinks is appropriate or benevolant. Tricia cannot easily participate in a relationship with Lydia that is meaningful to her. They each recognize an impending transition.

This illustration documents the context of family functioning that influences the nature of personal development. Lydia's attempt to rescue Ken by offering to be Tricia's mother and defending his spotty job performance have permitted Ken to remain childlike in his demeanor (a quiet and dependent script). Ken relinquishes complete parental authority to Tricia's grandparents. Jack continues to struggle with his fallen hopes for his son in the business while trying to muster enough compassion for his son's physical problems. The parent-child relationship in the older generations has influenced Tricia's personal development, a fear of her father's death, an anger about his lack of involvement with her, and a perception that her grandparents (or parents in effect) cannot adapt to her growing up. Family treatment required an examination of role images that could no longer be replicated. Lydia and Jack interacted with Ken in an imbalanced over- and underfunctioning dance. Ken was perceived as even more dependent than his daughter, Tricia. Ken needed to become more responsible as a guardian and begin to offer guidance to Tricia. While his health limited a physically active involvement, he was encouraged to become more emotionally invested with Tricia by reconciling the unresolved emotional confusion of Carol's (Tricia's mother) death and to be more responsible for the supervision of Tricia.

It would be naive to think that this negotiation is conducted in formal dialogue. Many negotiations by family members with one another are not formalized in the sense that one says, "I think we need to talk about this." Instead, a large part of this negotiation is done via a chosen behavioral change in an effort to correct the script (I speak by behaving). New meanings accompany a new class of action or behavior, which serves as a request or demand for a change in role image. For instance, a child may disobey rules more flagrantly as a message of desired autonomy. A middle-aged daughter may seek employment to convey her unwillingness to step up her caregiving responsibility for an ill older parent. A son may coax his distant father into a fishing trip to reestablish emotional ties. These behaviors convey meanings about the desire for how relationships might be experienced in more satisfactory ways.

Presented here are illustrations of dyadic adjustments. However, these movements resonate through the family system, as in the case of the wife of the distant father who is so pleased at her husband's new commitment to his relationship with his son that it improves their marriage. An adolescent who presses for more autonomy may foster an urgent need for the parents to revise their own parental role or role images. Cohler and Geyer (1982) report that "all too often, both parents and offspring see few alternatives other than rigid independence or continued dependence" (p. 210). What they mean by 'see' has to do with a mental process that contributes to a reforming of the self and other with a corresponding shift in the communication (of microevents) that organizes *and* reflects more functional role images.

Conclusion

The study of human relations requires an acknowledgment that there is always a context that influences the structure and interactional properties. This is akin to the artist's medium, whether it be an actor who inserts oneself into a script, the painter who selects the particular oil or water color for a creation and draws on life experience, or a dancer whose choreography is organized by the setting and particular talents. For parents and children, the context includes, but is not limited to, the history of shared experiences, other family relationships such as the marital, sibling, and other parent or child relationships, and environmental influences such as geography, work, and personal well-being.

This acknowledgement is important because it contributes to a more complete and useful explanation of the nature of a particular parent-child relationship. The mechanics of one's own relationship with a parent or child are associated with the mechanics or workings of the entire network of social relations. A parent's or child's marriage, additional sibling or parent or child relations, and extrafamilial relations all play a part in any dyadic association. Lucy's relationship with Sheila was influenced, partly in a dysfunctional manner from Sheila's standpoint, by Lucy's relationship with Little Nanny. The relationship of Sheila and Little Nanny was influenced by Lucy's relationship with Little Nanny. Sheila's memories of her father's physical punishment play a part in her emotional reactivity in interaction with her mother. In the Jameson family, Tricia's relationship with Ken (her father) is limited or constrained by Lydia's perceived parental responsibility of Ken.

Specifically, in the case of parent-child relations any intergenerational dyadic unit is influenced by other intergenerational dyadic units. Theoretical development, then, or intervention models pertaining to parent-child relations, require the consideration of other familial dyadic units.

This chapter described several selected phenomenon as they might be conceptualized to provide a fuller understanding of parent-child relationships over the life course. First, the nature of any parent-child relationship is influenced by a larger social context must be acknowledged. Second, the nature of any interaction in the parent-child relationship is a consequence of all constructed ideas of previous shared experiences. Thus, previous events such as bonding, playful interaction, guidance and advice, storytelling, and so on are contributors to any ongoing pieces of interaction and mental process pertaining to the relationship. More importantly, such mental process that influences the parent-child relationship is selectively being revised by the experencing person, and managed so as to be made viable in corroboration with another person (von Glasersfeld 1986). This contribution is the formation and reformation of what is called 'reality.' This notion sets an optimistic tone in that it implies change or revision, a particularly appealing possibility as it pertains to relationships of parents and children over the life course. Third, the reality that is constructed cooperatively by participants in a relationship leads to the organization of particular role images or scripts. This mental process leads to a shared reality that influences the dynamics of interaction and perspectives of self and other.

It is suggested here that what social scientists label as 'satisfaction' in relationships or what individuals perceive as a 'good' or 'bad' relationship is in essence the summation of observations each makes about the extent to which their mental constructions reflect or approximate those of the other. When parents and children substantially differ, in the case of filial expectations or responsibility, childrearing, frequency of interaction, goal attainment, or emotional expression, there is present a working hypothesis by each cognizing organism (parent and child) that subjective realities differ to the extent they are perceived as discrepant, or not 'objective.' When parents and children establish some 'objectivity,' it is a process in which "the constructs that constitute subjective reality will be considered 'objective' if they turn out to be viable also in the construction of the cognizing subject's models of others" (von Glasersfeld 1986, 114). Thus, the arena of study in parent-child relations is the association of mental processes, including role images and scripts, that influence transactional patterns and changes over time.

References

Aldous, J. 1987. New views of the family life of the elderly and the near-elderly. *Journal of Marriage and the Family, 49,* 227–234.

Boszormenyi-Nagy, I., & Spark, G. 1973. *Invisible loyalties.* New York: Harper & Row.

Bowlby, J. 1979. Self-reliance and some conditions that promote it. In *The making and breaking of affectional bonds* (103–125). London: Tavistock Publishing.

Bridges, W. 1980. *Transitions: Making sense of life's changes.* Reading, Mass.: Addison-Wesley.

Butler, R., & Lewis, M. 1982. *Aging and mental health* (3d ed.). St. Louis: C.V. Mosby.

Byng-Hall, J. 1988. Scripts and legends in families and family therapy. *Family Process, 27,* 167–179.

Cohler, B.J., & Geyer, S. 1982. Psychological autonomy and interdependence within the family. In F. Walsh (ed.), *Normal family process* (196–228). New York: Guilford.

Delia, J.G. 1977. Constructivism and the study of human communication. *Quarterly Journal of Speech, 63,* 66–84.

Demos, J. 1979. Images of the American family: Then and now. In V. Tufte & B. Meyeroff (eds.), *Changing images of the family* (43–60). New Haven: Yale University Press.

Ferreira, A.J. 1963. Family myth and homeostasis. *Archives of General Psychiatry, 9,* 457–463.

Firth, R.; Hubert, J.; & Forge, A. 1969. *Families and their relatives.* London: Routledge & Kegan Paul.

Gladstone, J. W. 1988. Perceived changes in grandmother-grandchild relations following a child's separation or divorce. *The Gerontologist, 28,* 66–72.

Hagestad, G. O. 1981. Problems and promises in the social psychology of intergenerational relations. In R. Fogel, E. Hatfield, S. Kilser, & J. March (eds.), *Aging: Stability and change in the family* (11–46). New York: Academic Press.

Jarrett, W. H. 1985. Caregiving within kinship systems: Is affection really necessary? *The Gerontologist, 25,* 5–10.

Mahler, M. 1972. On the first three phases of the separation-individuation process. *International Journal of Psychoanalysis, 53,* 333–338.

Mancini, J. A.; Quinn, W. H.; Franklin, H.; & Gavigan, M. A. 1980. Social network interaction among older adults: Implications for life satisfaction. *Human Relations, 33*, 543–554.

Metcoff, J., & Whitaker, C. 1982. Family microevents: Communication patterns for problem solving. In F. Walsh (ed.), *Normal family processes* (251–274). New York: Guilford.

Quinn, W.H. 1984. Autonomy, interdependence, and developmental delay in older generations of the family. In W.H. Quinn & G.A. Hughston (eds.), *Independent aging: Family and social systems perspectives* (21–34). Rockville, Md.: Aspen Systems Corp.

Quinn, W.H. 1983. Personal and family adjustment in later life. *Journal of Marriage and the Family, 45*, 57–73.

Quinn, W.H., & Keller, J.H. 1983. Older generations of the family: Relational dimensions and quality. *American Journal of Family Therapy, 11*, 23–34.

Segal, L.H. 1986. *The dream of reality*. New York: W.W. Norton.

Shanas, E. 1984. Old parents and middle-aged children: The four- and five-generation family. *Journal of Geriatric Psychiatry, 17*, 7–20.

Spark, G. M., & Brody, E. M. 1970. The aged are family members. *Family Process, 9*, 195–210.

Sprey, J. 1969. The family as a system in conflict. *Journal of Marriage and the Family, 31*, 699–706.

Stierlin, H. 1974. *Separating parents and adolescents*. New York: Quadrangle.

von Glasersfeld, E. 1986. Steps in the construction of "others" and "reality": A study in self-regulation. In R. Trappl (ed.), *Power, autonomy, utopia* (107–116). Plenum.

von Glasersfeld, E. 1984. An introduction to radical constructivism. In P. Watzlawick (ed.), *The invented reality* (1–29). New York: Norton.

Williamson, D.S. 1981. Personal authority via termination of the intergenerational hierachival boundary: A "new" stage in the family life cycle. *Journal of Marital and Family Therapy, 7*, 441–452.

5
Older Family Systems: Intra- and Intergenerational Relations

Sarah H. Matthews
Jetse Sprey

Regardless of the question posed, most research on relationships in older families deals with parent-adult child dyads (Brody & Schoonover 1986; Hagestad 1986; Mancini, Blieszner, & Thompson 1986; Thompson & Walker 1984). Questions rarely are asked about each member of a respondent's family, but instead about his or her relationship with a particular family member or, for a parent, with the adult children as a group. We know, for example, that most older parents live within an hour's drive of at least one child (Shanas 1979), but we know little about how many children live nearby, the implicit assumption being that one child is functionally equivalent to three or ten. As another example, we know that when a "frail" elderly parent is unmarried, the "primary caregiver" is most likely to be an adult daughter (Horowitz 1985), but we know almost nothing about the way her brothers and sisters, if she has any, participate. Or again, we know the degree to which elderly mothers and their daughters share beliefs about filial obligations (Lang & Brody 1983), but we do not know whether those beliefs are shared by the daughters' sisters and brothers; that is, whether it applies to other family members or only to the dyad selected for the research. Even studies in which information is collected from more than one adult child or sibling focus on dyadic relations and forego the opportunity to examine networks of ties (Hagestad 1981; O'Bryant 1988; Rosenthal 1988; Townsend & Poulshock 1988).

By singling out specific dyads within families or by treating adult offspring as a group, the existing research draws attention away from the fact that family relations are systemic. Relationships between any two members make sense only within the context of the network of bonds that constitutes the family (Kantor & Lehr 1975). The very idea of a "favorite child" is a

This research is supported by Grant AG03484 from the National Institute on Aging, "Dividing Filial Responsibility in Adult Sibling Groups."

case in point. We argue, then, that information about networks of family ties is essential for understanding the distinct process of its constituent units, including specific dyads. The conception of older families as systems, or networks of interdependent actors, may well complicate the analysis of familial process but ultimately will lead to better theoretical understanding. This brief essay offers a rationale for a more systemic and structural treatment of older families.

After identifying and defining the relevant concepts that guide our thinking, we begin with a discussion of the limitations of the family life cycle model because its main architects, demographers and social psychologists, are the only researchers who have attempted to conceptualize *whole* families and their members' ties to one another through time. We do not suggest this approach be abandoned, but rather that it be supplemented and its limitations clearly understood. The potential of conceptualizing families as networks of interdependent actors is then explored. Where appropriate, examples are drawn from an ongoing research project on how members of adult sibling groups interact with their parent(s) and one another to meet filial responsibilities when at least one of their parents is aged seventy-five or older.

Terms and Concepts

A parent is defined here simply as a person who has produced offspring, while a child is someone who knows at least one parent. Siblings are children who have at least one parent in common. Such terms identify social relationships, so that parenthood implies the actual existence of at least one child, childhood that of at least one parent, and siblinghood that of at least one brother or sister. In fact, of course, people do not stop being parents if they outlive their offspring, and every human always remains someone's child. Siblinghood, however, does not come automatically but depends on the birth of another. It is the relationships among these actors when they are adults on which this chapter focuses. These are the actors who are "directly" tied to one another, with other family members, for example, adult children's spouses and children, and parents' parents, being linked only "indirectly" to at least one of these actors.

The complexity of family ties is often dealt with by using the concept of "role," a descriptive label that, because it directs attention to dyadic ties, is analytically narrow and, for at least some purposes, counterproductive. The notion of role as a set of rights and obligations associated with a particular social position identifies a culturally prescribed and recognized range of tolerable behavioral variation. Such prescriptions can be analytically useful when interactional settings are quite specific, so that it makes sense to view certain changes as role "loss," "gain," or "conflict." However, the notion that parenthood, as a lifelong involvement, and "generation" as a "lineage descent position within families" (Bengtson et al. 1985, 305) can be understood as roles confuses the practice of labeling with conceptual thought. Defining parenthood or other kin bonds as multidimensional roles only adds another label.

There is, regrettably, no concise way in the English language to distinguish between someone who is a parent of one child and someone who is the parent of two, just as there is no way, in a word, to distinguish between someone who has a brother and someone who has a sister. Although it is usually assumed that the feminist slogan "sisterhood is powerful" applies only to women, in fact, strictly speaking, it does not. This presents one of the primary problems in talking about families as networks of interdependent actors. The kinship terms available in the language invite or, perhaps more apropos, seduce one to treat intragenerational as well as intergenerational relationships as interchangeable and symmetrical. This, in turn, tends to blur cognizance of the fact that, for example, being the only daughter among four siblings is quite different from being one of a brother-sister pair.

Although the language indirectly channels our focus toward dyadic ties, relationships like grandparent, parent, child, and sibling "implicate" or "entangle" humans not in the lives of only one other person but in the lives of a web of specific others. As argued before, the image produced in most research on parent-adult child relations is of essentially dyadic intergenerational ties. In fact, when there is more than one parent and/or more than one adult child in an older family, relationships are not dyadic and explanatory power is lost if such ties are the exclusive focus. A realistic understanding of how adult children are affected by and relate to their old parents requires seeing older families as "figurations" or "groupings of interdependent human beings" (Elias 1978, 13). At the extreme, even brothers and sisters who have nothing to do with one another for years remain "implicated" in a system from which there is no real exit short of death.

What is needed, then, are ways to think about social relationships and, in particular, family ties simultaneously as systemic *and* dyadic. This not only challenges the everyday language, but it also raises thorny methodological problems because in most research individuals remain the unit of enumeration and analysis. To clarify our own thinking on this matter, we view persons as linked to their social world or society in two ways: First, by means of their memberships—voluntary or involuntary—in social groups or collectivities and second, through their participation in social relationships with specific others (Breiger 1988). Of course, these two categories are in reality not mutually exclusive. It is clear, for example, that parenthood and other family positions combine membership statuses in institutionalized social arrangements and socially recognized interpersonal relationships. Age cohorts, such as the "baby boom generation," merely reflect a shared membership in a recognized social collectivity. Friends or acquaintances represent relationship positions but, as a type, lack a common membership status. The types referred to here are "ideal" ones, and, as such, not directly amenable to measurement. Their purpose, however, is to illustrate that bonds like parenthood, childhood, or sisterhood, are special in that they combine both membership position and relational status.

The Family Life Cycle Model

The considerable influence of demographers is evident in that almost without exception research on intergenerational relations (and in social gerontology in general) begins with a discussion of changing demographic patterns to provide an empirical foundation and justification. The data analyzed by demographers describe individuals who are categorized into age cohorts. For research on families, the important individual characteristics were identified by Glick (1947) in his initial formulation of the family life cycle model. *Actual* families, however, are not the unit of analysis. Instead, models of the progression of nuclear family members through the life cycle, with the married couple as the anchor, are constructed from cohort data. In Glick's original formulation, only one family life cycle, constructed using the median age at which members of specific age cohorts made transitions between stages, was presented to represent the population. Subsequent research has identified a variety of family life cycles, with the most recent work using computer simulation models to introduce enough variables to capture the complexity of individual decisions that eventuate in many family life cycles (Bongaarts 1987). The goal is to develop a "general, all-encompassing population model" (Hohn 1987, 73).

As significant as this research is, in our view, there are three limitations inherent in this conceptualization that distract scholars from recognizing that families are systems of specific, interdependent actors. The first is its focus on the composition of the household of the marital dyad, with the result that children are included only when they are young. In the initial formulation of the model, it was assumed that marriage ties would continue until the death of one of the spouses so that households and nuclear families were considered to be equivalent. Furthermore, only "stable" marriages are included. The model cannot easily accommodate childless marriages, divorces, single parents, or remarriages (Hohn 1987). Demographers have attempted to overcome these limitations. At this writing, however, the fact that individuals continue to be members of families when all members are adults and are likely to live apart remains outside all but the grossest demographic models and, as such, is ignored.

This conceptual framework, then, does not lend itself to the study of the continuing reciprocity among the aging parents and adult children. Albeit significant, relative to the total life span, the amount of time during which children are minors in relation to one another and their parents is small. Ties among members of nuclear families, however, continue throughout the lives of the members. The model is inadequate for elucidating the ongoing interaction among the offspring and, if there is more than one child, fails to draw attention to the exchanges between or among the adult children—individually and/or together—with the parents.

The second drawback to the family life cycle model is that it has led social psychologists interested in understanding family dynamics to focus almost exclusively on how individuals experience the *transitions* postulated in the model. Stages in the family life cycle are linked to "critical" role transitions primarily in the lives of married couples (Aldous 1978) and are seen as probable "turning points, markers, passages, and seasons—and continual developmental tasks to describe common changes in adulthood" (Berardo 1982, 9). The focus on transitions, of course, cannot be attributed solely to the family life cycle model. Concepts drawn from human development have been a part of social gerontology since its inception (Dannefer 1984). Filial maturity and disengagement are both cases in point.

For nuclear families in which all members are adults, the transition to the so-called "empty nest" stage has received a great deal of attention and serves as the exemplar for the discussion of this point. Much of this literature focuses on the adjustment to the departure of the last child from the parental home and, as such, involves questions concerning the mental states and coping behaviors of the parents (Glenn 1975). Although the "empty nest" is a new stage for both parents and their adult children, the family life cycle model presents it as a "developmental task" for individuals, almost always mothers.

This line of thinking encourages a focus on individuals in permanent "roles" rather than as members of networks whose structural characteristics change. The "role loss" often associated with the empty nest derives its content primarily from what researchers believe middle-aged parents are supposed to feel when an important segment of their so-called parental role is removed suddenly. Moreover, problems associated with the return of an adult child certainly cannot be explained within the narrow analytical context of lost and regained roles (Clemens & Axelson 1985; Shehan, Berardo & Berardo 1984).

A "nest," whether empty or filled to overflowing, may be an appropriate metaphor for a household (although we question that), but certainly is not synonymous with family. Parents, as a rule, remain in the lives of their adult children, and through them to grandchildren. Unlike most birds, which do not recognize their offspring or one another once the nest is empty, there is ample evidence that parent-adult child and sibling bonds rarely are severed completely. Findings from a comparative study of black, Hispanic, and white mothers, in fact, indicate that only among the last was there any evidence to support the notion of the "empty nest syndrome" (Borland 1982). Since not even all white women in the sample experienced distress, the author concluded that further research is needed "to determine whether or not the empty-nest syndrome actually exists" (p. 128). Ignoring the rather obvious reification of the "syndrome" in this conclusion, it seems warranted to suggest that the concept itself is a poor tool for the analysis of what actually happens in families when the last—youngest, younger, or only—child has become (residentially) independent. Even the strictly psychological implications of the departure of a member, therefore, requires analysis within a broader systemic context.

Without doubt, changes occur for parents as well as their offspring once all children are adults, but the reaction of the former must be understood as an adjustment to the structural reorganization of a household: A triadic household structure, for example, may be transformed into a dyadic one that, as Simmel noted many years ago, is likely fundamentally to affect its negotiated order of process. The *family*, however, does not change in size, although when family members do not share a residence on a daily basis, their ties to one another must be characterized differently.

A third drawback of the current family life cycle model is its use of cohort data to describe families. Its proponents seek to provide a blueprint of intergenerational relations based on past and current nuptiality, fertility, divorce, and mortality rates for age cohorts in relation to one another currently as well as in the past and future. A major limitation, then, is imposed by the type of information that is available. Data about characteristics of individuals and household composition are used to simulate family ties. Peter Uhlenberg (1980), for example, uses cohort data about the average age at parenthood and life expectancy to construct the probability of middle-aged sons and daughters having a specific number of surviving parents and parents-in-law. He concludes that in 1976, almost 50 percent of husbands aged fifty-five and wives aged fifty-two could expect to have at least two, up from 20 percent in 1940. The precision of such figures makes one forget that they do not describe actual groups but rather models of the "average" family. As helpful as these summaries are for understanding population structures, family members are affected by their family structure, which may be very far from "average." The use of arithmetic averages to describe attributes of families is questionable. It may make sense, for example, to use the mean purchasing power of categories of families as a basis for comparison. To assume, however, that knowing that the mean number of children for a given class of families is 2.4 would be of much help in the explanation of parent-adult child relations seems far-fetched.

For some purposes simulating families by means of cohort data is appropriate, but for many issues, especially questions pertaining to the dynamics of family process, there simply is no substitute for the study of actual family systems. Families may be characterized as "relations between age groups" (Bengtson et al. 1985), but this may be one of their least significant characteristics. They are sets of individuals who are permanently tied to one another throughout a major portion of their adult lives by dint of cultural prescription (Allan 1979). The "normalized" (Dannefer 1988) family life cycle is not particularly relevant. In fact, we would suggest that actual families whose members all develop "on time" and without hitches are almost always someone else's.

Although it is clear that the population structure of a society constrains the behavior of its members in many ways, it should be equally obvious that the structure of familial systems does this as well. That a much needed focus on the systemic characteristics of families has not been more vigorously pursued is largely because of the conceptual and research-technical difficulties encountered when moving to a level of analysis beyond that of the individual.

Families as Systems of Interdependent Actors

Contemporary proponents of structural analysis see patterned social relationships as a more powerful source of explanation than personal characteristics of system members (Wellman 1988). They interpret all dyadic bonds, for example, in light of the two individuals' additional relations with other network members, so that "to discover how A, who is in touch with B and C, is affected by the relation between B and C. . .demands the use of the network concept" (Barnes 1972, 3, cited in Wellman 1988, 36). It is clear that this way of thinking is directly relevant to most issues raised above.

Obviously, within the limited format of this chapter we cannot begin to solve the conceptual problems connected with the structural analysis of older family systems. We will, however, attempt to show what must be conceptualized and illustrate its complexity by means of examples drawn from an ongoing research project on the reciprocity between adult siblings and their aged parents.

It has been suggested that the *content* of ties between contemporary adult siblings is essentially voluntary. This, however, does not call into question their *relationship* status: Brothers and sisters continue to be related regardless of their feelings toward one another or their residential proximity (Allan 1979). This was supported by the experiences of the initial fifty pairs of siblings—all sisters—whose parent(s) were aged seventy-five or older who reported that *all* adult children in their families were implicated regardless of their actual participation. This affirms Riley's conceptualization (1983) of adult family ties as a "matrix of latent relationships" and directs questioning toward their mobilization under conditions of need or crisis.

One of the above fifty families, for example, included five siblings, of whom two sisters and one brother lived in the same town as their widowed mother. One sister (A) described her arrangement with the mother, who was unable to leave her apartment alone because of severe arthritis:

> She lives in an apartment by herself. She can take care of her personal needs [and] cooking. I see her every day. I take her shopping. She has no friends and she never did. All she has is family. She relies on us which, lately, I've been resenting mainly because I'm not the favorite and I'm the one who gives her the most help and attention. I don't begrudge it, but she doesn't appreciate what I do for her.

Her in-town sister (B) visited their mother regularly and shared many evening meals with her. However, her sister (A) complained:

> I have to go get the food. If my sister doesn't tell her she's not coming, Mother will call me worried sick. Once I called my sister to tell her that she should make a life of her own and not spend all her free time with Mother or else she'd better call Mother every time she doesn't come . . . She was angry when I said those things to her . . . I think I would like to divide up responsibilities with her, but I can't discuss that with her.

The in-town sister (B) told a different story:

> My sister's work schedule gives her freer hours in the daytime. She feels very responsible . . . Everyone does his fair share, but she does a lot. My out-of-town sister [C] says maybe she has taken on too much.

This sister (B) suggested, then, that her "overburdened" sister (A) had *chosen* to do "too much" for their mother. Furthermore, if the two had had a more amicable relationship, the evening meals with their mother might have been seen as a contribution instead of an additional burden (Matthews 1987b).

That a system's perspective is at least important if not essential for understanding the nature of the dyadic ties in this family is clear. Although one of these sisters might be described as subjectively burdened, the feelings of resentment expressed by sister A, are as much directed toward her sister as her mother. Moreover, if the mother had been asked to designate a primary caregiver, it is not clear which sister would have been selected. It is apparent, however, that the "findings" would have been quite different. This suggests that data collected from self-selected dyads within families must be interpreted with care. Furthermore, in this family the division of tasks appears to be based on personality factors—the motivation to do "too much"—as well as on contingency criteria, such as free time, marital status, and proximity. Finally, in attempts to explain why some family members participate and others do not, it is important to remember that if one sibling, for whatever reason, does a given job, others are excused or precluded from doing it. In this case, one sister was freed from grocery shopping because her sister did it. In this specific sample of fifty families, the twenty-three pairs of sisters who had no other siblings were more likely to report sharing equally than were those who had additional brothers or sisters (Matthews 1987a).

A somewhat different example comes from a family comprising a father, a mother, and three sons, two of whom resided in the same community as their parents, while the other lived about two hours away. The two in-town brothers were interviewed. According to one son, the father had Alzheimer's disease, which had caused the deterioration of their parents' longstanding poor relationship. His sympathy was with their father, while he described his brother as being very close to their mother. When she had a stroke, the decision was made to move them to separate board-and-care homes.

This proved unsatisfactory because their mother, once she had regained her strength, was unhappy and, after their father assaulted an aide, they were asked to remove him. The mother lobbied to return to her home without her husband. A compromise was reached: Both parents moved back to the house but into separate bedrooms. The unmarried brother quit his job to live with them, to look after his father, and to keep peace in the household. The married brother who lived nearby would be available to help. Careful monitoring of the parents, particularly of their eating habits, brought order to the household so that after a few months the brother was able to reenter the labor force, but in a job that did not require travel as did his previous one. The two brothers cooperated to ensure that the arrangement worked, although the married brother lost his job unexpectedly which, ironically, left him with less time to spend with their parents. The out-of-town brother apparently did very little, although according to one brother, if the current situation were to change, he expected him to be willing to take one of their parents to live with him, his wife, and three children.

This family illustrates that caring for old parents, in its actual process, is an interplay of contingencies and individual loyalties. It would be very difficult, if not irrelevant, to tease out what percentage of the behavior of the two in-town brothers reflects a feeling of solidarity with both parents, one particular parent, or one's brothers. It also is clear in this case that flexibility—the potential to deal with contingencies as they arise—must be considered a major, albeit difficult to measure, resource of family systems. The emphasis that some family scholars have placed on "predictability" of family members' life cycles as a major condition of familial stability (Hagestad 1986) seems somewhat misplaced. An orderly passage through individual and family life cycles may be something people hope for and, perhaps, naively take for granted because it is easier than living with the idea of randomness. In our study population, however, families whose members aged without incident were rare. Successful coping under such circumstances is not the outcome of planning or earlier learned skills as much as it is a matter of surviving in a more or less tolerable manner by selecting or inventing strategies that somehow work. This case shows that if such plans do *not* work or become impossible because of changed contingencies, something else is tried. This is not to deny, of course, that some families cope better than others, but rather to emphasize that chance events play a significant part in success.

The author of a comprehensive study of kinship interaction over the family life span (Leigh 1982) reports that "adults remain in fairly constant contact with relatives, especially with parents and grown children" (p. 205). In his research the "family life span variable" per se was not significantly correlated with the amount of such interaction but contingency variables, such as geographic propinquity, were. Furthermore, interaction with siblings was likely to depend on the demands of the respective family situations of those involved. Our research supports this view. In line with the argument presented here, siblings will remain, *nolens volens*, implicated in each other's lives, but the degree to which their ties remain or become active, depends on an everchanging progression of contingencies. A final example underlines this claim.

This family consists of a mother in her nineties who has been married for a long time to someone other than her daughter's and son's father. The daughter was fifty-two and the son seventy at the time of the interviews. The daughter lived within walking distance of their mother; the son lived in another state. The son had dissociated himself from their mother (but not from his sister) more than twenty years earlier. When asked when her brother had moved out of town, the daughter answered,

> Fifteen years ago. I haven't seen him since he moved. I have talked to him more since he got divorced [within the previous year] . . . He just called her [Mother] one day, about six months ago. I've always had contact with him over all the years . . . I've never discussed anything with my brother about my parents. We exchange cards every holiday. Every once in a while I send a family picture. My mother has never seen my brother's kids since they were young.

When asked about the division of filial responsibilities between her and her brother and whether it was fair, she answered that it was not shared.

> He hasn't talked to them for years and he is not here, besides. And I stayed here. [Is it fair?] I never really thought of it that way. It just became one of the things I've done all my life. I don't resent my brother. I just think that what he is doing is stupid—not talking to your parents. And now he blames his ex-wife. And now I don't think he is talking to his children . . . And I don't want him to come here. I don't want to have to take care of him *and* my parents. They're enough. Does that sound mean?

Apparently, then, "implication," as we use the concept, is understood by members of older families, and the potential that latent ties may become active is recognized as an ever present possibility.

In Conclusion

In this conceptual treatise the argument was presented during the course of the chapter and, therefore, does not require a long conclusion. Nevertheless, a few final comments are in order. First, we suggest that the "average" family implicit in demographers' abstract conceptions of inter-cohort relationships is potentially misleading because it suggests that the significant, structural characteristics of families are known. Family members as nonrelated, isolated entities, indeed, can be treated as cohort members. Conclusions drawn, however, do not pertain to family systems. Parents and children, brothers and sisters, see themselves as members of generations and families in *relation to very specific others*. Fitting them in birth cohorts may reveal aspects of the society of which they are a part, but does not provide clues to the way in which they see and interact with one another.

Second, we have used the term structure loosely and often synonymously with system and network. In the interest of brevity, any discussion of the complex research methodology of structuralism (Wellman 1988) was avoided. Instead, our main concern has been to convey an approach implicit in the analytical ideas of structure, network, and, more broadly, system. All these terms incorporate "individual perceptions of social structure into larger concepts that subsume these same individual perspectives" (Howell 1988, 62). We argued, for example, that belonging to culturally recognized membership and/or relationship positions implicates individuals. If one wishes to explain family members' behavior, collectively and individually, the social system of which they are a part first must be identified and described in its totality, even if not all of its members are to be questioned or observed. This will lead to more realistic and relevant explanations of why and how specific family members maintain their close relationships and provide clues to the circumstances under which familial ties become or remain active. For example, the cases cited earlier indicate that adult children who take a disproportionate share of the responsibility for an older parent are not necessarily participants in self-selected familial dyads.

Third, the past three decades of research above all have shown older families to be relatively stable even though the mutual ties of their members on both structural and affective dimensions tend to change continuously, sometimes in response to one another, more often, however, as a result of extrafamilial commitments. It is because of this adaptive potential that the image of families as sets of latent relationships (Riley 1983) is apropos. To it, however, we wish to attach an element of perpetual uncertainty and randomness, kept alive through contingencies and chance occurrences. Predictability and the expectation of being able to cope can be seen as reflecting perceptions—or illusions—of order and continuity. They manifest faith and hope that things somehow are bound to remain as they should be. This makes a perspective that proposes an orderly life cycle composed of recognizable transitions between predictable stages an appealing one to both participants in and students of the family. In reality, kinship ties are more complicated. Our own conceptualization and research design for studying older families reflect this.

Finally, the notion of "implication" perhaps best exemplifies the argument presented in this chapter. Its synonym—entanglement—is a term that captures our contention that family relations in our society create a web from which there is no escape. While individuals may neglect familial obligations, they cannot wish away family membership. This raises theoretically relevant questions. If we posit, for example, that the parental "nest" is never really empty, how do we explain what goes on between older parents and their departed offspring? If we discard overly simplistic explanations of parental caregiving as an essentially dyadic form of interaction, how do we approach the systemic nature of the continuing reciprocity among parents and adult children? Is it possible to place the realities of neglect and abuse in this systemic context? These questions cannot even be asked, much less answered, within a frame of reference that focuses on individual family members or one that sees the family life cycle as beginning with the marriage of a couple and terminating with the death of its surviving member.

References

Aldous, J. 1978. *Family careers*. New York: Wiley.

Allan, G. 1979. *A sociology of friendship and kinship*. Boston: George Allen and Unwin.

Bengtson, V. L.; Cutler, N. E.; Mangen, D. J.; & Marshall, V. W. 1985. Generations, cohorts, and relations between age groups. In R. H. Binstock & E. Shanas (eds.), *Handbook of Aging and the Social Sciences* (304–338). New York: Van Nostrand.

Berardo, F. M. 1982. Preface: Middle and late life transitions. *The Annals of the American Academy of Political and Social Science, 464,* 9–10.

Bongaarts, J. 1988. The projection of family composition over the life course with family status life tables. In J. Bongaarts, T. K. Burch, & K. W. Wachter (eds.), *Family demography: Methods and their application* (189–212). Oxford: Clarendon Press.

Borland, D. C. 1982. A cohort-approach to the empty-nest syndrome among three ethnic groups of women: A theoretical position. *Journal of Marriage and the Family, 44,* 117–129.

Breiger, R. L. 1988. The duality of persons and groups. In B. Wellman & S. D. Berkowitz (eds.), *Social Structures: A Network Approach* (83–98). Cambridge: Cambridge University Press.

Brody, E. M., & Schoonover, C. B. 1986. Patterns of parent-care when adult daughters work and when they do not. *The Gerontologist, 26,* 372–381.

Clemens, A. W., & Axelson, L. J. 1985. The not-so-empty-nest: The return of the fledgling adult. *Family Relations, 34,* 259–264.

Dannefer, D. 1984. Adult development and social theory: A paradigmatic reappraisal. *American Sociological Review, 49,* 100–116.

———. 1988. What's in a name? An account of the neglect of variability in the study of aging. In J. E. Birren & V. L. Bengtson (eds.), *Emergent theories of aging* (356–384). New York: Springer.

Elias, N. 1978. *What is sociology?* New York: Columbia University Press.

Glenn, N. D. 1975. Psychological well-being in the postparental stage: Some evidence from national surveys. *Journal of Marriage and the Family, 37,* 105–110.

Glick, P. C. 1947. The family cycle. *American Sociological Review, 12,* 187–202.

Hagestad, G. O. 1981. Problems and promises in the social psychology of intergenerational relations. In R. W. Fogel, E. Hatfield, S. B. Kiesler, & E. Shanas (eds.), *Aging: Stability and change in the family* (11–46). New York: Academic Press.

———. 1986. Dimensions of time and the family. *American Behavioral Scientist, 29*, 679–694.

Hohn, C. 1987. The family life cycle: Needed extensions of the concept. In J. Bongaarts, T. K. Burch, & K. W. Wachter (eds.), *Family demography: Methods and their application.* (65–80). Oxford: Clarendon Press.

Horowitz, A. 1985. Family caregiving to the frail elderly. *Annual Review of Geriatrics, 6*, 194–246.

Howell, N. 1988. Understanding simple social structure: Kinship units and ties. In B. Wellman & S. D. Berkowitz (eds.), *Social Structures: A Network Approach* (62–82). Cambridge: Cambridge University Press.

Kantor, D., & Lehr, W. 1975. *Inside the family.* San Francisco: Jossey-Bass.

Lang, A. M., & Brody, E. M. 1983. Characteristics of middle-aged daughters and help to their elderly mothers. *Journal of Marriage and the Family, 45*, 193–202.

Leigh, G. K. 1982. Kinship interaction over the life span. *Journal of Marriage and the Family, 44*, 197–208.

Mancini, J. A.; Blieszner, R.; & Thompson, L. 1986, November. The relationships that older mothers and fathers have with their daughters and sons. Paper presented in Research and Theory Workshop at the Annual Meeting of the National Council on Family Relations, Dearborn, Mich.

Matthews, S. H. 1987a. Provision of care to old parents: Division of responsibility among adult children. *Research on Aging, 9*, 45–60.

———. 1987b. Perceptions of fairness in the division of responsibility for old parents. *Social Justice Review, 1*, 425–437.

Matthews, S. H., & Rosner, T. T. 1988. Shared filial responsibility: The family as the primary caregiver. *Journal of Marriage and the Family, 50*, 185–195.

O'Bryant, S. L. 1988. Sibling support and older widows' well-being. *Journal of Marriage and the Family, 50*, 173–184.

Riley, M. W. 1983. The family in an aging society: A matrix of latent relationships. *Journal of Family Issues, 4*, 439–454.

Rosenthal, C. J. 1986. The differentiation of multigenerational households. *Canadian Journal on Aging, 5*, 27–42.

Shanas, E. 1979. Social myth as hypothesis: The case of the family relations of old people. *The Gerontologist, 19*, 3–9.

Shehan, C. L.; Berardo, D. H.; & Berardo, F. M. 1984. The empty nest is filling again: Implications for parent-child relations. *Parenting Studies, 1*, 67–73.

Thompson, L., & Walker, A. 1984. Mothers and daughters: Aid patterns and attachment. *Journal of Marriage and the Family, 46*, 313–322.

Townsend, A., & Poulshock, W. S. 1986. Intergenerational perspectives of impaired elders' support networks. *Journal of Gerontology, 41*, 101–109.

Uhlenberg, P. 1980. Death and the family. *Journal of Family History, 6*, 313–320.

Wellman, B. 1988. Structural analysis: From method and metaphor to theory and substance. In B. Wellman & S. D. Berkowitz (eds.), *Social Structures: A network approach* (19–61). Cambridge: Cambridge University Press.

Part 2
Parent-Child Dynamics and Interaction

6
Conceptualizations of the Parent-Child Relationship: Solidarity, Attachment, Crescive Bonds, and Identity Salience

Maxine P. Atkinson

I t is a common lament among family social scientists and social geron-tologists that much of our research is atheoretical. Without theoretical foundations, we can perhaps document facts, but those facts have little meaning without a context within which to evaluate them. Without theory we are left with "dated and situation-specific findings" (Blalock 1982) which at best may help us to face simple practical problems in one geo-graphic locale at one point in time. In addition to the paucity of theoretical work in aging and family research, we have also failed to conceptualize parent-child relationships as a life course phenomena. Parent-child relation-ships clearly change over time but our existing conceptualizations are more appropriate for static phenomena (see Hagestad 1984, 1987 for discussions of this issue).

Our most ambitious goal should be to construct theoretical models that allow us to understand the parent-child relationship over the life course. However, the first step in this process is to conceptualize this relationship so that we know what we need to measure. Once we have conceptualized and measured this variable, we can use it in theoretical models as a predic-tor or outcome variable. Until we can conceptualize and measure what it is about the parent-child relationship that we want to explain (or use to explain some other phenenomena), no causal model will be useful or valid. The purpose of this chapter is to document previous and provide new alternative theoretical conceptualizations of parent-child relationships appli-cable to parents and their children from birth of child to death of parent. I begin with a critique of the research program that has thus far contributed

I would like to thank Barbara J. Risman for her critique, and Viktor Gecas, Michael Schwalbe, and Eric Woodrum for advice and comments.

most to our understanding of the relationship between aged parents and their adult children. There is no comparable theoretical tradition for understanding the parent-child relationship at the later stage of the life cycle. I then offer suggestions for alternative conceptualizations of the parent-child relationships over the life course. These alternative conceptualizations include a consideration of the leading theoretical tradition concerned with earlier stages of the life cycle and the social psychological literature on dyadic bonds and self-concept.

As Hagestad (1984) points out, there are two distinct research traditions that address parent-child relationships. One, which Hagestad terms the "omega," focuses on aged persons and their adult children, and the other, termed "alpha," focuses on the relationship between young children and their parents. The two ends of the life course have never been linked, to say nothing of the years in between. However, one research program in the omega tradition has consistently worked toward developing a theoretical conceptualization of the relationship between family members using a life course perspective.

Critique of Family Solidarity

Theoretical Critique

Vern Bengtson and his colleagues propose the concept of family solidarity as the focus of studies of intergenerational family relations, including, of course, parents and children. In addition to its theoretical grounding and life course perspective, this work is important to consider for three reasons: 1) It is probably the most carefully tested and clearly articulated conceptualization currently available in the omega tradition; 2) It is a cumulative, ongoing program of research; and 3) It is a program of research centered on a concept that is well-known and often-used.

The family solidarity model is based on two classic theoretical traditions: structural functionalism and small group theory. The roots of family solidarity can be traced from Durkheim to Homans. Durkheimian notions of mechanical solidarity provide the structuralist roots; similarity among family members is seen as the basis for family solidarity. Initially, (Bengtson, Olander & Haddad 1976) family solidarity was seen as having three interdependent dimensions: associational solidarity, consensual solidarity, and affectional solidarity. Bengtson and his associates define associational solidarity as interaction, affectional solidarity as positive sentiment, and consensual solidarity as extent of agreement or similarity in values, opinions, and beliefs. More recent work (Bengtson & Shrader 1982; Mangen, Bengtson & Landry 1988) adds three more dimensions: the exchange of services or assistance (functional solidarity); norms of family solidarity (normative solidarity); and family size, roles, and propinquity (intergenerational family structure). In earlier work (Bengtson et al. 1976) the last three dimensions (functional solidarity, normative solidarity, and intergenerational structure) were used as predictors of family solidarity rather than as dimensions of the criterion variable.

Although this research program is important and has considerable merit, there are several serious theoretical issues that must be addressed. The notion of solidarity, either on the macro level as Durkheim proposed it or on the small group level as proposed by Homans, is limited in its relevance and utility for understanding family relationships. Bengtson et al.'s conceptualization of solidarity is based on Durkheim's notion of mechanical solidarity. Durkheim believed that in the preindustrialized world communities shared a common world view, and were unified by a collective conscious: a shared system of identities, values, and commitments. Durkheim called these bonds that held such culturally homogenous societies together mechanical solidarity. According to Durkheim's formulation, families shared a common world view not as members of a family but as individuals who were a part of one society. It is more consistent with Durkheimian logic to argue that even within preindustrial societies, interdependence of family members would form the basis of their cohesion or solidarity. The family as a group would more likely be held together because of a division of labor within the family and resulting mutual dependence (such as organic solidarity). Thus, it is the process of differentiation rather than processes of nondifferentiation or similarity that formed the basis of family solidarity even in preindustrial societies. (This concept of interdependence is characteristic of what Durkheim called organic societies.) It is even more problematic to assume that the basis of cohesion is the same for both modern families and preindustrial societies.

The most recent work in the program admits that viewing families as bonded only by mechanical solidarity is a limitation (Mangen et al. 1988). We differ in that I argue that the notion of mechanical solidarity is not simply limited but inapplicable. They do suggest that organic solidarity be "reintroduced." I agree that this would be an improvement.

In addition, there are other problems with the applicability of mechanical solidarity to families. Mechanical solidarity stresses that it is the similarities between group members that bond them together. Family members can be and often are very different from each other. By definition, family members differ in age, cohort membership and generational status. They may also differ on other basic criteria such as socioeconomic status and value orientations. They may also evidence similarity on some attitudinal domains but be dissimilar on others (Glass, Bengtson & Dunham 1986; Troll & Bengtson 1979).

Even theories of solidarity proposed for small groups, derived from Homans, are unlikely to provide clear insights. Families are intrinsically different from other small groups. While solidarity concepts could be relevant to Burgess's (1926) notion of family as "a unity of interacting personalities," families are not *only* a group of interacting personalities. Academic departments, football teams, and play groups of young children are units of interacting personalities; families are a great deal more. For example, the parent role is unique (Rossi 1969) because of its irrevocability. Another unique feature is that neither child nor parent chooses the particular person who will play such an important role in their life. When we consider that the parent-child relationship is both permanent and ascribed, it becomes apparent that theories proposed to describe voluntary and temporary associations are not likely to be fruitful. The relationships are indeed as different as the academic department versus family analogy would suggest.

Methodological Critique

The Bengtson et al. program also provides tests of their conceptualizations of intergenerational solidarity and it is important to consider their methodology to help evaluate the construct. In many ways, the most recent work in this program provides a model of carefully conceived and executed measurement techniques (see especially chapter 3 by Mangen in Mangen et al. 1988). Mangen, Bengtson, and Landry (1988) not only recognize the importance of carefully choosing units of analysis to measure family solidarity but also employ various procedures to compare 1) individuals at different generational positions (the generational level of analysis); 2) family members as a group (lineage level of analysis); and 3) dyads within the family (lineage level of analysis). Still, I believe that because solidarity is a group level concept it is only appropriate to measure it as group level phenomena. While Mangen et al. realize the value of various levels of conceptualization (and earlier work by others in the program clearly recognized that solidarity is a group level construct [Bengtson & Black 1973; Gilford & Black 1972]), they do not recognize the need for consistency between level of analysis in measurement and theory. While this research group has tested the validity of conceptualizing intergenerational relations as solidarity, these tests of a group level phenomena with dyadic measures are not adequate. Unfortunately, it is at the dyadic level where most of their emphasis is placed.

If the fit between the level of empirical analysis and theoretical conceptualization made no difference in the results, we would still need to see that the dimensions of solidarity are interdependent (mutually correlated) to accept the concept as an adequate empirical construct. Here I agree with Bengtson and Mangen's conclusion (1988, 237) that solidarity is not a "higher order construct." The dimensions of solidarity are not correlated nor do the dimensions share common predictors (Atkinson, Kivett & Campbell 1986). For example, Atkinson et al. (1986) found that affectional solidarity is not correlated either with associational solidarity or with concensual solidarity. Mangen and McChesney (1988) note that affect is weakly correlated with association and negatively correlated with geographic proximity.

Despite the recognition that solidarity is a failed empirical construct, Bengtson and Mangen (1988) maintain that solidarity is "extremely useful as a meta-construct designed to organize discussion and add parsimony" (p. 237). It is here that we differ. Given the lack of fit between the level of analysis in measurement and theory, and the inappropriately applied theoretical logic, solidarity is not useful. Solidarity does not help organize our thoughts about parent-child relationships nor more extended intergenerational ties. Thus, on the basis of theoretical and methodological/empirical grounds, I argue that the logic of using solidarity as a criterion variable to describe familial relationships is ultimately flawed.

Still, this research program has made important contributions to our understanding of parent-child relationships. I suggest that future research in this tradition focus on the individual dimensions of the hypothesized solidarity construct as independent concepts in their own right.

Alternative Conceptualizations of Parent-Child Relationships

Choosing Alternative Conceptualizations

Before we can consider parent-child relationships over the life course, we must clearly conceptualize exactly what it is we are going to study. We need a criterion variable. I believe that at this initial stage of research, our criterion variable should reflect dyadic or individual level phenomena for theoretical, methodological, and practical reasons. Theoretically, we need a criterion variable at the dyadic or individual level because we need to ask a basic question that has yet to be adequately addressed: what is the nature of parent-child relationships over time? It is important to understand how the family as a group changes over time and how the larger family network influences dyadic relationships. However, these more complicated questions necessarily follow understanding dyads.

Methodologically, we are not as yet able to adequately measure family level phenomena. Though using an individual as an informant for the group greatly simplifies our technical task, family sociologists have long argued that this tactic is unacceptable because of the lack of validity (Safilios-

Rothschild 1969). Handling data from multiple family members introduces another set of problems including deciding exactly who is to be defined as part of the family. Even if this conceptual issue could be resolved, we would still have the problem of cost for collecting such data and the measurement error and specification problems involved in aggregation (Blalock 1982; Mangen 1988). Thus, at this time, we need a dyadic or individual level criterion variable.

Our criterion variable could represent a number of possible relationship domains given the primary restriction that we must remain on a level of generality applicable over the life course (Hagestad 1984). I suggest we begin with the most basic of questions: What is the nature of parent-child relationships? What is it that motivates parents to continuously deal with their screaming infant, obstinate toddler, rebellious teenager, adult child who "returns to the nest," or middle-aged child who cannot keep a job? Why do adult children continue a relationship with a parent with whom they share no apparent interests and who insists on giving unsolicited advice? Why do adult children provide care for infirm parents even when providing this care disrupts their lives and the lives of their own children and spouse? I suggest that the basic domain we need to consider is that of affect. Within this domain we might consider three possible dimensions or criterion variables: attachment, crescive bonds, and identity salience. I will review each of these concepts and discuss their strengths and weaknesses.

Attachment. Although the concept attachment is most prominently associated with the infant-mother tie (Ainsworth 1967, 1973, 1982; Bowlby 1969, 1973, 1980), several scholars have proposed that the concept is also useful as a way of viewing adult dyadic bonds (for example, Antonucci 1976; Skolnick 1985; Thompson & Walker 1984; Troll & Smith 1976; Weiss 1977, 1982). Weiss (1977) provides the most general definition: attachment is a sense of connection. Weiss used the concept to explain why couples who were divorcing and no longer loved each other would still feel tied to each other. Skolnick proposes that attachment might be a useful way of viewing all dyadic bonds, but particularly the marital bond. She asserts that attachment theory has always been a life span theory that is "a way of conceptualizing the propensity of human beings to make strong affectional bonds to particular others" (Bowlby 1982, cited in Skolnick 1985). Skolnick (p. 2) further characterizes attachment as being "concerned with emotional security; an attachment figure is a person who is counted on to be predictably available, especially in a time of stress." Troll and Smith also suggest that attachment is useful to conceptualize parent-child relationships across the life cycle. They hypothesize that attachment may be the opposite of attraction. Attraction suggests strong interest but the object of the attraction may be easily replaced while the attachment figure may be less interesting but irreplaceable.

The use of attachment as one criterion variable to assess the affective quality of parent-child relationships has several advantages. It meets the two basic criteria of representing a dyadic (or individual) level variable and is applicable over the life course. The concept has intuitive appeal in that it clearly connotes affective ties. Attachment theory is well-established in the child development literature and has been used in research that addresses later life relationships (Thompson & Walker 1984). As a theory it is coherent and has been tested by several researchers (see Ainsworth 1982). Conversely, use of attachment has several disadvantages. There have been few attempts at measuring attachment at any life stage other than infancy. Thompson and Walker provide an exception (see also Troll & Smith 1976) but Walker (1988) cautions that although their measure exhibited high reliability, there was little variance with respondents consistently reporting strong attachment. There have been many problems identified (Antonucci 1976; Skolnick 1985) for this theory to explain infant-mother attachment, including difficulty in operationalization (Cohen 1974). Although the identification of problems is itself a necessary step for theory development, the weaknesses already apparent may be germane to other stages of the life cycle as well. Given that operationalization is difficult at any one life stage, it is difficult to imagine a comparable measure for all life stages. Another weakness of this theory is that it is already closely associated with the infant-mother attachment literature and all the attendant gender biases and political implications. For example, the initial theory and research deals only with infant-mother attachment rather than infant-parent attachment; therefore taking for granted and reifying the current stratified gender system. Authors (see Skolnick 1985) often assume attachment is important for child development and imply that mothers who work outside their homes may be irrevocably harming their children by weakening their maternal ties.

Crescive Bonds. The concept of crescive bonds is much less familiar than attachment although the general notion of bonding is common. Ralph Turner (1970), a contemporary sociological theorist, uses bonding to describe family relationships from mate selection to parent-child interaction and it is his work from which I will draw. Crescive bonds develop over time and exist when an individual feels bonded or connected to another, when no other individual can be substituted, and when the relationship is expected to be ongoing. In Turner's words, crescive bonds "link irreplaceable individuals" and "lock interacting individuals in a continuing relationship" (p. 89). Turner argues that crescive bonds are formed through the processes of identification or acquiring identity bonds. Identity bonds are either partial or complete and partial bonds may develop into complete identity bonds, which Turner calls crescive bonds. There are two types of partial bonds: identification bonds and response bonds. Both types of partial bonds are contingent upon interaction that enhances self esteem. Identification bonds are formed when a person assimilates the qualities of another into his or her self-conception. When these qualities are perceived to enhance that self-conception, a bond is formed. The sources of identification are external and internal. Children are likely to identify with their parents because others identify children in this way. Children will accrue the positive regard of others to the extent that the parents are respected and liked (external identification). Children may also identify with their parents because they see parents as having positive attributes and would like to think of themselves as having the same attributes (internal identification). Thus, if children gain self-esteem from identification with their parents, they form an identification bond with the parents. Response bonds are also partial identification bonds. Response bonds form when an individual reacts positively toward us. We feel good about ourselves when we are responded to in positive ways and we bond to the person who enhances our self-esteem. Parents will bond to their child when the child demonstrates admiration, love, loyalty, and so on. Over time, partial identification and response bonds may develop into complete or crescive bonds. A crescive bond exists when identification occurs regardless of the consequences for self-esteem. Thus, bonds based only on identification that makes us feel good about ourselves are not likely to be stable, while complete identification, which does not require rewards, produces crescive bonds.

Turner also provides a foundation for operationalizing crescive bonds when he suggests different dimensions or forms of crescive bonds. One of the dimensions of crescive bonds is investment in incomplete action; that is, a sense of looking forward to sharing future activities and accomplishments. Parents and children can be seen to invest in incomplete action in a variety of ways such as planning vacations together, dreaming about educational plan for a child, planning for the acquisition of a new home, or simply planning a special dinner or visit. Parents and children across the life cycle can be seen as future-oriented and committed to future joint activities. Another dimension of crescive bonds is a sense of responsibility for other. Turner conceives this sense of responsibility as based less on obligation than sympathy. That is, our behavior is restrained or motivated because of the pain we might inflict on others for committing an act or failing to behave in a certain way. For example, parents may defer trips together without their children because the child might be hurt by being left behind. Adult children may attend a particular church because their aged parents could be hurt by their "defection" to another denomination or religion. A third dimension of crescive bonds, applicable to the parent-child relationship, is the relaxation of inhibitions. Interaction outside the family is usually more formal and restrained than interaction that takes place between parents and their children. Parents and children are freer in their verbal and nonverbal behavior. Turner provides as an example the child who vents anger in the presence of the parent but who would be afraid to do so with a teacher. The child has learned that the parent's anger is temporary and he or she will not be rejected. Appearance rules are relaxed and aged parents may allow their children to see them in states that would humiliate them in the presence of others. (The removal of dentures is a good example.)

Using crescive bonds to conceptualize the parent-child relationship has several advantages. Crescive bonds can exist on a group level but they are also clearly applicable to dyadic relationships. Crescive bonds are consistent with a life course perspective because they connote continued interaction over time. Although Turner was trying to provide a framework for a variety of family relationships, we can certainly focus our attention on the parent-child dyad with this concept. Turner clearly explains how crescive bonds are formed and suggests that identification changes over the life cycle and often develops into crescive bonds as the child and the relationship matures. Thus, the bonding process can be seen as a dyadic developmental process.

Despite the theoretical relevance of Turner's conceptualization of crescive bonds for parent-child relationships over the life cycle, it has several disadvantages. Perhaps the most important is that this is a new direction for family research. I can find no empirical literature nor theoretical application of Turner's work in the family literature. Although the foundation for operationalizing crescive bonds is given, this is only a beginning. Turner clearly asserts that the bonding process is different between parents and children when the child is young, but there is no indication of exactly when crescive bonds could be formed. It is unclear how a young child's identification with a parent could be measured. In short, Turner's conceptualization is theoretically promising but no prior research exists to build upon. However, given the current state of the field, perhaps a fresh breath of air is called for.

Identity and Identity Salience. Using either attachment or crescive bonds as a criterion variable to understand parent-child relationships holds promise. I would like to suggest a third alternative based on the convergence of symbolic interaction and exchange perspectives (Mutran & Reitzes 1984). I see children and parents as being connected because they are a part of each other's self-concept; more specifically, each has an identity as a parent/child in relation to each other. Self-concepts are our definitions of who we are. The self-concept is a mental picture including feelings about the self. Gecas (1982, 3) defines self-concept as "the concept the individual has of himself as a physical, social, and spiritual or moral being." My position is that the self-concept includes components, or identities, based on parent and child roles. Identities are self-in-role meanings such as the self as parent, child, husband, wife, or worker. Identities within the self-concept are related to each other but are hierarchically arranged by their salience (Burke 1980; Burke & Reitzes 1981; Stryker 1980). Parents and children not only form but maintain connections because of the formation of this identity as a parent/child.

A child's self-concept is initially formed in the context of the family. Parents are main actors for the child in the process of defining himself or herself. Even when a child rebels against a parent, the parent is helping to further define the child's self-concept by providing a standard to oppose. Therefore the child is still defining himself or herself in relation to the parent. Indeed, the most rebellious of children (of any age) may be able to rebel because they have a clear and efficacious self-concept. Although socialization is a lifelong process, once the self has been constructed, subsequent interaction and redefinitions of self will be influenced by the initial self-concept (Stryker 1980). Once the self-concept has been established, the parent-child identity and relationship continues, to variable degrees, because of our continuing need for knowledge and affirmation of self. I use our continuing need for knowledge and affirmation of self to explain why we continue to include the identity of parent/child in our self-concept across the life cycle. Then, I use the concept of identity salience, which I suggest we use as a criterion variable, to explain how the quality of the parent-child relationship varies over the life cycle.

Let me explain. We maintain our identity as children/parents because we are intrinsically interested in self and parents/children are sources of important and relevant information about ourselves. Markus (1980) provides as an example of our self-interested focus what she calls the "cocktail party effect." In a crowded room with many simultaneous conversations going on, we pay attention only to the conversation in which we are involved. However, if someone mentions our name, we immediately hear it and are curious. Similarly, parents understand that information about the self is of interest to their children. Children learn about themselves from parents and vice versa. Parents keep "baby books" not only to remind themselves of important events but also to give their children information about themselves. In addition, parents provide information about the family lineage. Indeed, the popular appeal of constructing family genealogies can be interpreted as search for self-knowledge. Adopted children may feel a need to know their biological parents primarily because they want to know themselves. Parents also obtain information about themselves from their children. Not only do parents and children share a common history, children are often believed to reflect parental characteristics, to be "just like them." Children may share such characteristics as a temper, red hair, or mathematical talents. Parents can see themselves as they are and review their youth by interacting with their children. Therefore, one reason parents and children interact and maintain the identity of parent/child throughout their lives is because they reciprocally provide information about each self.

Children and parents may also choose to continue their relationship and maintain the identity of parent/child because they are a source of self affirmation for each other. Whereas Turner (1970) would argue that obtaining rewards from parent-child interaction is only a part of the early relationship, I see continuing rewards as a basis of interaction over the life cycle. Parents are inclined to see and emphasize their child's positive traits because they reflect well on the parent's self. To be an overly harsh critic of one's child is to deny oneself a sense of accomplishment for "successful parenting." This general tendency for parents to perceive their children positively is conveyed to children of all ages directly and indirectly. Thus, children are rewarded with positive evaluation during interaction with parents and choose to continue their identity as child relative to their parent. Parents find continued interaction rewarding because they are able to "see" the fruits of their labor and to forgo their parent identity would require that they give up this reward. The rewards of the parent-child relationship are not only accrued at the dyadic level. Parent-child relationships are valued in our society and parents and children receive rewards from others for behavior which indicates continued commitment to these valued relationships and identities.

I have emphasized the rewards of the parent-child relationship not because I do not see negative affect and conflict in such relationships but rather because my goal is to provide a framework for understanding why relationships continue for lifetimes. We know that most aged parents maintain a relationship with at least some of their children (See Mancini and Blieszner, in press, for a review of the refutation of the alienation hypothesis).

One of the major sources of variation in the quality of the parent-child relationship lies in the extent to which the identity of parent or child is a salient identity. The more salient an identity, the higher the identity is placed on an individual's hierarchy of identities. The salience of the identity should vary not only by individual but within individual self-concepts over time. Why would the parent identity be more salient for some than for others? The parent identity may be of low salience because other identities are more important subunits of the self-concept. Other identities may be more rewarding or less costly than the parent identity. For example, if the worker or spouse identity provides more rewards, then the parent identity may be less salient. Many of us know women who did not marry because they took care of aged or infirm parents. In this instance, the child identity may have been so salient as to preclude the spouse or parent identity. On the other hand the parent identity may be especially salient to us because of other consistent identities. For example, if the spouse identity is salient for a wife, and the parent identity is salient for the husband, the wife will be motivated to increase the salience of her parent identity.

A life course perspective provides us with major categories of variables that might predict the relative salience of the parent/child identity. Individual time, family time, and historical time may predict such variation within and between individuals. Individual time is developmental stage of the individual, family time is life cycle stage of the family, and historical time refers to historical era (Aldous 1978; Hareven 1977). For example, individual time suggests that the child identity may be the most salient at younger ages since children have few other identities. Family time suggests that the child identity may become less salient as an individual becomes a parent and then more salient again as children leave home and aged parents require assistance or attention. Historical time suggests that the era in which one is a parent/child provides the social setting for identity salience. During the 1950s the parent identity may have been more salient for most women than it is during the 1980s.

The concept of identity salience has many advantages as a criterion variable to understand one dimension of parent-child relationships across the life cycle. Identity salience is an individual level variable based on the strong theoretical tradition of symbolic interaction. My use of identity salience as a criterion variable to measure the affective quality of parent-child relationships across the life cycle draws on symbolic interactionism and exchange theory. Mutran and Reitzes (1984) argue forcibly that symbolic interaction and exchange perspectives are congruent and their empirical findings are interpreted using the logic of identity salience. There already exists a literature that addresses the measurement issues and uses the concept of identity salience in empirical research (Burke 1980; Burke & Rietzes 1981; Spenner & Atkinson 1985; Rosenfeld & Spenner in press). The concept can be used for much of the life course. However, its applicability to very young children may be its major disadvantage because preverbal children probably have not developed identities (Gecas 1980).

Conclusion and Implications for Future Research and Theory

It is critical that we develop theoretical conceptualizations of the parent-child relationship that are applicable over the life course. Then, we must devise measurement strategies which allow us to operationalize these conceptualizations. It is only at this point that we can construct theoretical models that allow us to understand parent-child relationships as a developmental phenomena.

This chapter includes a critique of the work that uses mechanical solidarity to conceptualize parent-child relationships. I argue that the theoretical logic for the use of this concept is flawed. I suggest that those who choose to remain within this tradition either focus on the individual dimensions of the construct or move toward conceptualizing parent-child relationships as characterized by organic rather than mechanical solidarity.

I have suggested three alternative conceptualizations based on useful theoretical perspectives that can be used across most, if not all, the life cycle. Attachment, crescive bonds, and identity salience hold promise for future research. As important, they share common characteristics that may enlighten future theoretical work. All suggest that affect is the most relevant general domain. They also share the notion that parents and children are linked because they are important sources of emotional security and are irreplacable actors in each other's lives.

Though we need not commit ourselves to a particular concept to the exclusion of others, it is time that we stop lamenting the absence of theory in family gerontology and proceed with the risky and difficult work of producing it.

References

Ainsworth, M. D. S. 1967. *Infancy in Uganda: Infant care and the growth of love.* Baltimore: Johns Hopkins University Press.

———. 1973. The development of infant-mother attachment. In B. M. Caldwell & H. N. Ricciuti (eds.), *Review of child development research* (Vol. 3, 1–94). Chicago: University of Chicago Press.

———. 1982. Attachment: Retrospect and prospect. In C. M. Parkes & J. Stevenson-Hinde (eds.), *The place of attachment in human behavior* (171–184). New York: Basic Books.

Aldous, J. 1978. *Family careers: Developmental change in families.* New York: Wiley and Sons.

Antonucci, T. C. 1976. Attachment: A life-span concept. *Human Development, 19,* 135–142.

Atkinson, M. P.; Kivett, V. R.; & Campbell, R. T. 1986. Intergenerational solidarity: An examination of a theoretical model. *Journal of Gerontology, 41,* 408–416.

Bengtson, V. L., & Black, K. D. 1973, October. *Solidarity between parents and children. Four perspectives on theory development.* Paper presented at the meeting of the National Council of Family Relations.

Bengtson, V. L., & Mangen, D. J. 1988. Family intergeneration solidarity revisited: Suggestions for future management. In D. J. Mangen, V. L. Bengtson, & P. H. Landry, Jr. (eds.), *Measurement of intergenerational relations* (222–238). Newbury Park, Calif.: Sage Publications.

Bengtson, V. L.; Olander, E. B.; & Haddad, A. A. 1976. The "generation gap" and aging family members: Toward a conceptual model. In J. F. Gubrium (ed.), *Time, roles, and self in old age* (237–263). New York: Human Sciences Press.

Bengtson, V. L., & Schrader, S. S. 1982. Parent-child relations. In D. J. Mangen & W. A. Peterson (eds.), *Research instruments in social gerontology* (115–186). Minneapolis: University of Minnesota Press.

Blalock, H. M., Jr. 1982. *Conceptualization and measurement in the social sciences.* Newbury Park, Calif.: Sage Publications.

Bowlby, J. 1969. *Attachment: Attachment and loss* (Vol. 1). New York: Basic Books.

———. 1973. *Separation: Anxiety and anger* (Vol. 2). New York: Basic Books.

96 • *Aging Parents and Adult Children*

———. 1980. *Loss: Sadness and depression* (Vol. 3). New York: Basic Books.

Burgess, E.W. 1926. The family as a unity of interacting personalities. *The Family,* 7, 3–9.

Burke, P. J. 1980. The self: Measurement requirements from an interactionist perspective. *Social Psychology Quarterly, 43,* 18–29.

Burke, P. J., & Reitzes, D. C. 1981. The link between identity and role performance. *Social Psychology Quarterly, 44,* 83–92.

Cohen, L. J. 1974. The operational definition of human attachment. *Psychological Bulletin, 81,* 207–217.

Gecas, V. 1982. The self-concept. *Annual Review of Sociology, 8,* 1–33.

Gilford, R., & Black, D. 1972. *The grandchild-grandparent dyad. Ritual or relationship?* Paper presented at the meetings of the Gerontological Society, San Juan.

Glass, J.; Bengtson, V. L.; & Dunham, C. C. 1986. Attitude similarity in three-generation families: Socialization, status inheritance, or reciprocal influence? *American Sociological Review, 51,* 685–698.

Hagestad, G. O. 1984. The continuous bond: A dynamic, multigenerational perspective on parent-child relations. In M. Perlmutter (ed.), *Minnesota symposium on child psychology* (Vol. 17). Hillsdale, N.J.: Erlbaum.

———. 1987. Parent-child relations in later life: Trends and gaps in past research. In J. B. Lancaster, J. Altmann, A. S. Rossi, & L. R. Sherrod (eds.)., *Parenting across the life span: Biosocial dimensions* (405–433). New York: Aldine De Gruyter.

Hareven, T. K. 1977. Family time and historical time. *Daedalus, 106,* 57–70.

Mancini, J. A., & Blieszner, R. In press. Aging parents and adult children. *Journal of Marriage and the Family.*

Mangen, D. J.; Bengtson, V. L.; & Landry, P. H., Jr. (eds.). 1988. *Measurement of intergenerational relations.* Newbury Park, Calif.: Sage Publications.

Mangen, D. J., & McChesney, K. Y. 1988. Intergenerational cohesion: A comparison of linear and nonlinear analytical approaches. In D. J. Mangen, V. L. Bengtson, & P. H. Landry, Jr. (eds.), *Measurement of intergenerational relations* (208–221). Newbury Park, CA: Sage Publications.

Mangen, D. J. 1988. Measuring intergenerational family relations. In D. J. Mangen, V. L. Bengtson, & P. H. Landry, Jr. (eds.), *Measurement of intergenerational relations* (31–55). Newbury Park, Calif.: Sage Publications.

Markus, H. 1980. The self in thought and memory. In D. M. Wegner & R. R. Vallacher (eds.) *The self in social psychology* (102–130). New York: Oxford University Press.

Mutran, E., & Reitzes, D. C. 1984. Intergenerational support activities and well-being among the elderly: A convergence of exchange and symbolic interaction perspectives. *American Sociological Review, 49,* 117–130.

Rosenfeld, R. A., & Spenner, K. I. In press. Women's work and women's career: A dynamic analysis of work identity in the early life course. In M. W. Riley (ed.), *Social structure and human lives.* Newbury Park, Calif.: Sage Publications.

Rossi, A. S. 1969. Transition to parenthood. *Journal of Marriage and the Family, 30,* 26–39.

Safilios-Rothschild, C. 1969. Family sociology? A cross-cultural examination of decision-making. *Journal of Marriage and the Family, 31,* 290–301.

Skolnick, A. 1985, November. *The ties that bind: Attachment theory and the social psychology of close relationships.* Paper presented at the National Council on Family Relations Pre-Conference Theory Construction and Research Methodology Workshop, Dallas, Tex.

Spenner, K. I., & Atkinson, M. P. 1985, September. *Work commitment, sex-role attitudes, and women's work: New evidence and a proposed resolution.* Paper presented at The International Sociological Association Research Committee on Stratification and Mobility, Harvard University, Cambridge, Mass.

Stryker, S. 1980. *Symbolic interactionism: A social structural version.* Menlo Park, Calif.: Benjamin/Cummings.

Thompson, L., & Walker, A. J. 1984. Mothers and daughters: Aid patterns and attachment. *Journal of Marriage and the Family, 46,* 313–322.

Troll, L., & Bengtson, V. 1979. Generations in the family. In W. R. Burr, R. Hill, F. I. Nye, & I. L. Reiss (eds.), *Contemporary theories about the family* (Vol. I, 127–161). New York: Free Press.

Troll, L. E., & Smith, J. 1976. Attachment through the life span: Some questions about dyadic bonds among adults. *Human Development, 19,* 156–170.

Turner, R. H. 1970. *Family interaction.* New York: Wiley & Sons.

Walker, A. J. 1988. Personal communication.

Weiss, R. S. 1977. The erosion of love and persistence of attachment. In A. S. Skolnick & J. H. Skolnick (eds.), *Family in transition* (333–341). Boston: Little, Brown & Co.

Weiss, R. S. 1982. Attachment in adult life. In C. M. Parkes & J. Stevenson-Hinde (eds.), *The place of attachment in human behavior* (171–184). New York: Basic Books.

7
Parent-Child Exchanges in the Middle Years: Attachment and Autonomy in the Transition to Adulthood

Constance L. Shehan
Jeffrey W. Dwyer

O ver the last three decades the proportion of young adults between the ages of eighteen and twenty-nine who live with their parents has increased (U.S. Bureau of the Census 1987). In 1987, more than one-third of all young adults shared a residence with their parents, compared to one-quarter in 1960. This trend represents a reversal of a two-decade decrease between 1940 and 1960 (Shehan, Berardo & Berardo 1984). These statistics suggest that the norms regarding the appropriate timing for the transition to adulthood may be changing (Hogan 1980).

Successful navigation through the transition to adulthood involves the development of functional and attitudinal autonomy from parents while maintaining positive relationships with them (Frank, Laman & Avery 1988; Kenny 1987; Moore & Hotch 1981; Moore 1987). Little research on young adults' attachment to and dependence on their parents has been conducted. What we do know about changes in attachment and autonomy during the transition to adulthood is largely based on clinical observations (Frank, Laman & Avery 1988). In this chapter we identify factors associated with college students' functional and attitudinal independence from their parents, their perceptions about the quality of the relationships they have with their parents, and their normative expectations regarding adult children's rights and parents' obligations during the transition to adulthood. Our analysis addresses basic research questions that emerge from a power-dependence framework (Emerson 1962). Our purpose is twofold: first, to provide information that will contribute to a greater understanding of parent-child relations in this stage of the life course; and second, to establish a foundation for the application of social exchange theory to the study of intergenerational relations across the life span.

Autonomy and Attachment Issues in the Transition to Adulthood

Research to date on the transition to adulthood has concentrated on specifying the components of parent-adolescent separation (Frank, Laman & Avery 1988; Hoffman 1984; Moore & Hotch 1981; Moore 1987). Several dimensions of autonomy have been identified. *Functional autonomy* is defined as the ability to manage and direct one's personal affairs with minimal assistance from parents. This concept includes such developmental tasks as graduating from school, getting a job, managing personal finances, and establishing a separate residence. *Attitudinal independence,* on the other hand, refers to the young adult's identification of herself or himself as independent from parents. *Emotional independence* is defined as the absence of an excessive desire for parental approval, closeness, and/or emotional support, and *conflictual independence* refers to the absence of excessive guilt, anxiety, or resentment in one's relations with parents (Hoffman 1984).

There is little empirical information available that addresses variation in rates of attainment of autonomy by social categories such as race and social class. However, there is a growing body of evidence that suggests that gender differences exist. On the emotional dimension, women develop a greater capacity for closeness and empathy and remain more involved with their family relationships (Chodorow 1978). Moreover, women have more frequent contact with their parents after leaving home (Troll & Smith 1976), communicate with them more frequently (Campbell, Adams & Dobson 1984), and feel more closely connected to them (Frank, Laman & Avery 1988; White, Speisman & Costos 1983).

Although gender differences in emotional independence have been established, factors that influence the development of functional and attitudinal independence are not as clear. In one recent study of gender differences in the separation of late adolescents from their parents, women did not differ significantly from men on items that addressed decision-making and feelings of independence (Frank, Laman & Avery 1988). However, census data reveal that young men are considerably less likely to maintain a separate residence. In 1987, among eighteen- and nineteen-year-olds, 83 percent of the men and 70 percent of the women were living with their parents. Among twenty- to twenty-four-year-olds, the figures were 52 percent and 33 percent, respectively (U.S. Bureau of the Census 1987).

Previous research has also found that there are age differences in attachment and autonomy to parents within the young adult period. Older young adults feel more connected to and have a more empathic understanding of their parents (Frank, Laman & Avery 1988). Moreover, the assumption of the adult roles of spouse and parent, which are correlated with age, contribute to young adults' ability to understand their parents.

The impact of parental divorce on children's separation from parents has also been examined in previous research. Children from single-parent homes undergo some of the transitions of the young adult period at earlier ages than those from intact homes (Mueller & Cooper 1986).

Other variables that will be included in our analysis include mother's employment status, respondent's employment status, race, and father's occupation. Mother's employment status is included because previous research revealed that young children of employed mothers are more independent. The impact of respondent's own employment status is important because it indicates the presence of an alternative source of financial resources and should affect young people's ability to maintain a separate residence. Race and social class (as measured by father's occupation) have not been systematically studied in previous studies and are included in this analysis for exploratory purposes.

Parent-Child Exchanges in Young Adulthood: Theoretical Considerations

In previous research, parent-child relations have been effectively examined through the application of various forms of social exchange theory. (See Mutran & Reitzes 1984.) The questions addressed in this chapter emerged from a consideration of central exchange concepts. Using data from an exploratory study of college students, our analysis focuses on parents as providers of valued resources and on young adult children as recipients. Ideally, an exchange analysis would seek information about the reciprocal provision of resources—in this case, by children as well as their parents. Where relevant, we will draw on findings from a study of parents' reactions to living with their young adult children to provide some insight about the costs and rewards identified by parents.

Following the theoretical framework developed by Emerson (1962), college students' dependence on their parents is defined in terms of their reliance on resources provided by parents. Several basic questions are addressed: What rewards are provided by parents to children at this stage of the family life course? What costs do children experience as a result of receiving these resources? What alternative sources are available to replace parental assistance? What norms govern parent-child exchanges during the transition to adulthood? What is considered a fair exchange between parents and young adult children (Blau 1964)? Do young adult children feel entitled to assistance from their parents? How satisfied are children with their relationships with their parents?

In general, this research is exploratory, so it is difficult to hypothesize about findings. Nevertheless, we expect that the basic resource provided by parents to their children while attending college is financial assistance and that college students have few superior alternatives other than scholarships, loans, and/or employment. As a result, they are not likely to be functionally autonomous. The norms governing parent-child exchanges during the transition to adulthood are not as clearly specified as the norms of filial responsibility that govern exchanges between adult children and elderly parents. However, we expect that the principle of equity, the belief that those who are better able to give should give to those less able, operate in these exchanges and that college students do, indeed, feel entitled to such assistance.

Methods

The data used in this analysis are from a convenience sample of 530 undergraduate students enrolled in several introductory-level sociology courses at the University of Florida in 1985. Self-administered questionnaires were distributed in the classrooms at the beginning of a lecture period. Respondents required an average of fifteen minutes to complete the questionnaire.

Variables

The purpose of this analysis is to assess gender differences in functional and attitudinal independence from parents, in perceived quality of relationships with parents, and in adherence to norms that specify parents' and young adult children's responsibilities during the transition to adulthood. Functional independence is a dichotomy indicating whether the respondent has established a separate residence. Those who maintain their own year-round residence are coded 1 and those who live with their parents year round or during summer vacations are coded 0. Attitudinal independence is also a dichotomous variable coded 1 when the respondent considers himself or herself independent from parents.

Respondents' perceptions of the quality of the relationships they have with their mothers and fathers are measured with the following question. "All things considered, how would you rate your relationship with your mother (father)?" Respondents were instructed to circle the number on a horizontal bar that best described their relationship with their mother (father). The left end of the bar, coded 1, was labeled "very poor," and the right end of the bar, coded 10, was labeled "very good."

Two indicators of the normative dimension of the transition to adulthood are included. Both were originally coded on a five-point Likert scale, but have been dichotomized for purposes of this analysis. The first asks whether the respondent believes that adult children who live with their parents for more than four months each year should pay for room and board. Those who agree or strongly agree with this statement are coded 1. Similarly, respondents were asked whether parents have an obligation to allow their adult children to live with them if they are having problems. This is coded 1 when the respondent agrees or strongly agrees that parents have such an obligation.

Also included are several dichotomous variables: gender (1 = female, 0 = male); race (1 = black, 0 = white); employment status (1 = employed, at least part-time, 0 = not employed); mother's employment status (1 = employed, 0 = not employed); father's occupation (1 = professionals and managers, 0 = all others); and parental divorce (1 = yes, 0 = no). Several continuous variables are also included: age (in actual years), number of brothers and number of sisters.

Results

There are 313 females and 217 males in our sample. The women are slightly younger, on the average (19.5 years versus 20.1 years), and are more likely to be employed (32 percent versus 25 percent, respectively). The majority of each group is white (89 percent) and from professional and/or managerial families (59 percent of the women and 62 percent of the men). Roughly two-thirds of the women and men in the sample have employed mothers and over one-quarter of each group are from divorced homes. They have, on average, one brother and one sister.

Descriptive data not shown here reveal interesting differences between women and men on various dimensions of the transition to adulthood. Men in this sample are more likely than women to maintain a year-round residence separate from their parents (47 percent versus 42 percent) and were more likely to identify themselves as independent (40 percent versus 34 percent). They are, however, less likely than the women to be employed (25 percent versus 32 percent), which suggests that they receive financial help from their parents and are not as independent as they would like to believe. Men are considerably more likely than women to believe that parents are obligated to provide a home for their young adult children if the need should arise (53 percent versus 41 percent) and are slightly less likely to believe that young adult children who receive such assistance should pay their parents room and board (29 percent versus 21 percent). Finally, women and men do not differ in their evaluations of the relationships they have with their parents. Both groups rate their relationships with their mothers more highly than their relationships with their fathers.

Some of our research questions will be addressed through qualitative data not presented in tabular form. Identification of the rewards and costs of functional dependence was obtained through open-ended questions that asked, "What benefits would there be from adult children's sharing a home with their parents?" and "What problems might arise if an adult child moved back in with his or her parents?" The pattern of responses to these questions reaffirms the perceived role that parents have in providing emotional and financial support for their young adult children. Half the students identified emotional support and companionship and financial assistance as the primary benefits accruing to young people who depended on their parents in this way. Interestingly, however, these students also mentioned potential benefits for parents who live with their adult children. More than 25 percent of the males and 33 percent of the females identified companionship for their parents as a benefit of the co-residence of adult children and their parents. Apparently, some college-aged children believe the myth of the empty nest syndrome and feel that the presence of adult children in the home has ameliorating affects. The findings of a study by Clemens and Axelson (1985), however, suggest that our respondents have a distorted view of the benefits of co-residence for parents. Over half the parents in that study who had adult children living with them had expected their children to be living away from home after age eighteen. A sizeable minority were unhappy about living with their young adult children and were generally unwilling to have this living situation continue indefinitely.

When asked what problems might arise when adult children live with their parents, the students in our sample focused primarily on the inconvenience to the adult child and failed to mention the problems experienced by the parents. Moreover, they failed to recognize that their own financial dependence could cause their parents worry and discontent. The number one problem from the young adults' perspective was their loss of freedom. Parental concern with schedules and presence at meal times, as revealed in the Clemens and Axelson study, would most likely be interpreted by the adult children as an infringement of their privacy. The students in our study concurred with the parents in Clemens and Axelson's study in anticipating increased parent-child conflict. However, few students anticipated the strain on parental marriages that Clemens and Axelson's respondents experienced.

Qualitative data about the normative aspects of the transition to adulthood are available from responses to open-ended questions that asked, "When is the best time for young people to leave their parents' home and set out on their own?" and "Under what circumstances, if any, is it acceptable for adult children to live in their parents' home?" The majority of students in our sample identified "conventional" ages of independence. Nearly 40 percent mentioned age eighteen or high school graduation and another 16 percent mentioned age twenty-one or college graduation as the ideal time for young people to leave home. There were no significant gender differences. Responses to the question concerning the conditions under which it is acceptable for young adults to live with their parents indicate that financial problems are the major factor allowing the violation of norms concerning the appropriate time for leaving home.

While the patterns revealed by these descriptive statistics are interesting, they do not take into account the influence of other variables. Thus, we present results from multivariate analyses that control for several additional variables associated with functional, attitudinal, or normative dimensions of the transition to adulthood. Logistic regression techniques are used to predict college students' likelihood of maintaining a separate year-round residence, of identifying themselves as independent, and of adhering to beliefs about parental obligations (reported in tables 7–1 and 7–3). Ordinary least squares regression is used to model students' perceived quality of relationships with their parents (table 7–2). Because our efforts are largely exploratory, all relationships significant at $p < .10$ will be discussed in the text.

As shown in Model 1 in table 7–1, there are no gender or racial differences in the likelihood of maintaining a separate residence (our measure of functional autonomy) when other variables in the model are controlled. Age, own employment status, and mother's employment status are significant, however. The older the young adult child, the more likely she or he is to maintain a separate year-round residence, as indicated by the coefficient of 0.44.

Employed college students are 2.89 times more likely to maintain a separate year-round residence than are their nonemployed peers. Students whose mothers are not employed are 1.58 more likely to maintain a separate residence than are children of employed mothers. Given the high proportion of respondents whose fathers are professionals, this finding may suggest that one-earner families in this sample can afford to both forego a second income and provide for separate living arrangements for college-aged family members.

To determine the magnitude of the effect of dichotomous independent variables in logistic regression analyses, as we have done in the preceding paragraph and throughout the remainder of the analysis, the coefficients can be transformed into a log odds ratio (shown in our tables as the middle number in the set of three presented for the effect of each independent variable) by taking its natural antilogarithm. Additionally, when the coefficients for the dichotomous variables are negative, it is more effective to discuss their effects in terms of their contrast or reference categories, which are coded as 0. In our models, for instance, nonemployed mothers (which are coded 0) are the reference category of mother's employment status. Coefficients for the effects of the reference categories can be calculated (for

Table 7–1
Logistic Regression Models for Functional and Attitudinal Aspects of the Transition to Adulthood

Variable	Nonresident	Independent
Intercept	-7.78^a	-3.22
	——	——
	(.001)	(.045)
Gender	-0.15	-0.29
	0.86	0.75
	(.530)	(.185)
Race	-0.28	-0.28
	0.76	0.76
	(.485)	(.433)
Age	0.44	0.13
	1.55	1.14
	(.001)	(.077)
# Brothers	-0.08	0.02
	0.92	1.02
	(.538)	(.884)
# Sisters	-0.23	0.34
	0.79	1.40
	(.058)	(.003)
Status	-0.31	-0.28
	0.73	0.76
	(.188)	(.192)
Mother employed	-0.46	0.03
	0.63	1.03
	(.054)	(.876)
Employed	1.06	0.51
	2.89	1.67
	(.001)	(.032)
Divorced	0.41	0.82
	1.51	2.27
	(.118)	(.001)
Like Mom	-0.09	-0.01
	0.91	0.99
	(.219)	(.928)
Like Dad	-0.04	0.01
	0.96	1.01
	(.440)	(.970)
Mean of Dependent Variable:	.362	.445
Sample Size:	419	426
-2 Log Likelihood:	466.21	541.81
Degrees of Freedom:	11	11

[a]The top number is the logistic regression coefficient, the middle number the odds ratio, and the bottom number the X^2 probability.

example, for mother's employment status, $e^{-(-0.46)} = 1.58$) but are not presented in the tables and, thus, are "implied coefficients."

There are no gender or racial differences in attitudinal autonomy as shown in Model 2 in table 7–1. The logit cofficient for age is 0.13, suggesting that the likelihood of the respondent defining himself or herself as independent increases with age. Employed respondents are 1.67 times more likely to consider themselves independent than are their nonworking counterparts. Moreover, as expected, respondents with divorced parents are 2.27 times more likely to be attitudinally autonomous than are respondents from intact homes. College students who work while in school and those who have experienced family difficulties may have more frequently dealt with situations usually associated with adulthood.

The covariance models reported in columns 1 and 2 in table 7–2 show that there are no gender differences in college students' perceptions of their relationships with their mothers and fathers, controlling for other variables in the model. When the quality of the relationship with mother is the dependent variable (Model 1), only the quality of the relationship with father has a significant positive effect. Conversely, race, age, parental divorce, and quality of the relationship with mother are significant in Model 2. Nonwhites rate their relationships with their fathers less positively. Older respondents report better relationships with their fathers, and children of divorced parents rate their relationship with their father less highly. Additionally, quality of the relationship with mother is positively related to attitude toward father.

Several variables have a significant impact on whether respondents believe adult children should pay room and board, as shown in Model 1 in table 7–3. Employed respondents are 2.03 times more likely to support paying room and board than those who are unemployed. On the other hand, the better the relationship between the repondent and their father, the lower the odds that they support payment of room and board.

Model 2 in table 7–3 shows that the odds of agreeing that parents are obligated to provide housing for their children are lower for women (or, conversely, greater for men). The implied logit coefficient for gender reveals that male respondents are 1.77 times more likely to feel that parents have such obligations. Similarly, nonemployed college students are 1.52 times more likely to support the assertion that parents should provide housing when their children have problems.

Conclusions and Implications for Further Study

The research reported in this chapter has examined the degree of dependence on and attachment to parents during the transition to adulthood and on normative expectations about parental responsibility among a sample of

Table 7–2
Covariance Models for College Students' Perceptions of their Relationships with their Parents

Variable	Mother	Father
Intercept	ᵃ 7.94 (.001)	2.21 (.118)
Gender	−0.04 −0.13 (.411)	0.06 0.29 (.154)
Race	0.02 0.08 (.747)	−0.08 0.60 (.068)
Age	−0.08 −0.07 (.123)	0.08 0.19 (.063)
# Brothers	0.01 0.03 (.754)	0.01 0.02 (.847)
# Sisters	0.04 0.06 (.408)	−0.05 −0.11 (.284)
Status	0.07 0.23 (.132)	0.01 0.03 (.870)
Mother employed	0.07 0.23 (.154)	−0.03 0.15 (.469)
Employed	−0.05 −0.16 (.354)	−0.06 −0.31 (.183)
Divorced	0.05 0.17 (.349)	−0.23 −0.15 (.001)
Like Dad	0.33 0.24 (.001)	——
Like Mom	——	0.31 0.42 (.001)
Adjusted R^2:	.101	.164
Sample Size:	433	433
F – Value:	5.85	9.47

ᵃThe top number is the standardized regression coefficient, the middle number is the unstandardized coefficient, and the bottom number is the p-value.

Table 7–3
Logistic Regression Models for Normative Aspects of the Transition to Adulthood

Variable	Should Pay Parents	Parents Obligated
Intercept	−3.57[a]	1.41
	(.037)	(.362)
Gender	0.33	−0.57
	1.39	0.57
	(.210)	(.006)
Race	0.01	−0.27
	1.01	0.76
	(.974)	(.423)
Age	0.05	−0.06
	1.05	0.94
	(.494)	(.371)
# Brothers	0.33	−0.04
	1.39	0.96
	(.015)	(.743)
# Sisters	0.07	−0.11
	1.07	0.90
	(.588)	(.281)
Status	−0.20	0.03
	0.82	1.03
	(.423)	(.891)
Mother employed	0.17	−0.16
	1.19	0.85
	(.523)	(.449)
Employed	0.71	−0.42
	2.03	0.66
	(.009)	(.073)
Divorced	0.07	0.11
	1.07	1.12
	(.799)	(.634)
Like Mom	0.12	0.10
	1.13	1.11
	(.136)	(.134)
Like Dad	−0.11	−0.07
	0.90	0.93
	(.070)	(.188)
Mean of Dependent Variable:	.202	.463
Sample Size:	431	430
−2 Log Likelihood:	413.24	572.49
Degrees of Freedom:	11	11

[a]The top number is the logistic regression coefficient, the middle number the odds ratio, and the bottom number the X^2 probability.

college students. There were no significant gender or race differences in college students' attainment of functional or attitudinal independence or in the perceived quality of their relationships with their parents. Our findings suggest it is becoming acceptable for young adults past the "conventional" age of independence to not only accept aid from their parents but to feel they have the right to expect such aid. The balance of exchange of goods and services between the college-aged children and their parents appears to be asymmetrical—going primarily from parents to children. The middle-aged parents of the students in our sample are probably at or near their peak earning power, whereas the children are at their lowest. (We have no information about the income of our respondents or of their parents, but as indicated previously, a very high percentage of the students have fathers who are professionals or managers and the majority have employed mothers. Only a minority of the students, on the other hand, are employed even part-time.) Thus, norms of equity seem to be operating. The parents of our respondents are in a superior position relative to their young adult children with regard to economic resources. As a result, they are apparently obligated to provide for them, even though many of the children consider themselves independent. The majority of students in this sample believe that parents are obligated to allow their young adult children to live with them if they have problems and that the adult children should not be expected to pay room and board in return. Males are significantly more likely to adhere to this belief than are women, when other factors are controlled. In general though, students expect financial benefits to accrue to them as a result of living in their parents' home. In fact, financial need is probably their primary motive for living with their parents. They save money while establishing themselves in the working world. Too often, however, they fail to appreciate the fact that the financial gains they feel entitled to may be burdensome to their parents.

What do young adult children offer to their parents in exchange for the instrumental resources they receive? In the short run there may be no direct instrumental return. The primary benefit for parents may be satisfaction in knowing that they are fulfilling their parental responsibility. To what extent are parents able to control their young adult children's behavior when they provide greatly needed resources? For the students in our sample the relevant power domains may include choice of college, dating and choice of mate, place of residence while at school, nonmarital heterosexual cohabitation, choice of major, and ultimately choice of occupation. What strategies can parents use to influence their young adult children's behavior? Threats to withdraw funds may be the only one available, although studies indicate that adult children can be manipulated by fear of loss of parents' love. On the other hand, what strategies can adult children use to circumvent parental authority? One approach is to restrict the amount of time they make available to spend with parents and/or conceal their activities from their parents.

Over the life course, the balance of dependence and power between parents and children shifts. At some point in the life cycle the norms of filial responsibility come into play and children begin to think of themselves as having a responsibility to provide for their parents who had provided for them earlier in life. Why does this reversal in the patterns of exchange and dependence occur? This question calls for a life span perspective on human development and intergenerational relations.

Dependence at the end points of the life span is largely biologically determined—fixed by birth and by any physical and mental deterioration associated with the aging process preceding death. The progression from total dependence in infancy to independence in adulthood to dependence again in old age, however, is governed not only by biological factors but by social factors as well. In our society, the dependence of children on their parents continues past the age at which independence is biologically and psychologically possible. Moreover, near the end of life, older adults often fight to maintain their independence beyond a point at which they are biologically and psychologically capable of sustaining themselves.

A critical issue in the examination of parent-child exchanges over the life span, then, concerns the legitimization of dependence. What factors enter into consideration of the legitimacy of dependency? Financial considerations? Emotional needs? Health? Do the same considerations apply to the elderly as to the young? Norms govern parent-child exchanges and, consequently, determine the legitimacy of children's dependence on parents as well as parents' dependence on children. Norms of equity dictate that family members most able to give should give to those most in need.

Another important issue surrounding parent-child exchanges across the life span concerns the relationship between dependence and power. The person who is more dependent in a relationship is also the relatively more powerless one (Emerson 1962). In infancy, for instance, the child is more or less totally dependent on her or his parents for all the necessities of life. But it is unrealistic to claim that he or she is totally powerless. The infant-parent relationship is truly one of exchange, insofar as the infant has behavioral responses that are valued by the parents. Parental behavior is shaped by parents' desires to elicit valued behavior (such as smiles and words) from their children. In general, though, the relationship between infant and parent is an unbalanced one in terms of power-dependence, with the parent being considerably more powerful.

The power of parents over children (and of children over parents) emerges from four sources (Rollins & Thomas 1979): the child's perception of parent's ability to reward and punish; the child's identification with parents; the child's perception that a parent has a right to control behavior and that the child has an obligation to comply; and the child's perception that the parent has some special knowledge or expertise.

Although intergenerational control or power relations follow a life course pattern, available data generally do not cover periods beyond adolescence (Troll & Bengtson 1979). Information about intergenerational patterns of exchange and affection available from three-generational studies such as *Family Development in Three Generations* (Hill, Foote, Aldous, Carlson & MacDonald 1970) can be applied to the questions outlined above. Most parents and children continue to provide each other with money, gifts, and/or personal services throughout life. The peak period of giving generally occurs in middle age, whereas the peak periods of receiving family aid occurs in childhood and late old age (Troll & Bengtson 1979). A shift in the balance of giving, from parents giving more to children giving more, may only occur when parents can no longer give. The oldest generation typically seeks help with illness and household management and is in a relatively dependent state, receiving more than giving. The middle generation looks for emotional gratification and generally gives more financially than it receives. And the youngest generation needs assistance with child care and financial responsibilities but is high in both giving and receiving other types of resources to other family members (Hill et al.). In regard to alternative sources of resources, all three generations preferred to get help from family members over other sources (Hill et al.). The Minneapolis study also provides information about normative aspects of intergenerational exchanges. The youngest generation tends to adhere most strongly to kinship obligations whereas the oldest generation adheres least strongly.

The foregoing discussion suggests questions that need to be addressed in a life span examination of exchange or power-dependence relations between parents and children. These questions can and should be applied to studies that examine intergenerational relations at all stages of the life course.

Several sets of questions pertain to the resources exchanged by parents and children. First, what is the *nature* of the rewards (resources) exchanged between parents and children? How does the nature of exchanged resources change over the life span? Second, what is the *quantity* of goods/services exchanged between parents and children? Who provides more resources—parents or children? How does the relative amount of resources exchanged between parents and children change over the life span? And third, what *alternative sources* of these valued resources do the children and their parents have at any given stage? How do their alternatives change over the life course? To what extent, then, is there a reciprocal dependency relationship between parents and their adult children?

Several sets of questions pertain to the other bases of family power. First, to what extent do children *identify* with their parents (and thus grant control to them) at any given point in the life cycle? Is the self-identity of children dependent on their ties with their parents? How does this identification change over the life cycle? Second, do children perceive their parents to have a *special knowledge or expertise* that justifies their having control over certain decision areas? How does this perception change over the life span? Do parents perceive their children to have some special knowledge or expertise that justifies their granting control over decision areas? How does this change over the life span? And third, to what extent do children believe that their parents have the right to exercise control over their behavior? Conversely, is dependence (or acceptance of the support offered by another) of children on their parents or parents on their children perceived to be *legitimate*? Is the right to control children's behavior inherent in the parent role and the right to be dependent and to accept parental support built into the offspring role? That is, do these normative aspects of exchange and dependence/power remain in effect throughout the life span of the family members, such that exchange is unilateral or asymmetrical from parents to children throughout the parent's life?

Finally, several other sets of questions pertain to family decision-making processes. First, what life or daily living decisions are negotiated between parents and children at each stage of the life span? Which decisions fall outside of the parent-child relationship? Does the number/proportion of decision areas negotiated outside the parent-child relationship determine the relative autonomy of these family members? How do the nature and number of decision areas negotiated between parents and children change over the family life cycle? And second, to what extent are children's decisions controlled by their parents at each stage of the family life cycle? How involved are parents in their children's decision-making processes? Conversely, to what extent are parents' decisions controlled by their children at each stage of the family life cycle? How involved are children in their parents' decision-making processes? What is the relative impact of the bases of power in determining the extent of parental involvement in children's decision-making and of children in parental decision making?

References

Blau, P. 1964. *Exchange and power in social life.* New York: Wiley & Sons.

Brody, E. 1981. Women in the middle in family help to older people. *The Gerontologist, 21,* 471–480.

Campbell, E.; Adams, G.; & Dobson, W. 1984. Familial correlates of identity formation in late adolescence: A study of the predictive utility of connectedness and individuality in family relations. *Journal of Youth and Adolescence, 13,* 509–525.

Chodorow, N. 1978. *The reproduction of mothering: Psychoanalysis and the sociology of gender.* Berkeley: University of California Press.

Clemens, A., & Axelson, L. 1985. The not so empty nest: The return of the fledgling adult. *Family Relations, 34,* 259–264.

Emerson, R. 1962. Power-dependence relations. *American Sociological Review, 27,* 31–41.

Frank, S.; Laman, M.; & Avery, C. 1988. Young adults' perceptions of their relationships with their parents: Individual differences in connectedness, competence, and emotional autonomy. *Developmental Psychology, 24,* 729–737.

Glick, P., & Lin, S.-L. 1986. More young adults are living with their parents: Who are they? *Journal of Marriage and the Family, 48,* 107–112.

Hill, R.; Foote, N.; Aldous, J.; Carlson, R.; & MacDonald, R. 1970. *Family development in three generations.* Cambridge, Mass.: Schenkman.

Hoffman, J. 1984. Psychological separation of late adolescents from their parents. *Journal of Counseling Psychology, 3,* 170–178.

Hoffman, L. 1974. Effects on children: Summary and discussion. In L. Hoffman & F. I. Nye (eds.), *Working mothers* (126–166). Chicago: Rand McNally.

Hogan, D. 1980. The transition to adulthood as a career contingency. *American Sociological Review, 45,* 261–276.

Kenny, M. 1987. The extent and function of parental attachment among first-year college students. *Journal of Youth and Adolescence, 16,* 17–29.

Moore, D. 1987. Parent-adolescent separation: The construction of adulthood by late adolescents. *Developmental Psychology, 23,* 298–307.

Moore, D., & Hotch, D. 1981. Late adolescents' conceptualizations of home-leaving. *Journal of Youth and Adolescence, 10,* 413–416.

Mueller, D., & Cooper, P. 1986. Children of single parent families: How they fare as young adults. *Family Relations, 35,* 169–176.

Mutran, E., & Reitzes, D. 1984. Intergenerational support activities and well-being among the elderly: A convergence of exchange and symbolic interaction perspectives. *American Sociological Review, 49,* 117–130.

Rollins, B., & Thomas, D. 1979. Parental support, power, and control techniques in the socialization of children. In W. Burr, R. Hill, F. I. Nye, & I. Reiss (eds.), *Contemporary theories about the family, Volume I* (317–364). New York: Free Press.

Shehan, C.; Berardo, F.; & Berardo, D. 1984. The empty nest is filling again: Implications for parent-child relations. *Parenting Studies, 1,* 67–73.

Troll, L., & Bengtson, V. 1979. Generations in the family. In W. Burr, R. Hill, F. I. Nye, & I. Reiss (eds.), *Contemporary theories about the family, Volume I* (127–161). New York: Free Press.

Troll, L., & Smith, J. 1976. Attachment through the life span: Some questions about dyadic bonds among adults. *Human Development, 19,* 156–170.

U. S. Bureau of the Census. 1987, March. Marital status and living arrangements (table 2). *Current Population Reports* (Series P-20, no. 423).

White, K.; Speisman, J.; & Costos, D. 1983. Young adults and their parents: Individuation to mutuality. *New Directions for Child Development, 22,* 61–76.

8

Elderly Parents and Their Children: Normative Influences

Gary R. Lee
Constance L. Shehan

With increasing proportions of our population living to older ages, more and more scholarly attention has been devoted to relations between older and younger generations. Issues involving interactional frequency, residential proximity, exchange of aid and services, and family caregiving for the frail or vulnerable elderly have been studied extensively and intensively. The cultural myth of the "isolated elderly" has been demolished for some time. Ethel Shanas (1979a, 1979b), for example, has shown that the majority of elderly parents in the United States live near at least one child, and see a child or children on a daily or weekly basis. Many other studies have demonstrated that older people who require assistance with the activities of daily living receive the vast majority of such assistance from their families, particularly their adult children (Brody 1981, 1985; Brody & Schoonover 1986; Chappell & Havens 1985; Cicirelli 1983; Hanson & Sauer 1985; Morris & Sherwood 1984; Stoller 1982, 1983).

American culture has always emphasized the import and value of family relations. This is not unique to our culture, of course, and many other cultures such as the Japanese (Palmore 1975) attach much greater value to intergenerational ties. Nonetheless, most Americans of all generations believe adult children should take some responsibility for the welfare of their aging parents (Brody, Johnsen & Fulcomer 1984; Brody, Johnsen, Fulcomer & Lang 1983; Cicirelli 1981; Seelbach 1984), and that families can provide emotional and affective support, along with instrumental assistance, that formal service agencies cannot provide (Chappell & Havens 1985; Quinn 1984).

To this point, our argument paints a rather pleasant picture of correspondence between values and behaviors. Americans value intergenerational relations highly, and for the most part manage to behave in accord with these values. Instances of older persons who are truly isolated from their families are very rare, and few older Americans who require aid or assistance are forced to rely solely on formal agencies.

There are, however, some dark clouds behind these silver linings. One indication of trouble comes from the burgeoning literature on the financial, physical, and emotional strains experienced by adult children who provide care to their aging and ailing parents (Brody 1981, 1985; Brody & Schoonover 1986; Cantor 1983; Horowitz 1985; Lee 1985a). Care of elderly parents is provided willingly, but not without considerable cost in most cases.

Interestingly, less empirical and theoretical attention has been devoted to the consequences of intergenerational relations for the elderly parents. Perhaps this is partly because of the widespread assumption noted earlier that families provide emotional and psychological support to their older members along with instrumental care when needed, and that family relations are therefore an unmixed blessing for them. After all, older persons who are the beneficiaries of care from family members experience the rewards of loving support while their children sustain the costs.

There is some evidence, however, suggesting that this point of view is more than a little simplistic and naive. Exchange theory (Dowd 1975, 1980; Lee 1985b) posits that the unreciprocated receipt of benefits from another is psychologically costly and damaging to self-esteem. Empirically, some recent research has shown that receipt of assistance from children is associated with lower morale and higher depression among older persons, while providing assistance to children increases morale and decreases depression (Scott & Roberto 1984; Stoller 1985). Mutran and Reitzes (1984) found somewhat opposite patterns among widows, who are perhaps more in need of assistance and less able to provide it to their children, but on balance it appears there may be adverse psychological consequences that accompany dependence on children for many older people.

Another related issue here involves the extent to which relations with grown children are really capable of providing emotional support to elderly parents. Quite a few studies have shown that frequency of interaction with children is either unrelated to morale (Blau 1981; Lee 1979; Mancini 1979) or negatively related to the morale of aging parents (Dowd & LaRossa 1982). Frequency of interaction is admittedly a very crude and partial indicator of the nature of intergenerational relations. However, frequency of interaction with friends is positively related to morale among older persons (Lee & Ishii-Kuntz 1987). The latter study also shows that frequency of interaction with friends affects morale positively because it diminishes loneliness; interaction with children has no such effect.

Lee and Ishii-Kuntz (1987) argue that friendship relations affect emotional well-being because these relations are voluntary and involve mutual choice. To be chosen as a friend indicates that one possesses characteristics or qualities that others find desirable; one is chosen as a friend from a virtually infinite field of eligibles. On the other hand, kinship relations, including parent-child relations, are bounded by norms of obligation. Inter-action is expected; alternatives are severely circumscribed or nonexistent. Interaction with kin thus carries few of the psychological benefits that attach to interaction with friends. Furthermore, the aging parent/adult child relationship can almost never be terminated if the costs to either party come to exceed the rewards. In exchange theory terms, there is a high probability that such relations continue even though they are no longer "profitable."

What might make these relations unprofitable, particularly from the point of view of the older generation? There is, of course, the ever-present possibility of conflict or strife, which is more pervasive in intergenerational relations than most of us would like to admit. Interaction may be unsatis-fying because of value conflicts, disagreements over a variety of issues, mutual disapproval, or a thousand other reasons, but must be continued nonetheless because of the norms of obligation noted above. In spite of some strong arguments to the contrary (Aldous 1987; Hess & Waring 1978), parent-child relations are not like friendship relations because we have only our own parents and/or children; they cannot be replaced by more satisfactory or profitable alternatives.

In addition, from the parental point of view, there is the ever-present spectre of dependency. Clark and Anderson (1967) established more than two decades ago that independence is probably the primary value among America's elderly, and that dependence, particularly dependence on their children, is the greatest fear. More recent research has done nothing to disconfirm this. Brody et al. (1983), in a comparison of three generations of women, found that members of the oldest generation were least likely to feel that children should help their elderly parents, most likely to agree that professional services can take the place of family care, most likely to say that they would rather pay a professional than ask a family member for help, and most likely to agree that older people could get everything they need if there were enough government programs.

Note how these dimensions of the value of independence conflict with the typical American emphasis on familistic values discussed above. Ameri-cans apparently believe that families should take care of their less capable members, and a tremendous volume of research indicates that families indeed do so (Brody 1985; Brody & Schoonover 1986; Cicirelli 1981, 1983; Morris & Sherwood 1984). But many people, and perhaps especially the elderly, are more willing to provide such care than receive it. We believe in family responsibility in the abstract, are willing to assume responsibility in concrete cases, but don't want to be a "burden" on our children. This creates something of a paradox: family members would rather sustain the costs than the benefits of family care.

But sweeping generalizations characterizing the normative system of a society as diverse and pluralistic as the United States are always hazardous, and inevitably wrong in some cases. While independence is a paramount value for older persons in our society, there is some dispersion around the central tendency. A few earlier studies have examined this variation, along with some of its antecedents and consequences. Kerckhoff (1966) classified older persons according to the norms they held regarding the degree to which older parents and their adult children should assume responsibility for one another's welfare. One of his more interesting findings was that older persons who espoused norms of nuclear family autonomy had higher morale than those who believed their children should care for them. A similar pattern was found subsequently by Seelbach and Sauer (1977; Seelbach 1977, 1978, 1984).

Note that these relations do not involve help or care actually received from children, but rather the endorsement of norms that say that aging parents are *entitled* to such help. In part, this may reflect the fact that belief in entitlement to family assistance is positively correlated with the need for such assistance (Seelbach 1977, 1978). It may be that older people who believe their children should help them feel less capable and less confident in themselves than do others, thus experiencing diminished morale.

Hypotheses

In the remainder of this paper, we present a new analysis of the antecedents and consequences of the filial responsibility expectations of elderly parents. We hypothesize that filial responsibility norms are held more strongly by those who actually have lower capacities for independence, as indicated by advanced age, poor health, being unmarried, being unemployed or retired, and low education.

We also hypothesize that those who expect greater support from their children have lower morale than others, for at least two reasons. First, higher expectations for filial support indicate little confidence in one's ability to be independent, which is a cardinal value and virtue among older persons. Second, higher expectations are more difficult to satisfy; those who hold them run a greater risk of disappointment.

Methods

The data for this study were obtained from a sample of residents of Washington state aged sixty and older in 1975. The sample was obtained in two stages. First, a "screening letter" was mailed to almost five-thousand households randomly selected from telephone directories covering the entire state. This letter asked whether any members of the household were aged sixty or older, and, if so, whether these persons would consent to receive a questionnaire. Affirmative responses were received from 750 households, containing names of 1,162 eligible individuals. Questionnaires were sent to all potential respondents, and 870 were ultimately returned, for a response rate of 74.9%.

In spite of the relatively high response rate to the questionnaire itself, the sample is neither random nor representative. An unknown number of eligible respondents did not return the original screening letter, so the sample in reality is highly self-selected. Furthermore, some of the respondents are married to other respondents. To minimize the problem of nonindependence of observations this causes, all analyses are conducted separately by sex.

This analysis is restricted to respondents who are or had been married, who have at least one child who does not live with the respondent, and who answered all items pertinent to the analysis. This leaves us with 209 males and 170 females.

The ultimate dependent variable in this study is morale, measured by a six-item Likert scale including items such as, "On the whole, life gives me a lot of pleasure" and "Things just keep getting worse and worse for me as I get older." Scale scores range from 6 (low) to 24 (high). The reliability of the scale (alpha) is .846. Means and standard deviations for this scale, and all other measures employed in this study, are given in table 8–1 below.

Filial responsibility is measured by four items taken from Heller's (1970) "familism scale." These items are: (1) If a person's father has a large medical bill he cannot pay, the son is morally obligated to pay it; (2) It is the responsibility of married children to be with their parents in time of serious illness, even if the children live some distance away; (3) As many activities as possible should be shared by married children and their parents; and (4) Children of elderly parents have as much responsibility for the welfare of their parents as they have for the welfare of their own children. Scale scores range from 4 to 16; higher scores reflect higher filial responsibility expectations. Unfortunately these items are not highly intercorrelated in this data set; the alpha coefficient representing internal consistency is only .548. This has the consequence of making our estimates of correlations involving this variable conservative, assuming that the error is randomly distributed, so our results should be regarded as more suggestive than usual.

Three measures of relations with children are employed here, all of which refer only to children who do not reside with the respondent. The first is an estimate of the frequency with which the respondent sees the most frequently seen child, on a seven-point continuum ranging from once a year or less to once a day or more. This simple measure is highly correlated ($r = .81$) with total number of visits with all children, and shows

Table 8–1
Means, Standard Deviations, and Bivariate Correlations among all Variables

Variable	Age	Education	Health	Employed	Married	Children	Seechild	Give	Receive	Filial	Morale	X̄	S
Age	—	-.05	-.10	-.38*	-.13	-.04	-.08	-.24	.11	.11	.01	68.1	5.9
Education	-.27*	—	.18*	.08	.15*	-.15*	-.04	.10	-.10	-.09	.21*	12.3	3.9
Health	-.19*	.34*	—	.09	.07	-.10	-.07	.00	-.19*	-.06	.39*	3.9	0.9
Employed	-.30*	.13*	.26*	—	.09	.07	.25*	.21*	.03	-.02	.02	0.3	0.5
Married	-.52*	.09	.07	.02	—	.02	.09	.06	-.06	-.03	.06	0.9	0.2
Children	.08	-.22*	-.07	.01	-.05	—	.22*	.14*	.17*	.07	-.04	2.7	1.6
Seechild	-.13*	.02	.07	.16*	.02	.24*	—	.45*	.32*	.06	-.13*	4.1	2.0
Give Help	-.18*	.18*	.14*	.11	.08	.17*	.47*	—	.48*	.10	-.05	4.3	4.0
Receive Help	.20*	-.14*	-.11	-.05	-.17*	.24*	.48*	.38*	—	.25*	-.17*	3.1	3.2
Filial	.15*	.09	-.03	-.05	-.07	-.09	-.02	.05	.12	—	-.07	9.1	1.4
Morale	-.05	.24*	.30*	.03	.09	.05	-.01	-.00	.03	-.08	—	18.6	2.3
X̄	68.1	12.2	3.7	0.1	0.7	2.7	3.9	4.4	3.9	9.1	18.4		
S	6.7	3.3	0.8	0.4	0.5	1.6	2.0	4.0	3.4	1.5	2.6		

Note: Males (N=209) above the diagonal; females (N=170) below the diagonal.

*p < .05 (one-tailed test).

similar relations to other variables in the analysis, so is used here for the sake of parsimony. It also has the advantage of being unaffected by total number of children.

Second, respondents were asked how often they received help from their child(ren) in six different areas: advice, illness, financial assistance, nonfinancial gifts, household tasks, and transportation. Third, they were asked how often they provided help to their child(ren) in each of these areas plus babysitting. Scores were then summed to provide estimates of the frequency of aid received and aid given. Because these estimates are moderately affected by total number of children, the latter variable is included as a control in our analyses.

The other variables included here are age and education (in years), self-rated health (a five-point continuum), and dummy variables representing marital status (1 = married) and employment status (1 = employed). Means and standard deviations for all variables are shown in table 8–1, separately for males and females.

Results

The bivariate correlations shown in table 8–1 lend little support to our hypotheses. Filial responsibility expectations (FILIAL) are positively related to age among women, and to aid received from children among men. Other than these, there are no significant correlations involving this variable. The correlations between filial responsibility and morale are negative as predicted, but very weak, and do not approach significance.

Morale is significantly related to education and health for both sexes. In addition, men who see their children less often and receive less aid from them have higher morale; these correlations are nonexistent among women.

Table 8–2 presents the regression analysis of our measure of filial responsibility, separately for males and females. The results are somewhat different than those implied by the correlation analysis, but again show that filial responsibility is essentially unrelated to most of the variables included here. For men, those with higher expectations actually receive more aid from their children, but this is not the case among women; the effect is in the same direction, but weaker and nonsignificant. Interestingly, women's filial responsibility expectations are negatively affected by number of children.

To some extent, the absence of support for our hypotheses may be caused by the low internal consistency of our scale of filial responsibility. However, the magnitudes of most relationships are so small that, even assuming perfect measurement, it is unlikely that any truly substantial effects would be observed. The safest conclusion from these data is that

Table 8–2
Regression Analysis of Filial Responsibility

Variable	Males		Females	
	B	Beta	B	Beta
Age	.022	.094	.028	.128
Education	.021	−.058	−.043	−.096
Health	.000	.000	.036	.021
Employed	.030	.010	−.003	−.001
Married	.002	.000	.027	.008
Children	.031	.034	−.131*	−.144
Seechild	−.022	−.032	−.052	−.071
Give help	.012	.036	.034	.093
Receive help	.094*	.216	.053	.122
R^2	.072		.060	

*$p \leq .05$ (one−tailed test)

those whose personal resources are limited are no more or less likely than others to expect support form their children in old age.

Table 8–3 presents our regression analysis of morale. This table is a bit more complicated. There are three parts to each panel (male and female). The first two columns show the coefficients (unstandardized and standardized, respectively) for the total sample. The second and third sets of columns differentiate the sample into those below and above the mean, respectively, on filial responsibility expectations. We will discuss these columns shortly.

The first two columns of table 8–3 show that only education and health are significant predictors of morale. Filial responsibility expectations do not affect morale. There are, however, some interesting patterns among coefficients that do not quite reach statistical significance. Women have higher morale if they have more children, receive more aid from their children, and give less aid to them. Although these effects are not significant, owing in part to the small sample size, the pattern they suggest is contrary to our hypotheses based on the value of independence among older persons. For men, the directions are reversed, but the magnitudes are much lower and do not approach significance.

A separate analysis (not shown) indicated significant interaction effects between filial responsibility norms and both frequency of interaction and exchange of aid with children. The four columns on the right of table 8–3 report regression analyses of morale for those below (columns 3 and 4) and above (columns 5 and 6) the mean on the filial responsibility scale. It would

Table 8–3
Regression Analysis of Morale

	Males					
	Total		Low Filial		High Filial	
Variable	B	Beta	B	Beta	B	Beta
Age	.028	.073	.027	.066	.008	.022
Education	.079*	.135	.115*	.210	.018	.027
Health	.885*	.351	.624*	.268	1.391*	.476
Employed	.091	.018	.102	.022	.066	.012
Married	.191	.020	−.457	−.049	.144	.015
Children	.065	.044	.155	.103	−.062	−.044
Seechild	−.104	−.090	−.183*	−.168*	.117	.092
Give help	.010	.018	.055	.095	−.086	−.148
Receive help	−.055	−.076	−.094	−.130	−.054	−.077
Filial	−.034	−.020	—	—	—	—
R²	.190		.209		.265	
N	209		137		72	

	Females					
	Total		Low Filial		High Filial	
Variable	B	Beta	B	Beta	B	Beta
Age	.019	.048	−.009	−.022	.037	.108
Education	.164*	.211	.154*	.202	.295*	.347
Health	.831*	.279	.918*	.311	.441	.144
Employed	−.221	−.032	−.371	−.055	.356	.041
Married	.648	.117	.519	.091	.474	.090
Children	.189	.119	.278*	.169	−.074	−.050
Seechild	−.084	−.066	−.254*	−.189	.321	.272
Give help	−.076	−.118	−.118*	−.178	−.041	−.068
Receive help	.112	.148	.125	.162	.075	.101
Filial	−.102	−.058	—	—	—	—
R²	.156		.187		.255	
N	170		117		53	

*p ≤ .05 (one-tailed test)

be preferable to look at the lower and upper quartiles, for example, but sample size is too small to permit this. Note that dividing the sample at the mean score does not divide the sample in half; there are more cases below the mean than above it. This indicates that the mean is distorted by some extremely high scores; many people who are above the mean are well above it. Nonetheless, this division produces some interesting patterns.

For men, those with low filial responsibility expectations have lower morale if they see their children more frequently. Giving aid to children increases morale, while receiving aid decreases it, although the latter two effects are not quite significant. For those with high filial responsibility expectations, visiting with children is positively related to morale while giving aid to children is negatively related to morale.

The morale of women with low filial responsibility expectations is negatively affected by interaction with children and giving aid to children; the effect of receiving aid is positive. For those with high expectations, the effect of interaction with children is positive, but the effects of aid exchanged with children are smaller. Several of these effects fail to reach significance because of the small sample size, but comparing the effects between the two halves of the sample clearly produces some suggestive patterns.

Women appear more comfortable with being on the receiving end of exchange patterns than men, particularly when their filial responsibility expectations are low. The effects of receiving aid from children, although generally small, are always negative for men and positive for women. Perhaps men are more concerned with independence, while women are gratified by their children's willingness to support them. Although our results are only suggestive, because of the small size of the sample as well as measurement problems, they identify some possibilities that may be worth more systematic attention.

Conclusions and Implications

Norms regarding adult children's responsibilities to their aging parents turn out to be important in a number of ways, but not in the ways we anticipated. They do not affect morale directly, but instead influence the ways in which other factors affect morale.

One of the more interesting patterns in table 8–3 above involves the effects of frequency of interaction with children on morale. As noted earlier, previous studies have reported no relationship between these variables. This analysis suggests that there may be different relationships among different segments of the elderly population, depending on filial responsibility norms. Among those who do not feel entitled to a great deal of support from their children, interaction and morale are negatively related. Among those who do feel entitled to such support, there are indications that the relationship may be positive. The latter effects are not significant in this sample, but significance is difficult to attain with so few cases; among women, particularly, the effect is fairly substantial (*beta* = .272), second in magnitude only to the effect of education.

These findings suggest that those who hold highly familistic norms are gratified by frequent interaction with their children, while those who value independence or autonomy more highly are negatively influenced by such interaction. Close relations with children may raise the spectre of dependence for these persons. But dependence on children is less threatening if one feels entitled to filial support. This is a minority pattern among older Americans, but nonetheless real.

In spite of some promising beginnings in the earlier work of Kerckhoff (1966) and Seelbach (1977, 1978, 1984; Seelbach & Sauer 1977), too little attention has been paid to the normative underpinnings of intergenerational relations. Sweeping generalizations about the norms and values of older persons in our society gloss over important variations. It is clearly insufficient to argue either that older Americans value their independence or that they feel entitled to support from their children; each generalization is true for some and false for others. These two values are to some extent contradictory, although each has been reported to be characteristic of the elderly population.

To understand the meaning and significance of the behavioral dimensions of intergenerational relations, we need to understand the normative context within which these behaviors occur. We have assumed too much and documented too little about these norms. More systematic analyses of normative beliefs, their relations to behaviors and to psychological outcomes, are sorely needed.

Such analyses, of course, must be oriented toward the development and testing of explanatory theory to be meaningful. The perspective of exchange theory (Dowd 1975, 1980; Lee 1985b) has been invoked frequently in this chapter, and its application to intergenerational relations presents an interesting case. Exchange theory is premised on the assumption that actors are motivated to participate in social relations by the desire for "profit"—the excess of rewards over costs. However, as we argued earlier, in a dyadic relation in which the flow of valued resources is exclusively or primarily unidirectional, the "beneficiary" of the exchange actually experiences substantial costs: the costs of dependency.

These costs take at least two interrelated forms. One is that dependency, or the inability to reciprocate, is psychologically uncomfortable, especially for older persons, since it is contrary to the strong value placed on independence in our culture. Second, according to what is perhaps the central premise of exchange theory, the dependence of Actor B on Actor A is equivalent to the power of Actor A over Actor B. As Dowd (1975, 587) has noted succinctly, the older person with few resources has nothing to exchange but "the humble capacity to comply." This is why there is a strain toward balance in exchange relations; neither the provider nor the recipient of resources in an unbalanced exchange is likely to be satisfied with the relationship. Dependence is inherently costly.

It follows that if the costs entailed by a relationship exceed the rewards emanating from that relationship, the actors involved are motivated to either (a) change the parameters of the relationship, or (b) withdraw from that relationship and, perhaps, seek more profitable alternatives. As we noted above, however, actors cannot simply withdraw from family relations. Even if exchanges are unbalanced, as they often are in the case of elderly parents receiving care, assistance, and support from their middle-aged children, they must be maintained. The literature on family caregiving makes it clear that, for most types of services, most older people have few alternatives to their families.

But, as Brody et al. (1983) have shown, family members may be more willing to provide assistance to one another than to receive it. This suggests that, within the family context, the profit motive may be quite secondary to something else, which might be called "altruism" for want of a better term. Altruism, however, cannot explain why older recipients of services from their grown children are not more distressed by their dependency than they appear to be from the data reported here.

Two possibilities suggest themselves. One is that this sample does not contain a good representation of older persons who are truly dependent on their children (or others, for that matter), since it requires a substantial amount of independence to participate in a mailed questionnaire survey. This implies that most parent-child relationships in which the members of this sample participate are fairly close to balanced. We might expect more and stronger negative psychological outcomes in a sample of less capable older persons whose exchanges with their children are more unbalanced.

The second possibility involves the potential inapplicability of exchange principles to intergenerational relations, owing to the nature of family norms. Balanced or equal exchanges, particularly if viewed in small segments, are not necessarily *equitable* exchanges. It may be that, at least in certain circumstances, older persons experience few adverse psychological consequences of dependence on their children because they perceive their children's contributions as equitable compensation for the costs they sustained themselves as parents earlier in their families' histories. In other words, intergenerational exchanges may be unbalanced at both ends of the family life cycle, but balanced and equitable over the entire course of the life cycle. Older persons who have high filial responsibility expectations may be asserting their feelings of entitlement to a return on their investments in their children.

This may explain why the effect of frequency of interaction with children on the morale of their elderly parents is negative for those with low filial responsibility expectations, but positive for those with high expectations (table 8–3). The patterns exhibited by our measures of aid given and aid received are less interpretable in this context, but clearly these variables have no dramatic effect one way or the other. Again, this may be because the truly dependent are missing from our sample.

Exchange patterns within families, and particularly in intergenerational relations, may be different than those involving unrelated persons. This is because the norms pertaining to them, defining appropriate expectations for returns on investments and limiting options for the resolution of unprofitable exchanges, are different. Theorists and researchers need to be aware of the possibility of these differences. Further exploration of the norms surrounding intergenerational relations in the later years of the family life cycle, and of the consequences of these norms for both behaviors and psychological outcomes, is sorely needed.

References

Aldous, J. 1987. New views on the family life of the elderly and the near-elderly. *Journal of Marriage and the Family, 49*, 227–234.

Blau, Z. S. 1981. *Aging in a Changing Society*. New York: Franklin Watts.

Brody, E. M. 1981. Women in the middle and family help to older people. *The Gerontologist, 21*, 471–480.

———. 1985. Parent care as a normative family stress. *The Gerontologist, 25*, 19–29.

Brody, E. M.; Johnsen, P. T.; & Fulcomer, M. C. 1984. What should adult children do for elderly parents? Opinions and preferences of three generations of women. *Journal of Gerontology, 39*, 736–746.

Brody, E. M.; Johnsen, P. T.; Fulcomer, M. C.; & Lang, A. M. 1983. Women's changing roles and help to elderly parents: Attitudes of three generations of women. *Journal of Gerontology, 38*, 597–607.

Brody, E. M., & Schoonover, C. B. 1986. Patterns of parent-care when adult daughters work and when they do not. *The Gerontologist, 26*, 372–381.

Cantor, M. H. 1983. Strain among caregivers: A study of experience in the United States. *The Gerontologist, 23*, 597–604.

Chappell, N. L., & Havens, B. 1985. Who helps the elderly person: A discussion of formal and informal care. In W. A. Peterson & J. Quadagno (eds.), *Social bonds in later life: Aging and interdependence* (211–227). Beverly Hills, Calif.: Sage Publications.

Cicirelli, V. G. 1981. *Helping elderly parents: The role of adult children*. Boston: Auburn House.

———. 1983. Adult children's attachment and helping behavior to elderly parents: A path model. *Journal of Marriage and the Family, 45*, 815–825.

Clark, M., & Anderson, B. G. 1967. *Culture and aging: An anthropological study of older americans*. Springfield, Ill.: Charles C. Thomas.

Dowd, J. J. 1975. Aging as exchange: A preface to theory. *Journal of Gerontology, 30*, 584–594.

———. 1980. Exchange rates and old people. *Journal of Gerontology, 35*, 596–602.

Dowd, J. J., & LaRossa, R. 1982. Primary group contact and elderly morale: An exchange/power analysis. *Sociology and Social Research, 66*, 184–197.

Hanson, S. L., & Sauer, W. J. 1985. Children and their elderly parents. In W. J. Sauer & R. T. Coward (eds.), *Social support networks and the care of the elderly* (41–66). New York: Springer.

Heller, P. L. 1970. Familism scale: A measure of family solidarity. *Journal of Marriage and the Family, 32,* 73–80.

Hess, B. B., & Waring, J. M. 1978. Changing patterns of aging and family bonds in later life. *Family Coordinator, 27,* 303–314.

Horowitz, A. 1985. Sons and daughters as caregivers to older parents: Differences in role performance and consequences. *The Gerontologist, 25,* 612–617.

Kerckhoff, A. C. 1966. Family patterns and morale in retirement. In I. H. Simpson & J. C. McKinney (eds.), *Social aspects of aging* (173–192). Durham, N.C.: Duke University Press.

Lee, G. R. 1979. Children and the elderly: Interaction and morale. *Research on Aging, 1,* 335–360.

Lee, G. R. 1985a. Kinship and social support of the elderly: The case of the United States. *Aging and Society, 5,* 19–38.

Lee, G. R. 1985b. Theoretical perspectives on social networks. In W. J. Sauer & R. T. Coward (eds.), *Social support networks and the care of the elderly* (21–37). New York: Springer.

Lee, G. R., & Ishii-Kuntz, M. 1987. Social interaction, loneliness, and emotional well-being among the elderly. *Research on Aging, 9,* 459–482.

Mancini, J. A. 1979. Family relationships and morale among people sixty-five years of age and older. *American Journal of Orthopsychiatry, 49,* 292–300.

Morris, J. N., & Sherwood, S. 1984. Informal support resources for vulnerable elderly persons: Can they be counted on, why do they work? *International Journal of Aging and Human Development, 18,* 81–98.

Mutran, E., & Reitzes, D. C. 1984. Intergenerational support activities and well-being among the elderly: A convergence of exchange and symbolic interaction perspectives. *American Sociological Review, 49,* 117–130.

Palmore, E. 1975. *The honorable elders: A cross-cultural analysis of aging in Japan.* Durham, N.C.: Duke University Press.

Quinn, W. H. 1984. Autonomy, interdependence, and developmental delay in older generations of the family. In W. H. Quinn & G. A. Hughston (eds.), *Independent aging: Family and social systems perspectives* (21–34). Rockville, Md.: Aspen Systems Corp.

Scott, J. P., & Roberto, K. A. 1984. Older rural parents and their children. In W. H. Quinn & G. A. Hughston (eds.), *Independent aging: Family and social systems perspectives* (182–193). Rockville, Md.: Aspen Systems Corp.

Seelbach, W. C. 1977. Gender differences in expectations for filial responsibility. *The Gerontologist, 17,* 421–425.

———. 1978. Correlates of aged parents' filial responsibility expectations and realizations. *Family Coordinator, 27,* 341–350.

———. 1984. Filial responsibility and the care of aging family members. In W. H. Quinn & G. A. Hughston (eds.), *Independent aging: Family and social systems perspectives* (92–105). Rockville, Md.: Aspen Systems Corp.

Seelbach, W. C., & Sauer, W. J. 1977. Filial responsibility expectations and morale among aged parents. *The Gerontologist, 17,* 492–499.

Shanas, E. 1979a. Social myth as hypothesis: The case of the family relations of old people. *The Gerontologist, 19,* 3–9.

———. 1979b. The family as a social support system in old age. *The Gerontologist, 19,* 169–174.

Stoller, E. P. 1982. Sources of support for the elderly during illness. *Health and Social Work, 7,* 111–122.

———. 1983. Parental caregiving by adult children. *Journal of Marriage and the Family, 45,* 851–858.

———. 1985. Exchange patterns in the informal support networks of the elderly: The impact of reciprocity on morale. *Journal of Marriage and the Family, 47,* 335–342.

9

Factors Influencing Intergenerational Consensus in Adulthood

Jennifer L. Glass
Charlotte Dunham

F amilies are often considered the major agents through which religious beliefs, moral values, and social attitudes are transmitted through the generations. While debate still rages over what "functions" the modern family has lost (Lasch 1977; Shorter 1975), there is still considerable consensus that the family is, or should be, the chief influence on individuals' religious and social ideologies. While we now know that intergenerational influence on sociopolitical attitudes is often indirect (occuring through the inheritance of social status) or reciprocal (occuring through the mutual accomodation of parents and children), it is nevertheless true that parents and adult children exhibit greater similarity in their sociopolitical attitudes than one would expect from chance alone (Glass, Bengtson & Dunham 1986; Glass & Polisar 1987). Given the evidence of persisting family influence on social ideologies in adulthood and the widespread belief that families (rather than other social institutions) *should* have control over the sociopolitical socialization of their members, the important question then becomes under what conditions is such family socialization successful? Or, in other words, can we explain variability in the extent to which parents and adult children agree on religious and social issues? Are there family characteristics or relationship characteristics that foster intergenerational influence? Are these causal forces stable over the life course and over successive generations? These are some of the issues this chapter will address. We will begin, however, with a discussion of theories of family functioning that attempt to explain variability in intergenerational similarity, followed by a brief overview of some of the conceptual and methodological problems encountered in studying parent-child influence.

This research was supported by grants from the National Institute of Aging (#AG-04092) and the National Institute of Mental Health (MH-38344), Vern L. Bengtson, Principal Investigator.

Theoretical Considerations

Because families are both institutions that structure and place individuals in the larger social order and intimate environments where psychological and physical needs are met, both sociodemographic and psychological characteristics of families have been considered important determinants of family influence over individual members. Unfortunately, no comprehensive theories consider both simultaneously, so we are left to speculate whether the two forces interact to produce similarity or dissimilarity among members of successive generations. Among those who emphasize the structural characteristics of families are stratification theorists, critical Marxists, and family demographers. These perspectives all contain an implicit, but vague, social psychology of how structural characteristics affect family interaction. In contrast, psychoanalytic and family systems theorists emphasize the internal affective or emotional climate in the family as the primary determinant of family similarity in attitude, temperament, or behavior, without much explicit regard for class, structure, or religious differences among families.

Let us turn first to the structural theorists. Many scholars in both mainstream stratification and critical Marxist literature have pointed out how educational attainment and/or social class affects family interaction and family influence (Bernstein 1975; Goslin 1969; Kohn & Schooler 1978; Sennett & Cobb 1973; Zaretsky 1976). Both perspectives emphasize the way in which the larger culture (including educational institutions and the mass media) disparage and belittle the belief systems of working and lower-class parents. Even when specific beliefs are not addressed, children see that their parents are in general held in low esteem by others of higher status, and might therefore view their parents' beliefs with distrust. Kohn and Schooler (1978) and Bernstein (1975) have pointed out an additional way in which class hampers intergenerational similarity. By restricting the complexity and quantity of interaction parents are likely to have with their children, working-class employment hampers parents' efforts to accurately and consistently communicate their social and religious beliefs to their children. In contrast, parents of higher status both enjoy the respect of the larger culture and command more attention and approval of their sociopolitical beliefs. They may also wield more power over their children well into adulthood, through the promise of goods, services, or future inheritance. Highly educated parents also tend to have jobs that encourage good communicative skills and attention to complex social issues, and provide parents with the time and energy to transmit their attitudes accurately to their children.

While that picture seems relatively straightforward and simple, the actual relationship of social class to family functioning is likely to be much more complex. First of all, middle-class parents, while marshalling more material and educational resources to the influence process, are also more likely than working-class parents to value independence and critical thinking in their children (traits that are not likely to induce rote internalization of parental beliefs and attitudes in subsequent generations). In addition, we cannot forget that parents and children reciprocally influence each other. It may be that middle-class parents are less susceptible to their children's influence attempts than working-class parents whose children often exceed them in education or income. Finally, while the larger culture may fail to support the beliefs of lower-status parents, those parents and their children are often bound more closely by ties of loyalty and mutual need precisely because they are relatively more isolated in working class or ethnic subcultures than are their more affluent counterparts. While social theorists have emphasized the relative advantages of social class for enhancing family similarity in belief systems, these other factors may outweigh the obvious advantages of greater material and social resources. Empirically, it has yet to be demonstrated that socioeconomic status has a major role in enhancing the intergenerational transmission of attitudes.

Another structural characteristic of families most closely examined by demographers is family size. While theorists have long suspected that the dynamics of large families differed from small families, recent empirical evidence more conclusively demonstrates that child outcomes are often linked to family size. Judith Blake (1987) has shown significant differences in academic achievement and socioeconomic attainment among children from small and large families after controlling for a variety of background characteristics. Her explanation of these findings is relevant for the study of attitude transmission as well. She believes children get less individual attention from parents and other adults in large families, and that children spend proportionately more time in the presence of siblings or peers. Since more of their socialization is nonparental, it stands to reason they will exhibit relatively fewer of the attitudes and behaviors of their parents. This greater diversity in large families also affects the process of reciprocal influence, since parents in large families are influenced by the experiences of a greater number of children who have each been exposed to a number of external influences. Both these forces should decrease parent-child attitude similarity for any particular dyad from a large family.

A similar type of reasoning can be applied to differences in family composition. Single parents also have less time for one-to-one contact with their children, and this may again produce larger parent-child differences in adulthood than are evident in two-parent families. However, countervailing forces may dilute this effect. Unless both parents share the same beliefs, two parents may present inconsistent beliefs to their children, undermining similarity between each parent and child. Single parents do not share the role of primary socializer, and may actually spend more time with children in their adulthood if they are not involved in a spousal relationship.

One might also hypothesize gender differences in parent-child similarity. Because adults today were primarily raised by mothers on a day-to-day basis, mothers surely had greater opportunity to make their values and beliefs known to their children than fathers. Mothers may also continue to be more involved in their children's lives in adulthood, making mothers the target of influence attempts by children more often than fathers. These patterns should decrease mother-child attitude differences in adulthood. The chance of empirically validating this claim is weak, however, because of the tendency toward homogamy among spouses. Because husbands and wives tend to share similar belief systems and mutually influence each other over time, greater mother-child similarity will indirectly produce greater father-child similarity as well, even though the father-child similarity occurs through the mother's intervention.

The last structural characteristic to be considered in this analysis is religious affiliation. Not only does religious participation encourage family discussion of religious beliefs and values, but religions themselves provide sometimes detailed positions on sociopolitical issues to which adherents are expected to attend. Those parents without religious affiliation do not have such extrainstitutional support for their beliefs. Religions differ, however, in the extent to which they emphasize a strong familistic orientation and espouse strict religious or social doctrines. Mormons, Fundamentalists, and (to a lesser extent) Catholics exhibit more of these latter characteristics than mainline Protestants or Jews. It may be reasonable to expect greater parent-child similarity among members of those religious groups.

Turning now to the psychodynamic or family systems theorists, we see pronounced emphasis on the affective bonds between parents and children. In various forms, it has been proposed that individuals identify with and internalize the beliefs of others with whom they have warm empathic relationships (Goslin 1969). Social learning theorists have maintained that parental warmth and nurturance are crucial for effective attitude and value socialization which produces parent-child consensus in adulthood. Extending this reasoning and following the original formulation of Homans (1950), several scholars have posited a relationship between parent-child association, affect, and consensus in adulthood (Bengtson, Roberts & Boyd 1987; Datan, Greene & Reese 1986). That is, family members who feel strongly bonded are more apt to associate with one another and to agree with one another on major issues. These three characteristics then become mutually reinforcing; increased association brings pressure toward consensus, increased consensus induces greater positive sentiments and satisfying interactions, etc.

But families, unlike other small groups, are not voluntary associations whose members can always choose their level of participation or involvement. Moreover, the emotional bonds established earlier in life may be more resistant to change than the attitudes or values that are being constantly reshaped or influenced by diverse adult experiences. Some empirical work shows little support for the idea that affective bonds are related to consensus on sociopolitical attitudes among parents and adult children (Atkinson, Kivett & Campbell 1986). While it certainly makes sense to hypothesize that parents and children with strong positive relationships should share religious and social ideologies, the issue is far from resolved.

In sum, the following family characteristics have been identified as contributors to diversity in parent-child attitude similarity in adulthood: social class, parent's education, marital status, gender, family size, religious affiliation, and closeness of parent-child bond. These characteristics represent structural and psychological forces thought to encourage parent-child similarity.

Conceptual Issues in the Study of Parent-Child Influence

While theories of family socialization focus on the childhood years, it is extremely difficult to verify the importance of primary parental socialization in the formation of individuals' social ideologies in adulthood. Parents' and childrens' social ideologies change over time, in response to normative life cycle events and historical changes, as well as the influence of family members and peers. For these reasons, it makes more theoretical sense to view family similarity in adulthood as a dynamic process in which parents and children mutually influence each other through their continued association and accumulated knowledge of each other's experiences. Rather than ask who influences whom, this chapter will assume that attitude consensus is always the product of mutual compromise. If this process continues throughout the children's adult years, then similar forces should predict parent-child similarity in later life as both parents and children age. However, it is possible that either cohort specific experiences or normative changes of aging will alter the characteristics that produce parent-child consensus on sociopolitical issues. For example, as religious institutions themselves change over time, parents and children of the same religious affiliation may find themselves in different "religious generations," making what was once a force for solidarity become a source of dissensus. As an example of age-related change, the advantages of social class may be quite important influences on children's attitudes when they are struggling young adults, but have little effect as they mature and become independent. In the analysis to be presented here, data from contiguous generations followed over time will be used to address these questions of stability across generations and over time in the determinants of parent-child similarity.

In addition to the conceptual difficulties encountered in studying dynamic processes of influence between parents and children, methodological issues must also be addressed. Sociopolitical attitudes cannot be measured without error, although reliable multi-item scales can be constructed to approximate such attitudes. Ensuring that those scales are both age invariant and reliable over time in longitudinal assessments is more difficult. Language use changes over time, and period effects alter the perceived meaning of even the most explicit words.

The problem of measurement error is compounded when the object of analysis is the difference between parents and children in imperfectly measured attitudes. The lack of complete precision in the identification of parent-child differences means that statistically significant predictors of those differences will be difficult to confirm. This suggests the use of liberal rather than conservative standards of statistical significance, under the assumption that measurement error occurs randomly across dyads and is uncorrelated with the family characteristics modeled as determinants of parent-child attitude differences.

On top of problems in measuring parent-child similarity are problems in identifying and measuring family characteristics. While theorists often assume that family characteristics are stable and identifiable, in reality these characteristics vary over time, sometimes differ across parents, and often differ between parents and children. Take religious affiliation as an example. A Lutheran parent may have Catholic-reared children, or a Catholic parent with Catholic-reared children may convert to a Fundamentalist faith after children reach adulthood. Similar problems exist in identifying socioeconomic status, marital status, and family size. Because parent-child influence is conceptualized as dynamic and continuous, our approach has been to focus on parent characteristics at the time of measurement as our primary independent variables. The decision to focus on parent characteristics rather than parent and child characteristics needs to be elaborated. Parent characteristics are emphasized here solely on methodological ground. Since parent and child characteristics are often correlated, including both produces multicollinearity and/or spurious effects of child characteristics on the extent of parent-child similarity. Because parent characteristics (like education, income, religious affiliation, number of children) are minimally affected by child influences, while child characteristics are difficult to purge of parental influences, parent characteristics are more exogenous to the processes generating parent-child attitude similarity. Resolving each of these methodological quagmires necessitates a compromise between the complexity of dynamic family processes and the simplicity of the data and methods we have available to study them. While imperfect, the simple statistical models used here provide a beginning point for the exploration of family characteristics that can explain variability in parent-child attitude similarity.

Data and Methods

The data to be used here come from the USC Longitudinal Survey of Three Generation Families (see Miller & Glass 1988, for details of sample design). Grandparents, parents, and adult grandchildren were first surveyed in 1972, then followed -up in 1985. This longitudinal sample is almost exclusively Caucasian, economically prosperous compared to national norms, but religiously and politically heterogeneous. Average age of each generation in 1985 was seventy-eight for the grandparents (G1), fifty-seven for the parents (G2), and thirty-three for the grandchildren (G3). Fifty-eight percent of the 1985 sample was female, in part because of differential mortality between survey waves. Because the original sampling frame was a large health care plan in southern California, most of the oldest generation still lived in that area. However, a third of the parents and more than half the grandchildren lived outside the area in 1985.

Because differential attrition in longitudinal samples is a potential source of bias, longitudinal respondents were compared to those who participated only in the original survey. No differences were found on most variables, with the exception of family income and education, which were higher in the longitudinal sample. Importantly, there were no differences in mean parent-child attitude similarity between the two groups.

In each wave, family members were asked to rate their agreement with a series of statements reflecting political, gender, and religious ideologies. The political ideology scale contained the following four items: 1) It is man's duty to work; it is sinful to be idle; 2) Most people on welfare are lazy; they just won't do a good day's work and so cannot get hired; 3) The most important task facing our society today is to maintain law and order; 4) The United States should be ready to answer any challenge to its power anywhere in the world. The reliability of this scale for each of the three generations in descending order was .64, .69, and .63 in 1972. Those numbers barely changed in 1985 to .63, .68, and .65, respectively.

The gender ideology scale contained only two items: 1) Some equality in marriage is a good thing, but by and large the husband ought to have the main say in family matters; 2) It goes against nature to place women in positions of authority over men. That scale produced reliability coefficients of .63, .52, and .67 for the three generations in 1972, compared to .62, .73, and .73 in 1985.

The religious ideology scale contained three items: 1) This country would be better off if religion had a greater influence in daily life; 2) Every child should have religious instruction; 3) God exists in the form in which the Bible describes Him. This scale produced high reliability coefficients of .86, .83, and .75 for the three generations in 1972, while remaining stable at .84, .82, and .85 in 1985.

Two types of parent-child dyads were constructed from the longitudinal data, grandparent-parent dyads and parent–adult-child dyads. Because the middle generation appears in both dyad types, the two samples are not independent. Moreover, respondents may appear in more than one dyad within samples because many families had more than one parent or more than one child participate in the survey. Not to have included the partially replicated dyads would have the effect of under-representing two-parent families and families with larger numbers of children.

To construct the dependent variable of parent-child similarity, the absolute value of the difference between the parent's and child's scale score was taken for each dyad for all three attitude scales. The parent-child attitude differences have a range from 0 to 3, with 0 indicating perfect agreement and 3 indicating the largest difference of opinion possible. While there conceivably may be analytic differences between dyads in which parents are more conservative and dyads in which children are more conservative, these groups have been pooled in the present analysis by taking absolute values.

The independent variables selected to test the theoretical propositions mentioned earlier are household income (in thousands), occupational prestige score if employed (20-100 range), education (in years of schooling), total children in family, parent's gender (female = 1), marital status (married = 1), and religious affiliation. Religious affiliation was divided into a series of dummy variables with mainstream Protestant as the omitted category. Finally, parent's age in years was added as a control variable to all analyses since generations often span a considerable number of birth cohorts in this sample.

To test the effects of parent-child emotional closeness on attitude similarity, two complementary scales were used. One measured parent's affect toward the child, while the other measured child's affect toward the parent. Each scale was constructed by summing responses to a series of Likert-scaled items on perceived closeness, understanding, communication, and compatibility between dyad members. Since children were asked about all living parents, but parents were only asked about one designated child, the number of dyads available for this analysis was significantly reduced.

Results and Discussion

Affective Closeness

Regressions were run on parent-child attitude differences for each scale at both time periods. Initial regressions on the reduced dyad samples that contained measures of affective closeness consistently showed no relationship between reported affect of either parent or child and parent-child attitude similarity (Bengtson, Roberts & Boyd 1987 report these findings in greater detail). Part of the failure to find any significant association may be caused by the lack of variability in the measures of affective closeness. As is common in large mailed surveys, most parents and children reported uniformly close and positive relationships with each other. Aside from social desireability, it is also possible that survey participation was affected by family closeness; that is, members of the sampling frame with parent-child conflicts chose not to participate. At any rate, the survey results obtained here show no support for the contention that affective closeness is related to similarity in social or religious attitudes among parents and adult children.

Structural Characteristics

Results for the structural variables are displayed in table 9–1. The differences in results between older and younger dyads are taken to reflect cohort/generational differences in the determinants of parent-child similarity, while the differences in results within dyad type over time (1972 to 1985) are taken to reflect aging and life cycle changes in the relationships of parents and children as they travel together through time. Results of all regressions will first be discussed as a group to evaluate the hypothesized relationships between sociodemographic characteristics and parent-child similarity. After that, explicit generational and longitudinal comparisons of results will be made.

Regarding our two indicators of social class, parent's household income and occupational prestige, the results are mixed. In nine of the twelve regressions, neither variable was significant. In two instances, social class indicators were associated with larger parent-child differences, while in only one instance (religious ideology among older dyads in 1985) did parents' occupational prestige reduce parent-child differences. Clearly, the results failed to support the contention that class-based resources increase intergenerational similarity.

The effects of parents' education are more consistent. While ten of the twelve models showed no significant effect, two equations showed negative effects of education on the size of parent-child differences. While not over-

Table 9–1
Regressions of Parent-Child Attitude Disagreement on Parents' Sociodemographic Characteristics

Older and Middle Generations	1972			1985		
	Politics	Gender	Religion	Politics	Gender	Religion
Income	.08	−.03	.01	.08**	.05	−.02
Occ. prestige	.01	−.00	−.00	.00	.00	−.01**
Education	−.01	.01	−.00	−.01	−.02	−.01
No. of children	−.02	.03	−.03	.04**	.07 **	−.02
Marital status	.00	−.11	−.16	.05	.12	.08
Gender	−.08	−.04	−.16*	.02	−.16	−.01
Jewish	.26**	−.08	.41**	.30**	−.15	−.23
Mormon	−.20	−.21	.00	−.52**	−.44	−.11
Fundamentalist	.01	.04	.33**	.18	−.22	.33**
Catholic	.17*	−.25**	.07	−.09	−.06	−.18
Other	.43**	−.58**	.24	.30	.74 **	−.10
No religion	.27*	−.24	.00	.12	−.09	.03
Age	−.01	−.00	−.01**	.00	−.01	−.01
R^2	.07	.08	.07	.10	.12	.10

Middle and Younger Generations	1972			1985		
	Politics	Gender	Religion	Politics	Gender	Religion
Income	.02	−.01	−.02	.01	−.02	.01
Occ. prestige	.00	−.00	.00	−.00	.004**	.00
Education	−.02**	−.00	−.01	−.00	−.02	.00
No. of children	.01	.04**	.04**	.02**	.02 **	.06**
Marital status	.01	−.07	−.12	−.05	−.11	.01
Gender	−.12**	.03	−.01	−.05	−.20 *	.02
Jewish	−.10	−.08	−.02	.09	−.14	.10
Mormon	−.13	−.11	−.49**	−.22**	−.01	−.30**
Fundamentalist	−.12	.04	−.40**	−.04	−.00	−.19
Catholic	.01	.09**	.06	.04	.16 **	.01
Other	−.28**	−.01	−.14	.10	−.10	.14
No religion	−.18*	−.15*	.02	.04	−.12	.01
Age	.00	.00	.02**	.00	.01	.01**
R^2	.05	.05	.11	.03	.08	.04

Note: N = 293 for older dyads
N = 647 for younger dyads
*$p \leq .10$
**$p \leq .05$

whelming in number, these effects are at least consistent with the hypothesis that educated parents achieve greater consensus with their children on sociopolitical issues. Importantly, these effects only appeared among the younger parent-child dyads, never among the older dyads in which mean educational attainment was much lower.

The strongest pattern of effects occured for family size. Total number of children reported by the parent is significantly associated with larger parent-child differences in six of the twelve equations. The effect is seen in both younger and older dyads and in both time periods, and occurs more than once for each attitude scale. The family size effect does appear more often among the younger parent-child dyads, but is found in the 1985 results for older dyads as well. The appearance of this effect across different sociopolitical ideologies, across time, and across generations makes this finding rather robust—children from large families are less likely to share their parents' religious and social beliefs.

No effects of parent's current marital status were found in any equation. However, divorce, remarriage, and widowhood in adulthood makes current marital status a poor proxy for single parenthood during the childhood period of dependency. Nevertheless, the failure to find any marital status effects even for the youngest dyads in 1972 (when the children's mean age was nineteen) indicates that single parents are not less likely to have the time and involvement necessary to produce attitude consensus between parents and children.

Regarding parent's gender, three scattered effects indicated that mothers had smaller attitude differences with their children than fathers. This is consistent with Acock and Bengtson's (1978) earlier regression analysis of the first wave of this data, in which they found that mother's attitudes predicted children's attitudes better than father's attitudes among the complete mother-father-child triads. Two of the effects shown here were weak, however, and most of the equations showed no effect of gender, so the bulk of the evidence does not support the contention that mothers exhibit greater attitude similarity with their children than fathers.

Religious Affiliation

Let us turn to religious affiliation. Clear religious differences emerged, but they were often inconsistent across time or generation. Jewish parents in the older dyads showed larger-than-average parent-child differences in political ideology at both time periods and in religious ideology at the 1972 measurement. But no effects of Jewish affiliation ever appeared among the younger dyads. While it is tempting to explain these effects by way of cultural stereotypes of argumentative families in which intellectual independence and achievement are highly prized, the reality is probably more complex. Many of the Jewish grandparents were first-generation immigrants to the United States (some were socialists or Zionists fleeing persecution in eastern Europe). Unfortunately, these data cannot disentangle the extent to which religious affiliation served as a proxy for immigrant status, but such a confound would explain why the Jewish effects were restricted to the older dyads.

With respect to the three most traditional religions (Mormons, Fundamentalist Protestants, and Catholics), which we hypothesized would produce greater parent-child similarity, the evidence is decidedly mixed. Mormon affiliation was significant in four of the twelve equations and uniformly reduced parent-child attitude differences. Three of the four significant effects were concentrated among the younger dyads, and three of the four effects occured in the later time period (1985). While Mormon affiliation positively affected consensus on political and religious matters, it never affected consensus on gender ideology (an area in which the Mormon church has taken several controversial positions). Thus, Mormon affiliation does seem to increase parent-child consensus on some issues, but more strongly in recent years and among younger generations.

Fundamentalist affiliation affected only consensus on religious ideology, but the effects changed over time and generation. Among the younger dyads in 1972, Fundamentalism reduced parent-child religious differences, but by 1985 the effect was no longer significant. Among the older dyads at both points in time, Fundamentalist affiliation significantly increased parent-child differences. One interpretation of this pattern might be that parental Fundamentalism increases consensus early in life, but erodes consensus as children age and are continually exposed to less rigid beliefs.

In contrast to Mormon and Fundamentalist affiliations, Catholic affiliation did not generally affect consensus on political or religious matters, but showed significant effects in three of the four gender ideology equations. Once again, the effects were inconsistent across generations. Among the older dyads in 1972, Catholicism decreased parent-child gender differences. In the younger dyads at both time points, Catholicism increased parent-child dissensus on gender issues. Since the Catholic Church's most conservative teachings occur in the area of gender relations and reproduction, it is perhaps not surprising that Catholic affiliation increased dissensus among younger parent-child dyads whose children were continuously exposed to more liberal views on gender relations over this time period.

The findings for parents who reported no religious affiliation are interesting as well. While we had tentatively suggested that parents without the institutional backing of religion might have trouble achieving attitude consensus with their children, these results showed mostly no effect of nonaffiliation. In fact, of the three weak effects found, two indicated *smaller* parent-child differences among the younger dyads in 1972. These may be revealing potential advantages to nonaffiliation during periods of social and political turmoil. Overall, we can conclude that affiliation with the traditional familistic religions at least as often increased parent-child attitude differences as decreased them (with the exception of Mormonism), while mainstream or non-affiliation appeared to have little effect on parent-child attitude consensus.

The unanticipated positive effects of parent's age in three of the four religious ideology equations warrant discussion. Age was included to control for age heterogeneity within each parental generation. Because these effects are not confounded with age differences between parents and children (that is, older parents tend to have older children as well), we have concluded that these age effects are best interpreted as cohort effects among parents. If that is the case, parents in more recent birth cohorts consistently have smaller religious differences with their children than parents in earlier birth cohorts. While we suspect that the rapid liberalization of religious beliefs earlier in this century may have something to do with this phenomenon, we have no ready explanation for these age effects, nor why they are concentrated among the religious ideology equations.

Conclusion

We began this chapter by asking whether sociodemographic or relationship variables could explain why certain parents and adult children exhibit more agreement on religious and social issues than others. Using data from a longitudinal survey of three generation families, results showed that affective closeness between parents and children had little to do with their consensus on sociopolitical issues, but that certain structural characteristics did. Most importantly, consensus was higher in families with fewer children. Weaker evidence suggested greater similarity in attitudes between educated parents and their children and between mothers and their children. While Mormon religious affiliation decreased some parent-child differences, Fundamentalist and Catholic affiliation more often increased parent-child differences. Generational differences in the determinants of parent-child similarity seemed more pronounced than life cycle differences within the same generation, but both types of differences were found.

The findings presented here reiterate several important points for social theorists. One is that structural forces, such as family size, affect human behavior through their impact on ordinary daily interactions between people. While speculation on the social psychological impacts of changing family structures is common, contextual theories that link structure to ordinary behavior are still rare. Another point is that radical views, or views that differ markedly from mainstream public opinion, are both difficult to sustain over time and to transmit over generations because they are not reinforced through ordinary interaction. In this case, religions that organized social ideologies into an antimodern viewpoint were less successful in helping families transmit their beliefs across the generations. Mormons represent the interesting exception to these principles. While maintaining both large families and very conservative social ideologies, they compensate for these potential threats to consensus by emphasizing family interaction through exhortation and ritual.

While these results represent an intriguing start, data limitations preclude full answers to the question of what produces attitude consensus between parents and adult children. We explained little of the total variability in intergenerational consensus on these social ideologies, and ruled out more causal explanations than were verified. Suggestions for future work in this area include greater focus on parent's religiousity or religious behavior as opposed to religious affiliation, per se. More attention should also be paid to refined measures of parent-child interaction in adulthood (particularly extent and types of contact) since measures of emotional closeness seem both unreliable and possibly unrelated to patterns of influence. Finally, it may be wise to delve more deeply into childhood characteristics of the family, since longitudinal assessments reveal as much change as stability in parent characteristics such as religious affiliation, marital status, class, parent-child affect, etc. Change versus stability in these characteristics from childhood to adulthood may be equally important in determining attitude consensus between parents and adult children. Families experiencing discontinuities and rapid changes may find themselves with fewer resources with which to build consensus in adulthood.

References

Acock, A. C., & Bengtson, V. L. 1980. Socialization and attribution processes: Actual vs. perceived similarity among parents and youth. *Journal of Marriage and the Family, 43*, 501–518.

Acock, A. C., & Bengtson, V. L. 1978. On the relative influence of mothers and fathers: A covariance analysis of political and religious socialization. *Journal of Marriage and the Family, 40*, 519–530.

Atkinson, M. P.; Kivett, V. R.; & Campbell, R. T. 1986. Intergenerational solidarity: An examination of a theoretical model. *Journal of Gerontology, 41*, 408–416.

Bengtson, V. L.; Roberts, R. E.; & Boyd, S. 1987. Is family solidarity a useful construct? A replication and a revised conceptualization. Paper presented at annual meeting of the Gerontological Society of America, Washington, D.C.

Bernstein, B. 1975. *Class, codes, and control.* London: Routledge & Kegan Paul.

Blake, J. 1987. Differential parental investment: Its effects on child quality and status attainment. In J. B. Lancaster, J. Altmann, A. S. Rossi, L. P. Sherrod (eds.), *Parenting across the life span* (351–375). New York: Aldine.

Datan, N.; Greene, A. L.; & Reese, H. W. (eds.). 1986. *Life-span developmental psychology: Intergenerational relations.* Hillsdale, N.J.: Lawrence Erlbaum Associates.

Glass, J. L.; Bengtson, V. L.; & Dunham, C. C. 1986. Attitude similarity in three-generation families: Socialization, status inheritance, or reciprocal influence? *American Sociological Review, 51*, 685–698.

Glass, J. L., & Polisar, D. 1987. A method and metric for assessing similarity among dyads. *Journal of Marriage and the Family, 49*, 663–668.

Goslin, D. A. 1969. *Handbook of socialization theory and research.* Chicago: Rand McNally.

Homans, G. 1950. *The human group.* New York: Harcourt, Brace.

Kohn, M. L., & Schooler, C. 1978. The reciprocal effects of substantive complexity of work and intellectual flexibility: A longitudinal assessment. *American Journal of Sociology, 84*, 24–52.

Lasch, C. 1977. *Haven in a heartless world.* New York: Basic Books.

Miller, R. B., & Glass, J. L. 1988. *Parent-child similarity across the life course.* Unpublished manuscript, University of Southern California.

Sennett, R., & Cobb, J. 1973. *The hidden injuries of class.* New York: Random House.

Shorter, E. 1975. *The making of the modern family.* New York: Basic Books.

Zaretsky, E. 1976. *Capitalism, the family, and personal life.* New York: Harper & Row.

10
The Parental Role and Parent-Child Relationship Provisions

Janie K. Long
Jay A. Mancini

While the aging-parent–adult-child relationship has been examined numerous times over the past thirty or so years, it appears that the expectations attached to the role of parent by parents themselves are not well understood, nor do we know the particulars of how the parent-child relationship functions in the life of the older parent (Blieszner & Mancini 1987; Mancini & Blieszner in press; Ward 1985). The qualitative analysis we undertake seeks to provide information on how parents perceive their role, how they describe the relationship they have with an adult child, the meanings they attach to the relationship, and how that relationship functions to their betterment. Important to us is an understanding of what the older parent gains through a relationship with an adult child.

The work of Robert S. Weiss (1969, 1974) has influenced our approach to the question of what a relationship with an adult child means to an older parent. In the middle to later 1960s Weiss had studied Parents Without Partners groups and was attempting to test a theory about the functional specificity of relationships versus the "fund of sociability." The *fund of sociability* idea suggests that one's needs for intimacy, social support and the like can be met by any number of personal relationships. The hypothesis of *functional specificity* suggests that particular relationships are relatively unique in their ability to meet an adult's interpersonal needs. In his study of Parents Without Partners members Weiss found more support for the hypothesis of functional specificity. However, he has noted that "there is reason to suspect that attachment relationships, partly because they sponsor continuing proximity, tend toward multiplicity of provision" (Weiss 1974, 23). One primary attachment relationship is marriage; another involves parents and their children. Of significance to our interests are the relationship provisions identified by Weiss: attachment; social integration; opportunity for nurturant behavior; reassurance of worth; reliable alliance; and guidance. The point of departure in this study is to examine what parents say about how they relate to their children within the framework of the provisions. We are also interested in noting how these parental responses may suggest aspects of the relationship not previously elaborated. At the same time we also desire to identify those provisions discussed by Weiss that are not viable in this sample of older parents.

The character of these relationship provisions are as follows (Weiss 1969, 1974): *attachment* (feelings of intimacy, peace, and security and place); *social integration* (a sense of belonging to a group with which one shares common interests and social activities); *reliable alliance* (knowing that one can count on receiving assistance in times of need); *guidance* (having relationships with persons who can provide knowledge, advice, and expertise); *reassurance of worth* (a sense of competence and esteem obtained from a social role); and, *opportunity for nurturance* (being responsible for the care of others, a sense of being needed). The presence and strength of these relationship provisions vary across persons and across the life cycle; however, they are considered essential for adequate personal adjustment.

The Study

In the fall of 1984 we conducted 494 structured, in-home interviews with older parents who resided in Roanoke, Virginia. Funding was provided by the Andrus Foundation, American Association of Retired Persons. In the winter of 1985 we interviewed fifty-two of the original sample, using open-ended, conversational methods. Funding for this phase was provided by the Educational Foundation of Virginia Polytechnic Institute and State University. The following discussion is based upon these interviews.

Because the sample under study is derived from the first phase of the project, we will briefly review that initial sampling design. The procedure is a modified random, multistage design that has been used successfully in earlier research on older people (Mancini 1979; Quinn 1983). Its components are: (1) use of census tract data and block statistics; (2) application of a sampling multiplier; (3) derivation of cumulative sampling units; (4) formation of sample "paper" zones; (5) random selection of sampling units; (6) use of a compact (canvassing) sampling procedure. This resulted in 635 potential interviewees. Those that were completed (N = 494) represent a 78 percent response rate. From this sample was taken a subsample that would participate in follow-up, conversational interviews. When respondents were initially interviewed they were asked about their willingness to participate in a future study, and it is from this group the sample of fifty-two was drawn. Simple random selection was used, and 90 percent of those contacted for the second interview agreed to participate.

The subsample on which this study is based had an average age between seventy-two and seventy-three years, had lived in their neighborhoods an average of twenty-four years, and 60 percent were women. Fifty-two percent were married and 42 percent were widowed. Eighty-seven percent were Caucasian, and 73 percent were employed at age fifty. The average number of living children was just under three, and average years of education was eleven. This sample approximates the larger one from which it was drawn. Characteristics of that larger sample compare favorably with state and national census data on people sixty-five years of age and older.

The data were generated by the use of several leading questions intended to parallel those used in the structured interview study. The first question was very general: "I would like for you to talk about your present relationship with (_____). Perhaps the easiest way for you to begin would be to discuss the first things that come to mind when you think of (_____)." While the ensuing discussion was allowed to take any number of forms, the following questions were used as probes and as guidelines for the responses: "Would you talk about how you tell (_____) what you are thinking and feeling? For example, how would (_____) know if you are happy, sad, or angry? Can you give me an example of a specific situation you can recall?"; "Let's assume that a friend knew you and (_____) very well. Are there any particular words that he or she might use to describe that relationship between you and (_____)?"; "Even when we try hard not to, there are times when members of a family argue and disagree with each other. It is a common thing that happens. Would you tell me what you and (_____) say or do when you argue? When you disagree? Can you give me examples of specific arguments or disagreements?"; "What is the most important thing that (_____) does for you? Do you think you give as much to (_____) as she or he gives to you? Can you give me some examples of things you do for each other?" Older parents were asked to respond with regard to the child to whom they felt the closest. Of course those with just one child could make no such choice. Those parents with more than one child who could not or would not say to whom they felt the closest talked about the adult child with whom they had the most contact. While the methods of identifying the adult child varied, statistical tests of the level of affection and of antagonism in the relationships did not reveal significant differences.

Character and Provisions of Relationships

All the relationship provisions described by Weiss were reflected in the comments of the older parents. Those mentioned most often by our interviewees were attachment, reliable alliance, and opportunities for nurturant behavior. Reassurance of worth, social integration, and guidance were discussed less often.

Attachment

The function of attachment is a gain in feeling secure and connected with another; if this provision of the relationship is not met it is likely to lead to emotional isolation or loneliness. Many of our respondents spoke of attachment in terms of feeling close to and having contact with the adult child. The comments of these two fathers are exemplary:

> We've always been close. I talk with her two or three times a day. She always calls me in the mornings and asks how I'm feeling. She keeps me happy. I know I can depend on her for anything. If I need her, I have her.

> We do a lot of talking two or three times a week (on the phone). I think she loves me very much. She always tells me, "I love you." She has a heckuva phone bill and so do we.

Intimacy is one of the domains of attachment. An intimate relationship is one in which individuals can express their feelings freely and without self-consciousness. One mother spoke of this kind of exchange with her son:

> When he comes in at night he'll sit down and talk to me about things that have happened or things that he is interested in. The fact that he does come home and talk to me and tell me things helps me feel that we have a close relationship.

Being able to share a mutual respect for each other's opinions was expressed by some parents:

> A lot of parents say they couldn't live with their children . . . of course we have our arguments. Everybody has their ups and downs. I tell her what I think and feel. We just tell each other things.

> We've never had an argument in our life. We don't have the same opinions. We may disagree. I express what I think about it, and he does, too.

Several expressed a sense of security just knowing their children would be there if needed:

> I don't know what I would do without her. I enjoy having her right across the street. Since I lost my husband, I don't know what I'd do if I didn't have her. She can usually tell how I'm feeling. The most important thing she does for me is just being there.

Many of our respondents reported feelings of closeness, intimacy, mutual respect, security, and comfort in their relationships with their adult children. Their comments reflected feelings of attachment and seemed to help in minimizing perceived isolation and loneliness.

Reliable Alliance

Reliable alliance is the provision of services and resources, and its absence may provoke feelings of anxiety and vulnerability. Many parents in our sample reported a wide array of behaviors indicative of this relationship provision:

> He's done so much for me that you wouldn't believe. He furnished a car for me. He's moved me. If anything needs fixing while he's here he'll help.

> She furnishes me with a place to live, and she furnishes me food. When I'm sick, she's right with me.

> She lives up the street here about six houses. She looks after me and takes me places since my wife died. She has had me up for meals and offered to do anything she could. I call her or she calls me every morning to see if I'm all right.

> He gives me money. That's most important because I need it to help pay my bills. He's very nice about helping me.

Other comments from these parents demonstrate how their adult children support them in an instrumental, practical manner, including: providing groceries and produce out of their garden, sewing, picking up the parent's medicine, providing clothing, and providing transportation to pay the bills or to medical appointments. Many parents felt assured their needs would be taken care of by their children regardless of the time, energy, or finances needed. These feelings appeared to foster their sense of security.

Opportunities for Nurturance

The opportunity for nurturant behavior is provided by relationships in which the adult has responsibility for the child's well-being. When the adult child leaves home the parent's opportunities for nurturant behavior dramatically decrease. A minority of the parents in our sample felt that their contributions to their children were minimal. For example, consider this statement by a mother who had previously suffered a stroke: "I don't give as much to my daughter as she gives to me because I don't have nothing to give." However, the preponderance of comments indicate that nurturance still occurs, though it is different from early life patterns.

Most respondents felt they gave as much or more to their adult children as their adult children gave to them. This response supported the notion of a mutual exchange of services and/or resources among older parents and their adult children. Many middle-aged children provide assistance to their parents, and older parents often reciprocate with their own forms of assistance to their adult children. This interdependence is reflected in these comments:

> I think we go very well together. I couldn't do without her, and I don't think she could do without me.

> I suspect giving is a reciprocal thing . . . pretty evenly balanced.

Some were able to feel a sense of nurturance in some areas but not in others. One mother had the following to say when asked if she gave as much to her son as he gave to her: "Not really; Well, in love . . . yes; Materially, no." She believed that even though she could no longer provide certain services for her son that she had other ways to nurture him. Another mother had found ways to continue to give materially to her son: "Yes, I give as much to my son as he gives to me . . . like I give him the silverware."

Some parents felt they were doing more for their adult children than they were receiving from the adult children. These feelings were often true when the adult child was a single parent:

> Well, in the past few years, I might say the early years of her divorce, it became necessary for me on lots of occassions to help her with finances, and she has always let me know that she is very grateful for helping her out of lots of financial difficulties.

> His wife left him when the children were eight and three years old. He raised those girls all by himself with my help. If we really needed help, he would be willing to help. The help has been more the other way because he has really needed it, and we don't need any help.

Our respondents also provided evidence that women's participation in work outside the home provides opportunities for older parents to provide both nurturance and assistance. One seventy-year-old mother spoke of the assistance she provides for her daughter, a mother of four, who works outside the home:

> I help her with her housecleaning. I do things for her especially if she's going to have anyone coming in. She doesn't have time with working. I go in on Friday and get her housework done so that helps her.

Some of the parents in our sample also spoke of caring for adult children who were ill or handicapped in some way:

> She went into a deep depression after her husband died, and we had to help her a lot then. We're always doing things for her.

The father of a daughter who was diagnosed as schizophrenic explained that his daughter was terribly dependent on him and his wife. Another mother spoke of caring for her daughter who had a congenital heart disease and was mentally handicapped:

> She has spent half her life in bed. She can't do much because she gets completely out of breath. She's my only child, and I've been a widow for five years. We enjoy being together.

The divorce of the adult child, an adult daughter who worked outside the home, and children who were sick or disabled provided renewed opportunities for nurturance or a life with purpose for several members of our sample. Also, many parents felt they were able to give to their adult children on a continuing and equal basis, which provided them with a sense of fulfillment. Terms that typify the comments involving nurturance are interdependence, selective nurturance, marital and family status, the daughter's employment status, and the adult child's health.

Reassurance of Worth

Reassurance of worth is provided by relationships that attest to an individual's competence in some role. Many parents derive a great sense of pride and satisfaction from their parental role. The continued recognition of this role is important:

> I think she still respects me as her father.

> Of course they need our support. At least they let us think they need our support, and that's good, too. We all need to be needed. A wise child will let Mama and Daddy still feel like they are needed.

> She doesn't butt in on anything I want to do for myself.

> I love to have her opinion, so she'll give me her opinion. Then she'll say, "Now you're going to have to think that over for yourself, Mother."

Being able to do things on their own, thinking for themselves, and continuing to be accepted in their parental role were ways of being recognized for their value and competence. This recognition was thus important in maintaining higher levels of self-esteem for our respondents.

Social Integration

Social integration provides a person with a sense of belonging to some group. These relationships provide the sharing of experience, information, and ideas and often revolve around common interests or activities.

We have a very good relationship. He has a number of friends and when they have a get-together, very often I am invited, which means an awful lot. One girl asked my son why I was always invited, and my son told her I was his friend, and he loved me.

We go out at least twice a week for lunch. I also go over there real often to eat. They're always taking me with them when they go places and of course the past three Sundays we've been on picnics.

We've always hunted and fished together and done lots of things together. We always celebrate Christmas and birthdays together.

This function is usually provided by friends. The lack of comments related to this provision seems to support this idea at least as far as the older parent-adult child relationship is concerned.

Guidance

Persons who can provide knowledge or expertise are relied upon to supply guidance. This function is often provided by professionals such as therapists, social workers, and ministers or priests. However, we feel that guidance can be from an informal source (such as a family member) as well as from a formal source (such as a helping professional). Only a few spoke of their adult children as providing guidance:

I enjoy it most when he talks about his business (law). He's been very good on helping with family problems. He's been willing to help me at no charge legally with my will and some other financial problems that he gave me advice on.

He tries to give advice, which I think is all right to do.

Overall, the comments did not indicate that they sought or received a lot of guidance from their adult children. All things considered, the relationship is more significant with regard to instrumental, nonprescriptive assistance, and nurturance.

While the social integration, guidance, and reassurance of worth provisions were less evident in these relationships, three other characteristics not found in Weiss' typology were very evident. We have labeled these domains as noninterfering involvement, recognition of independence, and protection.

Noninterfering Involvement

Even though most older parents in the sample saw themselves as involved in their children's lives to some degree, many were very careful about drawing boundaries. Noninterfering involvement was the theme of many of the respondents. They wanted to be involved in their children's lives and to feel needed, but they did not see it as appropriate to give their adult children unsolicited advice. This may be why so few of their comments reflected the provision of guidance.

> You must learn to let your children go. You must learn to stay out of their hair. After all, the influence has long ago been made. The roots and foundations of life were made before she became fully adult. She is our extension, the extension of ourselves. But we do not, cannot, control or decide for her. It's good to live nearby, fifty or sixty miles, where we don't know what kind of cereal they eat for breakfast.

Several parents expressed their hestitation about offering unsolicited advice. Their sentiments indicate the realization that they were no longer the primary influence in their children's lives:

> They live in their own home. I don't bother them. Some mothers want to know everything that is going on . . . that's their business.

> I can see problems that he has, and it gets me sometimes. I don't always talk to him about his problems because I'm not a meddler.

> As far as her personal affairs with her children or her style of handling them, both my wife and I work at keeping our mouths shut.

> What's happened since she's been married and had a family and on her own is we consider she is on her own. We shouldn't interfere unless we're asked.

These aging parents have managed to remain involved with their children without becoming enmeshed in their lives. They remain willing to contribute when asked but do not see it as necessary to continue to provide guidance for their adult children.

Independence

The issue of independence permeates all the relationship provisions. Because independence was a dominant theme throughout the interviews and because it did not seem to be adequately covered by any one of Weiss's functions, we have chosen to separate it as another prominent aspect of the aging-parent–adult-child relationship.

Some respondents expressed a desire to remain independent in regard to housing arrangements. One son had suggested to his mother that she needed to go and live with his family. Her thoughts about the possible move were as follows:

He was almost certain that I had to go live with him. That's what he wanted, but I couldn't. I've lived here for so long, and this is my home.

Another woman spoke of her fear of cluttering up her children's lives. This woman's mother had lived with her, and she did not desire the same experience for her own children:

Your life is really not your own when you have somebody in the house with you, and I don't want to clutter up my children's lives with me.

Older adults often rely on age-peers to fulfill many of their needs. Many elderly feel more comfortable relying on friends than on family, especially in certain areas of their life. One woman spoke of her independence from her son in this way:

I'm not the kind of mother that's going to say, "Call every single day. You've got to call me, or I've got to call you." I have other friends that I interact with so it's not the fact that I'm dependent on him.

When older parents are dependent on their adult children they often recognize the pull of the adult child in many directions. One respondent acknowledged that she had to wait until her son could do whatever she needed doing because he had other obligations. Another woman spoke of recognizing her daughter's need for time with her husband:

I think she has her own life to live. Her husband comes first. We don't ever talk at night unless something has happened. I think that is her time with her husband.

Some parents recognized their own and their children's independence as prohibitive to any form of disagreement:

That's something we don't do (argue). They're always telling me what to do, and I've got to the age where I don't say anything. I just let it go on and then do what I want to do.

We don't have no reason to argue. She's on her own, and we're on our own. So we don't do no arguing. She lives her life, and we live ours. I don't have nothing to argue with her about, really.

Two explanations for a lack of arguments focused on the advanced age of the adult child:

We don't argue because I won't argue with him. We disagree on things, but that's it. We just drop it right there because he's forty-two years old.

An eighty-five-year-old mother had this to say about her adult daughter:

We don't disagree very much. I don't bother. She's an old lady now and knows her own business. I don't interfere at all.

Parents value and prefer independence but recognize the necessity of dependence under certain conditions and circumstances. This parent prefers independence but would choose dependence on his children over a move to a nursing home if it were feasible for him to do so:

> I'm trying to stay here as long as I can do for myself. When it gets to the time I can't do, I don't know what will come of me then; go to a nursing home, I reckon. I don't want to, but I guess I'll have to 'cause ain't none of them (the children) able to take care of themselves.

One woman indicated relief after talking about the possibility of moving into a nursing home with her daughter:

> I was telling my daughter that I would rather go in a nursing home than bother them. She said, ". . . not as long as she lived she wouldn't let me go in a nursing home." So you couldn't ask for nothing more than that I wouldn't think.

Except for these comments related to a possible move to a nursing home, all the parents advocated a certain amount of separateness between themselves and their adult children. This independence was portrayed as a natural occurrence between the two generations of adults.

Protection

Many parents indicated a desire to protect their adult children from their problems or needs. The aged parent is seen as providing for the adult child rather than putting himself or herself in a position of having to receive from the child. This protectiveness then serves to preserve the place of the aged parent as the nurturant one. Several talked about ways they attempt to cover up their feelings in front of their adult children:

> I don't discuss my inner feelings with her to any great extent. I know she can tell when something is bothering me . . . she always asks me whether everything is all right. The stock answer is, "Yes, everything is going all right."

> He can tell about feelings by a person's actions. If I didn't have a smile and a really warm welcome for him, he'd think something was wrong.

> I don't discuss my health because I know that worries her. I have a lot of medical problems. I usually just tell her I'm feeling well so she won't worry about it.

> I don't guess he ever thinks I get lonely or sad. Even when I'm tired or worn out. I don't try to show it.

I don't complain to my sons about anything. I never have and especially since I've been living alone because I don't want them to feel obligated that they've got to be running to see about me all of the time.

He's mighty helpful to me as far as doing things when I need help, but I try not to call on him too much. I try not to burden him.

These comments support the idea that older parents seek to protect their adult children, and also reflect their independence needs. They shield them from health concerns, from their anger and other strong feelings, and from feelings of obligation.

Implications

The fact that all of Weiss's relationship provisions were mentioned by members of our sample supports the use of this model as a viable one for looking at the aging parent-adult child relationship. Three of the provisions—attachment, reliable alliance, and opportunity for nurturance—were more central to our respondents than were social integration, guidance, and reassurance of worth. None of our sample had all the provisions filled by the adult child and this indirectly supports Weiss's idea that different kinds of relationships provide different functions. There were three other important aspects of the aging parent-adult child relationship: noninterfering involvement, independence, and protection. These aspects of the relationship were as important as attachment and the like. However, there is some degree of overlap across the six relationship provisions identified by Weiss, as well as noninterfering involvement, independence, and protection. A number of the relationship descriptors were pertinent to more than one relationship characteristic.

This exploratory and impressionistic account of how older parents view the relationships they have with their adult children has demonstrated the breadth of what they receive from these relationships. At the same time it has been shown that provision is reciprocal. Moreover, the comments have shown the role that individual needs play. The theme of personal independence was sounded throughout the interviews, so much so that we believe this need to be prepotent. An open-ended study such as this tends to confirm particular expectations and often raises a series of questions that cannot be addressed by the data. For the moment the questions raised by this analysis involve: reconciliation of needs for independence and dependence; history of parenting styles; the influence of gender; marital and family characteristics; and emotional health.

The need for *independence* expressed by our respondents causes us to wonder how these desires are reconciled with the practical realities of having to depend on others. What enables an older parent to feel psychologically comfortable with dependence? Does parent-child interdependence mitigate the negative feelings that may be associated with dependence? Often, cross-sectional research causes us to wonder about the *history and life cycle of a family relationship*. How have these relationship provisions changed over time? For example, how has the nurturance provision evolved, and why are some parents protective of their mature children's feelings? Is it left over from early parental roles or is it an artifact of current parental independence needs? Social scientists have taken a greater interest in the role *gender* plays in how parents and children relate. We have not been able to assess how the social provisions might vary by the parent's or the child's gender. However, we would expect there to be differences and would imagine that, on average, the provision linkages are stronger between mothers and daughters. Because the content of the provisions varies, we wonder if certain of them are more sensitive to gender? Relatedly, do parents have a clearer sense of their parental role with daughters more so than with sons? Are they more protective and nurturant of their daughters, and are sons more important on matters of reliable alliance (practical assistance)? Several *marital and family characteristics* should also influence what a relationship provides. For example, marital status of parent and child, their relative economic resources, and their physical proximity ought to come into play. Are the provisions more germane when a parent has no living spouse? How does the extent of geographical distance influence such provisions as reliable alliance, and how does it promote independence? Are parents as apt to rely on children when their own resources are ample, or when those of the child may be deficient? Indirectly we examined how the comments made by our sample indicated *psychological and emotional well-being*. However, this was by no means examined systematically. One of the questions often asked about the family life of older people involves how well-being is enhanced by the family. Do particular characteristics of the relationship or particular provisions have a greater impact on well-being? Which provisions are peripheral to well-being?

We have sought to discuss what an older parent gains through a relationship with an adult child. We began by examining Weiss's typology of relationship provisions. We also explored other significant dimensions of the relationship, and in that regard noted the pivotal role of personal independence. For this sample of older parents the relationship with an adult child is typified most by attachment, reliable alliance, opportunity for nurturance, noninterfering involvement, independence, and protection. We have provided some support for the viability of these relationship dimensions as being important avenues for subsequent studies of aging parents and their adult children.

References

Blieszner, R., & Mancini, J. A. 1987. Enduring ties: Older adults' parental role and responsibilities. *Family Relations, 36,* 176–180.

Mancini, J. A. 1979. Family relationships and morale among people sixty-five years of age and older. *American Journal of Orthopsychiatry, 49,* 292–300.

Mancini, J. A., & Blieszner, R. In press. Aging parents and adult children: Current and prospective social science research themes. *Journal of Marriage and the Family.*

Quinn, W. H. 1983. Personal and family adjustment in later life. *Journal of Marriage and the Family, 45,* 57–73.

Ward, R. A. 1985. Informal networks and well-being in later life: A research agenda. *The Gerontologist, 25,* 55–61.

Weiss, R. S. 1969. The fund of sociability. *Trans-Action, 6,* 36–43.

Weiss, R. S. 1974. The provisions of social relationships. In Z. Rubin (ed.), *Doing unto others* (17–26). Englewood Cliffs, N.J.: Prentice-Hall.

11
Helping Relationships in Later Life: A Reexamination

Victor G. Cicirelli

W hen parents become old and frail, it is their adult children who help them most. Although older people often receive much help from their spouses, they also receive help from their adult children, especially after widowhood. Adult children do maintain contact and provide care to elderly parents when needed (Cicirelli 1980, 1981; Horowitz & Dobrof 1982; Troll 1971). Indeed, parent caring is so widespread that Brody (1985) termed it a "normative family stress." In spite of the widespread availability of long-term care services to families of the elderly, only 5 percent of the elderly live in institutions at any given time. The proportion of bedfast and housebound elderly being cared for at home is twice that of those cared for in institutions (Shanas 1979), while the proportion of those living at home with some assistance is three times the number living in the community. Further, some 62 percent of all medical and personal care to elderly in the community has been found to come from family members; this percentage would have been much higher if other types of help had been included (National Center for Health Statistics 1972; Brody 1978). Cantor (1975) found that about two-thirds of the elderly received help from their adult children. In a study focusing on elderly who required assistance with personal care or daily activities (Noelker & Townsend 1987), 92 percent of daughters and 62 percent of sons interviewed were caregivers. In short, family members still provide the brunt of help to elderly parents for ordinary everyday living, as well as extraordinary help involving long-term care during illness, disability, impairment, and immobility. The extent of informal family care far exceeds formal help from the public sector, such as formal home care, day care, nursing homes, hospices, and so on.

Within the family, there is a continuous reciprocal process of giving and receiving involving children and parents across the life span. However, there is usually an imbalance in the reciprocity of giving and receiving at any particular time. During the early part of an individual's life span, the child's parents provide food, clothing, guidance, love, and the like. In these childrearing years, there is an imbalance in the exchange of help whereby the greater help flows from the parents to the child. During the early adulthood of the child, the exchange is more balanced, with middle-aged parents babysitting with grandchildren, helping with finances, and so on, while young adult children are helping parents with home maintenance, occasional transportation, shopping, and the like.

In the latter part of the parents' life span, when the child has grown to middle adulthood, the exchange of help is likely to shift more in favor of the elderly parent as the earlier process becomes reversed. However, there is always an exchange of help; it is the degree of imbalance that is shifting.

If one conceives of this exchange as a necessity for the survival of both the young and the old, childrearing and parent-caring may be viewed as an inextricable part of family life. Keeping these aspects of mutual help at the appropriate level of *imbalance* over the life span would seem to be important for the family as well as the species, although the degree to which this happens has varied from culture to culture and across time, depending on the social forces operating, and the unique experiences of family members.

Explanations of the Exchange of Help across the Life Span

Although there are various possible explanations of the exchange of help between children and parents, three theories stand out as the most prominent today.

Equity Theory

Equity theories have been most successful at explaining help exchanged between friends and neighbors but less successful at explaining help from family members. Equity theory states that in a helping situation, two people will strive to maintain a balance between help received and help given. If an imbalance occurs, both parties will experience distress, and attempt to reduce the imbalance. The underbenefited party will reduce giving and the overbenefited party will increase giving until a balance is restored. However, such a prediction does not seem appropriate to the exchange of help between children and parents where imbalance predominates. Although the theory predicts that the overbenefited party will experience distress, Ingersoll-Dayton and Antonucci (1988) found that elderly did not feel distressed at receiving unreciprocated instrumental care from adult children as they did from other caregivers.

Obligation Theory

Theories of obligation hold that adult children believe it to be their duty or responsibility to care for parents in old age, based on gratitude for parents' help earlier in life and/or on cultural norms that one is expected to help elderly parents. Such a theory may help to explain extraordinary care (Kingson, Hirshorn & Cornman 1986) where provision of help is very demanding because of the frailty and dependency of the elderly parent. Perhaps a child's sense of duty or responsibility motivates the continuation of care under such burdensome conditions. However, much help exchanged by children and parents throughout the life span deals with the ordinary needs of everyday living (such as babysitting, shopping, transportation, household activities, and so on). Surely, such an exchange of help does not depend on sense of duty alone, as little enjoyment would be experienced under such conditions.

Jarrett (1985) has argued for obligation as the basic motivation for caregiving of the elderly. His argument is based partially on rejecting attachment theory and its concomitant feelings of closeness as a motive for caregiving. He argues that feelings of closeness are likely to fade over the decades of adulthood, that caregiving itself is accompanied by caregiver strain that leads to dissipation of closeness and psychological distancing (Johnson & Catalano 1983), and that absent or diminished feelings of closeness lead to guilt and despair in the caregiver. Responses to this criticism will be considered in the light of attachment theory.

Attachment Theory

Briefly, the concept of attachment refers to an emotional or affectional bond between two people; it is essentially being identified with, having love for, and having the desire to be with the other person, and represents an internal state within the individual (Ainsworth 1972; Bowlby 1979, 1980; Cicirelli 1983). Initially, a child becomes attached to its caregiver (typically the mother) and this primary attachment is assumed to continue throughout the life span. Attachment behavior is overt behavior by which the child attempts to maintain physical closeness and contact with the mother. Such initial attachment behaviors as crying, smiling, or cooing signal the mother to respond to the needs of the infant. Usually the mother is sensitive and responsive, and provides the needed care and love. Attachment between child and mother is thus formed, and further attachment behaviors (such as crawling) are used to maintain proximity and closeness to the mother.

The existence of an internal state of attachment is inferred from attachment behavior. When the mother responds consistently and appropriately, a secure attachment is formed. Given such secure attachment, the infant responds positively to reunion with the mother after a short separation, and, using the mother as a base, the infant explores the environment to further develop knowledge, personality, and social adjustment.

In addition to attachment and attachment behavior, the adult model of attachment involves protective behavior; that is, behavior to protect the attached figure. The adult child is concerned with preserving or restoring the threatened existence of the attached figure (Bowlby 1979, 1980). In the latter part of life, the attached figure (the parent) becomes increasingly vulnerable to loss through aging and death. For most adult children, preserving the bonds of attachment to members of the primary group becomes increasingly important as the adult grows older. Thus, attachment leads adult children not only to attempt to remain in contact and communication with parents but also to protect them from destruction. Caregiving is an aspect of this protective behavior. One modification of the theory has been made (Cicirelli 1983). In adulthood, the maintenance of the attachment bond over separations in distance and time when reunions are unlikely needs to be explained. The child's propensity for closeness and contact with the attached figure continues into adulthood and throughout life, but can be satisfied on a symbolic level when overt attachment behavior such as visiting, writing, or telephoning is not possible. The individual can use covert thoughts to symbolize or represent the attached figure, and thereby experience closeness and imagined communication on a psychological level (Bank & Kahn 1982; Ross & Milgram 1982). This symbolic attachment behavior might involve the individual's review of the close relationship to the attachment figure, but it could involve such other dimensions as an adult child's preoccupation with thoughts about a parent, a yearning to be with the parent, and feelings of anxiety or concern about being away from the parent.

In other words, symbolic attachment is an important concept to explain continued attachment that cannot be reinforced by overt attachment behavior in adulthood. It also justifies the inference of attachment from direct verbal behavior rather than only from overt attachment behavior.

Let us return to Jarrett's (1985) criticism of attachment theory. One indicator of attachment is the degree of felt closeness to the attached figure. However, there may be other relatively independent indicators that are based on symbolic attachment. For example, an adult child who lives independently in another city may measure low on felt closeness (as Jarrett argues), but measure high on preoccupation with thoughts about the parent. In studies of infants, Ainsworth, Blehar, Waters, and Wall (1978) identified three types of attachment. The first was secure attachment, which has already been discussed. They also identified (for a smaller percentage of the population) avoidant attachment and resistant (or anxious/ambivalent) attachments. Both are forms of insecure attachment in which the mother was not sufficiently sensitive and responsive to the infant, thereby leading to a maladaptive attachment relationship. In avoidant attachment, the infant appears to avoid or ignore the parent rather than seek interaction, especially upon reunion after separation; this is a relatively weak attachment bond. In resistant attachment, the infant mingles proximity- or contact-seeking behaviors with angry, rejecting behavior. If such types of attachment can be measured in adulthood, perhaps they might be related to caregiving that occurs without a conscious feeling of closeness or with diminishing closeness. If so, this would explain Jarrett's data without resorting to the concept of duty or obligation.

Although the issue of feelings of attachment versus feelings of obligation as motives for caregiving of elderly parents is not yet settled, two studies by the present author bear on this question. In the first (Cicirelli 1983), when feelings of attachment and obligation were included as variables in a path model of caregiving to elderly parents, feelings of attachment were found to have both direct and indirect effects on adult children's commitment to provide future help while filial obligation had only an indirect effect on future help. In the second study (Cicirelli 1986), divorced adult children were asked to indicate on a three-point scale how important each of fourteen reasons for helping elderly parents was for them. Reasons based on love for the parent and on desire to protect the parent from need were regarded as most important, while reasons based on feelings of duty or obligation were much less important. Reasons based on long-term reciprocity (gratitude for parent's help in the past) were of intermediate importance. Although attachment appears to be the strongest motive for helping in these studies, filial obligation also seems to have some effect. Kivett's (1988) finding that obligation characterized adult sons' relationships with rural elderly fathers suggests that obligation may be a more important motivation for sons than for daughters. It is possible that parent caregiving behavior is multiply determined, so the issue is not whether caregiving is motivated by attachment or obligation (or equity) but how and under what conditions each contributes to stimulate and maintain caregiving and what kind of motivation leads to an optimal quality and duration of care.

Another issue raised by Jarrett (1985) was that attachment is an undesirable motivation for caregiving since continued caregiving leads to decreased closeness of feelings. Yet others (Horowitz & Shindelman 1983; Sheehan & Nuttall 1988) have found that affectional closeness to the elderly parent buffers caregivers from negative effects of caregiver strain and burden. This question needs to be examined in further research.

Another aspect of the adult model of attachment that is relevant to the care of elderly parents involves an elaboration of secondary attachment. If there is more than one child in the nuclear family, the children all form attachments to the parent. However, the siblings also form secondary attachments to each other (Dunn & Kendrick 1982; Hartup & Lempers

1973; Stewart 1983; Troll & Smith 1976) and display both attachment behaviors (contact and communication) as well as protective behaviors. The result of such a secondary attachment system is that each adult child not only is motivated to protect the elderly parent by the attachment to the parent, but also tends to coordinate with adult siblings to provide care for the parent as a result of their own attachment to each other. This sibling subsystem, characterized by mutual attachment for each other and attachment to their parents, has heretofore been overlooked as a coordinated caregiving group in favor of a concentration on the primary family caregiver. A notable exception is Matthew's recent work on shared sibling caregiving (Matthews 1987; Matthews & Rosner 1988).

Social Change and Parent Caring

Admittedly, the forgoing conception of the helping relationship between adult children and elderly parents is somewhat incomplete. Attachment between children and their parents is not uniformly close; likewise, the bond of attachment between siblings can vary depending on sibling structural factors (such as age difference between siblings, sex combinations) as well as the context or external situation (Senapati & Hayes 1988; Stewart & Marvin 1984). Even in the case of secure attachment, the strength of such attachment will vary over time and for different situations.

Unfortunately, social forces operating today may disrupt the attachment bond more than in any previous decade or century (Kingson et al. 1986; Treas 1977; Ward 1978). As these authors and others have pointed out, women are entering the employment force in greater numbers; geographic mobility increases distance between child and parents; differences in lifestyles between generations may reduce the contact between them; adult children's commitment to their own spouses and children may limit resources; increases in divorce, remarriage, and reconstituted (or blended) families lead to more complex family relationships as well as diminished resources for parent caregiving (Cicirelli 1984); and new family forms such as single parent families, cohabitators, gay relationships, and shared homes are on the increase with as-yet-unknown effects on parent caring. In addition, families are smaller than they were in earlier times, with fewer adult children to provide care; elderly parents are living longer and have a longer period when care is needed; there are greater numbers of both parents and parents-in-law needing help; adult children are themselves older at the time help is needed and have their own problems of retirement and ill health; and there are increased numbers of multiple-generation families. These factors not only limit children's capability to help parents but also may weaken the attachment bond to the extent that there is much less willingness to help. For example, reconstituted families may involve stepmothers and step-siblings or half-siblings. How does this influence the attachment to the original mother and siblings, and to what extent do new attachments form that are strong enough to lead to caregiving for new family members?

In the face of such forces, a new phenomenon may be developing. The unwillingness or lack of commitment of some adult children to help their parents may be caused by filial anxiety (Cicirelli, in press). Anxiety is generated when adult children anticipate the care of an elderly parent and worry about their own ability to assume such a task.

Future Research on Attachment Theory

Many areas of research need to be investigated to fully understand the relationship of attachment to caregiving. However, certain areas are of particular interest.

Symbolic attachment would seem to be an important concept for an adult attachment model. However, more precise identification of underlying dimensions is needed to go beyond conscious closeness to understand the full meaning of attachment. Subsequently, paper-and-pencil measuring instruments need to be developed for such a definition.

Second, Ainsworth's classification of secure and insecure attachment (Ainsworth et al. 1978) should be extended to adult attachment. This is being done in the area of romantic love considered as an attachment process (Hazan & Shaver 1987). It certainly should be investigated in relation to psychological closeness and degree of caregiving.

Third, studies should be carried out comparing equity, obligation, and attachment as motives for children's caregiving. It is important to determine which motive predominates and if or how they might work together to determine caregiving behavior. It is also important to determine the relationship of these motives to the quality, quantity, level, and duration of caregiving. For example, secure attachment may be more strongly related to duration of caregiving, while obligation is more related to level of caregiving and equity to quantity of caregiving. Also, predominant motives may depend upon other aspects of the caregivers and situation.

Fourth, research needs to be done to determine how adult children as a sibling subsystem act together to provide care. Also, ways should be developed to promote more effective coordination of sibling caregiving. This is becoming more important as the number of siblings declines and the number of elderly requiring care increases. Effective and efficient mobilization of sibling resources as a caregiving system based on the strength of their attachment has barely been explored.

Fifth, it is important to know the effects of many of the social forces operating today on the attachment process. How do female employment, divorce, remarriage, and reconstituted families affect attachment? If adult children experiencing such conditions still showed strong attachment and provided caregiving (ordinary or extraordinary), it would be important to know, as well as which conditions weakened attachment. If some children showed strong attachment to parents and others showed weak attachment while reared under the same conditions, what other factors might account for this?

It has been argued here that attachment theory can best account for the motivation of adult children to help elderly parents, and therefore much research needs to be done either to verify this position or determine its limitations. But in any event, if family caregiving is to provide a sufficient quantity of caregiving, with the quality needed, the level expected, and the duration required, then the understanding of motivation for caregiving is essential.

Policy Speculations

The relationship between childrearing and parent-caring is important for the optimum development of each as well as for maintaining the survival of both. As independent as the elderly want to be, it is important that they learn to accept help when they become frail and dependent. And as much as children want to keep their own independence, it is important for them to learn the necessity of giving under sacrifice. For both child and parent, caregiving and care-receiving increases their understanding of each other and themselves and the appreciation they have for each other. As a developmental phenomenon, it leads to an increase in maturity and wisdom, and it should not be destroyed by the social forces operating today.

Informal family care should remain the core of long-term care. Care from the public sector should supplement but not substitute for informal family care, except when extraordinary care is required beyond the limits of family resources. This should never lead to premature dependency on the public sector. When formal care is indicated, adult children should be the care managers of a parent's use of formal home care, adult day care, hospices, and so on. This whole approach can be strengthened with further development of adult children as an organized sibling caregiving system.

Governments and private institutions may wish to re-think their approach to family planning. If caregiving and care-receiving over the life span are essential to the optimal development of the mature personality, then those who have the resources to raise children should be encouraged to have two children, rather than having a single child or remaining childless. Giving and receiving along with siblings in the intimacy of the parent-child relationship throughout the life span is hypothesized to be an important developmental process in danger of being entirely overlooked in modern society.

As a final thought, it is appropriate to consider helping in another connection than for direct aid (instrumental or emotional support) or care management. As previously mentioned, caregiving is an example of protective behavior. If one wants to protect another from destruction, one can provide aid when the need arises. But one can also anticipate future vulnerability, and attempt to delay it for as long as possible as a way of protecting the individual.

With this in mind, adult children can be growth facilitators for their parents. The need of older people to remain self-sufficient and independent is well-known, but ways in which adult children can help their parents achieve this have not been given sufficient attention. Instead of concentrating on "support strategies" for meeting parents' care needs, adult children can help parents stay involved with life, ignore negative stereotypes about aging, learn new skills, take risks, and reach out for new experiences in life. And above all, adult children should show as much respect for their parents' autonomy as possible, allowing them to make their own decisions even when they are frail or dying.

If the goal of life is to live as fully as possible until death rather than to decline slowly for years, then adult children's protective behavior can and should include ways to promote parents' self-help and opportunities to maximize their quality of life.

References

Ainsworth, M. D. 1972. Attachment and dependency: A comparison. In J. L. Gewirtz (ed.), *Attachment and dependency* (97–137). New York: Wiley.

Ainsworth, M. D.; Blehar, M. C.; Waters, E.; & Wall, S. 1978. *Patterns of attachment:. A psychological study of the strange situation.* Hillsdale, N.J.: Erlbaum.

Bank, S., & Kahn, M. D. 1982. *The sibling bond.* New York: Basic Books.

Bowlby, J. 1979. *The making and breaking of affectional bonds.* London: Tavistock Publications.

———. 1980. *Attachment and loss*: (Vol. 3) *Loss, sadness, and depression.* New York: Basic Books.

Brody, E. 1978. The aging of the family. *Annals of the American Academy of political and Social Science, 438,* 13–27.

Brody, E. M. 1985. Parent care as a normative family stress. *The Gerontologist, 25,* 19–29.

Cantor, M. 1975. Life space and the social support system of the inner city elderly of New York. *The Gerontologist, 15* (Part 1), 23–27.

Cicirelli, V. G. 1980. Sibling influence in adulthood: A life span perspective. In L. W. Poon (ed.), *Aging in the 1980s* (455–462). Washington, D. C.: American Psychological Association.

———. 1981. *Helping elderly parents: Role of adult children.* Boston: Auburn House.

———. 1983. Adult children's attachment and helping behavior to elderly parents: A path model. *Journal of Marriage and the Family, 45,* 815–825.

———. 1984. Marital disruption and adult children's perceptions of their siblings' help to elderly parents. *Family Relations, 33,* 613–621.

———. 1986. The relationship of divorced adult children with their elderly parents. *Journal of Divorce, 9,* (4), 39–54.

———. In press. A measure of filial anxiety regarding anticipated care of elderly parents. *The Gerontologist.*

Dunn, J., & Kendrick, C. 1982. *Siblings: Love, envy, and understanding.* Cambridge, Mass.: Harvard University Press.

Hartup, W. W., & Lempers, J. 1973. A problem in life span development: The interactional analysis of family attachments. In P. B. Baltes & K. W. Schaie (eds.), *Life-span developmental psychology: Personality and socialization* (235–252). New York: Academic Press.

Hazan, C., & Shaver, P. 1987. Romantic love conceptualized as an attachment process. *Journal of Personality and Social Psychology, 52,* 511–524.

Horowitz, A., & Dobrof, R. 1982, May. *The role of families in providing long-term care to the frail and chronically ill elderly living in the community.* New York: Brookdale Center on Aging of Hunter College.

Horowitz, A., & Shindelman, L. 1983. Reciprocity and affection: Past influences on current caregiving. *Journal of Gerontological Social Work, 5,* 5–19.

Ingersoll-Dayton, B., & Antonucci, T. C. 1988. Reciprocal and nonreciprocal social support: Contrasting sides of intimate relationships. *Journal of Gerontology: Social Sciences, 43,* S65–73.

Jarrett, W. H. 1985. Caregiving within kinship systems: Is affection really necessary? *The Gerontologist, 25,* 5–10.

Johnson, C. L., & Catalano, D. J. 1983. A longitudinal study of family supports to impaired elderly. *The Gerontologist, 23,* 612–618.

Kingson, E. R.; Hirshorn, B. A.; & Cornman, J. M. 1986. *Ties that bind: The interdependence of generations.* Washington, D.C.: Seven Locks Press.

Kivett, V. R. 1988. Older rural fathers and sons: Patterns of association and helping. *Family Relations, 37,* 62–67.

Matthews, S. H. 1987. Provision of care to old parents: Division of responsibility among adult children. *Research on Aging, 9,* 45–60.

Matthews, S. H., & Rosner, T. T. 1988. Shared filial responsibility: The family as the primary caregiver. *Journal of Marriage and the Family, 50,* 185–195.

National Center for Health Statistics. 1972. *Home care for persons fifty-five and over.* Vital and Health Statistics, Series 10. (DHEW Publication No. (HSM) 72-1062). Washington, D. C.: National Center for Health Statistics.

Noelker, L. S., & Townsend, A. L. 1987. Perceived caregiving effectiveness: The impact of parental impairment, community resources, and caregiver characteristics. In T. H. Brubaker (ed.), *Aging, health, and family: Long-term care* (58–79). Newbury Park, Calif.: Sage Publications.

Ross, H. G., & Milgram, J. I. 1982. Important variables in adult sibling relationships: A qualitative study. In M. E. Lamb & B. Sutton-Smith (eds.), *Sibling relationships: Their nature and significance across the lifespan* (225–249). Hillsdale, N.J.: Erlbaum.

Senapati, R., & Hayes, A. 1988. Sibling relationships of handicapped children: A review of conceptual and methodological issues. *International Journal of Behavioral Development, 11,* 89–115.

Shanas, E. 1979. The family as a social support system in old age. *The Gerontologist, 19,* 169–174.

Sheehan, N. W., & Nuttall, P. 1988. Conflict, emotion, and personal strain among family caregivers. *Family Relations, 37,* 92–98.

Stewart, R. B. 1983. Sibling attachment relationships: Child-infant interactions in the strange situation. *Developmental Psychology, 19,* 192–199.

Stewart, R. B., & Marvin, R. S. 1984. Sibling relationships: The role of conceptual perspective-taking in the ontogeny of sibling caregiving. *Child Development, 55,* 1322–1332.

Treas, J. 1977. Family support systems for the aged: Some demographic and social considerations. *The Gerontologist, 17,* 486–491.

Troll L. E. 1971. The family of later life: A decade review. *Journal of Marriage and the Family, 33,* 263–290.

Troll, L., & Smith, J. 1976. Attachment through the life span: Some questions about dyadic bonds among adults. *Human Development, 19,* 156–170.

Ward, R. A. 1978. Limitations of the family as a supporting institution in the lives of the aged. *Family Coordinator, 27,* 365–373.

12
Intergenerational Economic Obligations in the Welfare State

Judith Treas
Michele Spence

E
conomic obligations between adult generations are no longer
thought to figure prominently in intergenerational relations, in part
because the state and private insurance have taken over this economic support function. Research has generated conflicting evidence about
how Americans view the respective roles of the family and the state in the
support of aging parents and grown children. Despite some normative
ambiguity, intergenerational economic assistance has been amply documented, often as a complement to public assistance. Recent cost-conscious
public policies even attempt to shift some economic responsibility back
onto the family. These public/private tradeoffs have highly personal meanings for the middle generation of Americans, as they are called on to meet
uncertain obligations to aging parents and grown children.

In this chapter, we investigate beliefs about what the middle generation
owes its grown children and aging parents in the context of the developed
welfare state. Are elderly mothers and grown daughters the responsibility of
the middle generation or is the state expected to pick up the tab in the
absence of family assistance? Is the state seen as a complement to family
efforts or as a substitute—a safety net guarding against occasional failures
of intergenerational support systems? Our analysis is based on data from
a national sample of 1,470 Americans in 1986. This chapter moves beyond earlier studies to bring a large and representative national sample
to bear simultaneously on perceived obligations to older and younger
generations.

Family and State Responsibility in Historical Perspective

Although the appropriate balance between family and state responsibility
has come in for new interest, this relationship has been under negotiation in

the United States for at least two centuries. In the first half of the nineteenth century, for example, many older persons could command filial responsibility by virtue of their control over inheritance and work partnerships (Schorr 1980). Although the American Poor Law acknowledged that some elderly were destitute, it enforced family obligations by giving community assistance only after all kin resources were exhausted. By midcentury, economic responsibility began to shift from the family to the more public spheres of the workplace and the state. Industrialization and urbanization undermined the senior generation's traditional sources of power while giving offspring wages that offered considerable independence from parents (Thornton & Fricke 1987). With a decline of home production and greater competition in the urban labor force, more older people found themselves turning to charity. Retirement pensions were a response to the needs of the aged, but also to the demands of industrialists seeking worker compliance and scientific managers urging a younger, more "efficient" workforce (Haber 1978; Atchley 1982).

With the advent of social security in the 1930s, families were freed from some responsibility for elderly kin. The 1960s witnessed further expansion of state responsibility with the development of Aid for Families with Dependent Children, food stamps, Medicare, and Medicaid. Social scientists came to define the family as an increasingly specialized institution focusing on childbearing and socialization (Parsons & Bales 1955). The late 1970s, however, prompted a retrenchment of the welfare state. Under the spectre of budget deficits, more economical programs to assist the needy have been sought.

One economizing approach assumes that Americans remain favorable to family helping, which can be encouraged and complemented by modest incentives and supports such as respite care to assist middle-aged caregivers of elderly kin. At least thirty-five states permit relatives to be paid for providing home care under some circumstances (Linsk, Keigher & Osterbusch 1988). A second approach assumes that state assistance to the needy has so undermined norms of intergenerational support that coercion is necessary to guarantee help. In 1985, Wisconsin enacted a law requiring parents of teenaged sons and daughters to support any grandchildren until the unwed teenaged parents turned eighteen (Cherlin & Furstenberg 1986). In Hawaii, Massachusetts, and Colorado, legislation has been proposed to require Medicaid copayments by kin (Daniels 1988).

The coexistence of these two approaches suggests that questions remain about whether families continue to feel strong economic obligations to kin or whether they have abdicated financial responsibility to the state. Before turning to an empirical consideration of these questions, we briefly review previous findings on economic assistance between kin and normative expectations about intergenerational financial obligations.

The Behavioral Structure: Do Families Help?

The age pattern of economic assistance from family members is U-shaped, with more help received by young families and households headed by an aged person. This pattern strongly implies dependence on the middle generation, who have a life cycle income advantage over younger and older generations. Two to 3 percent of the aged report getting regular cash contributions from a child in a given year, a decline since 1961 when 5 to 10 percent received such contributions (Schorr 1980).

Economic assistance flows down the generation ladder more than it flows up, particularly in industrialized societies (Caldwell 1982). In other words, grown children get more help than aging parents. A 1975 Louis Harris poll found that 45 percent of the public aged sixty-five and older help their children and grandchildren with money. Furthermore, parents are selective in their attentions to grown children. Assistance is concentrated on those children in greatest need, those who are single, and those divorced with children of their own (Aldous 1987).

Assistance is often in the form of gifts and lump-sum payments for college tuition, down payments, and provisions for young grandchildren (Belsky & Rovine 1984; Cantor 1979; Hofferth 1984, 1985; Taylor 1986). Gifts of money or goods may be favored because they avoid the dependency feelings associated with regular payments. The financial independence of adult children is valued both by them and by their parents (Kingson, Hirshorn & Cornman 1986). Similarly, aging parents generally do not wish to draw on their children's financial resources. Although economic assistance between adult generations persists, it is carried out in a manner that preserves values of economic independence.

The Normative Structure: Should Families Help?

Evidence on norms of intergenerational economic obligations is mixed. On the one hand, Americans believe in familial economic support. Two-thirds of family heads in 1960 felt that relatives should be responsible for old people in need (Baerwaldt & Morgan 1973). When asked about their preferences for family versus nonfamily sources of assistance (financial and other forms), a random sample of 450 respondents voiced preference for family, regardless of age, cohort, gender, education, and marital status (Sanders & Seelbach 1981). In another study, respondents aged seventy-two and older, those widowed or divorced, those with low incomes, and those in poor health had greater expectations of support from their children (Seelbach 1978). These studies suggest both a preference for family support and general norms of family economic obligations, although they may be situationally defined by need.

On the other hand, there is evidence that economic support of adults—at least older adults—is seen as the responsibility of the state rather than the family. In 1974, 96 percent of the public agreed that the government should provide income for older people when they are no longer working (Louis Harris & Associates 1975). Fully 91 percent of adult children in Cicirelli's (1981) sample saw their parents as having no need for "income services" from them, and 45 percent of the children expected regular government income assistance for their parents in the future. Brody (1981) found that middle-generation women were very much less likely than older and younger generations to choose a child to furnish financial help even though they felt that, in principle, it was all right for older people to get help from their children.

To summarize these somewhat contradictory findings, there is support for the notion of family as the "best" or "ideal" source of general assistance. Americans agree that kin have some general obligations, but they accept the government's role and do not, in practice, expect to have to help out financially. Indeed, independence is valued.

While intergenerational family obligations are still a part of the picture, it is not clear how Americans see the appropriate balance of family and state. Are government income maintenance efforts seen as a complement to family efforts or is the state viewed as a substitute for families who can't or won't help needy kin? Results from a unique data set offer some clues.

Data and Methods

Analysis is based on data from a special supplement to the 1986 NORC General Social Survey (Davis & Smith 1986). This supplement consists of a set of vignettes designed to measure American public opinion regarding government income support payments to needy young families and elderly women. The survey is based on a full probability sample of 1,470 noninstitutionalized Americans. Respondents each read ten hypothetical vignettes that describe the financial and social situation of either a young family or an elderly woman living alone. For example, a respondent might be informed that "a seventy-seven-year-old woman lives alone and is in good health. She has a married son who is not financially well off. She rents her housing. She has five thousand dollars in savings. Her total income from social security, interest earned on her savings, and a private pension amounts to three hundred dollars per week." After viewing a line graph showing the weekly income attributed to the family, respondents were asked to mark the graph in response to the question, "What should this woman's [or family's] income be?" Respondents were told to include "both the money already available from sources other than the government and any public assistance support you think this family should get." They were reminded that allocating benefits could affect their taxes.

Each vignette is composed of several dimensions. In the young family vignettes, the dimension of interest is "Parent's Help," consisting of four categories measuring the ability and willingness of the parents to assist their daughter financially. "Children's Situation" is the dimension of interest in the elderly woman vignettes. There are nine categories indicating whether the woman has children and, if so, whether the adult child is a son or daughter, financially well off or not, and married or single.

The use of vignettes, more accurately called the factorial survey method, is unique in that the values on the various dimensions are randomly assigned. Because these dimension values are independent of one another, we can analyze the family responsibility variables without "controlling" for other vignette dimensions that might confound the results in real life.

T-tests have been used to identify statistically significant differences in mean benefits assigned. In addition, F ratios are used to determine differences in the variances of the benefits. This is an indication of the degree of consensus on a norm: the lower the standard deviation, the greater the agreement among respondents about the appropriate benefit level.

Findings on Benefit Levels

The parents of young families and the grown children of elderly women represent a broad middle-aged generation whose family accountability may color respondents' judgments of how much public assistance the young and old deserve. Respondents may respond to the vignettes in three ways. 1) They may choose to reward family support with higher benefits, a pattern consistent with viewing the state as a complement to family assistance. 2) Alternatively, respondents may choose to reduce public assistance benefits when families help out financially or when they are at least in a financial position to do so. This is consistent with the view that the state is a substitute for family assistance. 3) Respondents may choose to ignore family economic support patterns altogether in assigning benefits—a finding that would suggest that public assistance has come to be seen as something to which the needy are entitled regardless of kin's ability and willingness to help.

For the young families, the contrast is between cases in which the parents help and those where parents can't help, where they refuse to help, or where the daughter won't ask for help. Of interest is whether young families with helpful parents get significantly higher benefits, lower benefits, or the same benefits as families in which intergenerational support systems fail to provide assistance. For the older women, there are two important contrasts. One is between women who do and do not have children. Another is between women with a child who is or is not well off. Because different expectations may obtain for daughters and sons as well as for married and single offspring, we also consider the impact of these vignette components.

Mean benefits awarded in response to family characteristics are shown in table 12–1. For the young family vignettes, lowest average benefits are given to grown daughters whose parents help out financially ($\overline{X}$ = $269.91). While consistent with the notion of public assistance as a substitute for family support, families with helping parents do not receive significantly lower benefits than do young families without intergenerational assistance. Elderly women are given highest benefits if they have no children ($\overline{X}$ = $257.35) and lowest benefits if they have a married son who is financially well off ($\overline{X}$ = $235.67). Again, the differences are not statistically significant at the .05 level although their patterning is consistent with the view that the state is a substitute for families who can't help.

Because the family situation described does not significantly influence the level of benefits awarded, there is support for the hypothesis that public assistance is seen as an entitlement for which intergenerational obligations are irrelevant. There may, however, be some subgroups in the population for whom family economic obligations are more salient. Subgroups traditionally characterized as having a strong sense of family identification and loyalty include women and blacks.

Female respondents may allocate benefits differently than males since they are the traditional "kinkeepers" (Cantor 1983; Horowitz 1985). Studies have shown that daughters tend to provide day-to-day services to parents, whereas sons are most involved in decision-making and providing financial help (Stoller 1982; 1983). Differing sex roles within the family may mean men and women hold different expectations of economic responsibility for the middle generation. On the one hand, female respondents may give lower benefits than males if they hold greater expectations for family assistance. On the other hand, females may award higher benefits, because they usually have lower personal incomes to support needy kin, and, hence, may be more tolerant of government support. Previous research, however, has not found women to be significantly more supportive of public assistance than men (Cook 1979).

The black family system is regarded as a unique resource in meeting physical, emotional, and economic needs of its members (Hays & Mindel 1973; Hill 1972; Stack 1974). Much economic assistance is in the form of in-kind transfers (McAdoo 1980). Studies of monetary assistance indicate, however, that blacks are less likely than whites to expect and/or receive economic assistance from kin (Hanson, Sauer & Seelbach 1983; Hofferth

Table 12–1
Mean Benefits Awarded to Categories of Family Assistance

Young Family Vignette*	Benefits	
	$\overline{X}$	N**
Parents' Help		
Financially help	$269.91	324
Unable to financially help	276.29	332
Could help, but she won't ask	270.50	313
Could help, but refuse	276.64	317

Old Woman Vignette*	Benefits	
	$\overline{X}$	N**
Children's Situation		
No living children	$257.35	142
Married son, financially well off	235.67	143
Married son, not financially well off	242.66	144
Unmarried son, financially well off	247.25	151
Unmarried son, not financially well off	255.64	158
Married daughter, financially well off	235.86	136
Married daughter, not financially well off	248.80	157
Unmarried daughter, financially well off	242.48	154
Unmarried daughter, not financially well off	250.88	135

Note: Zero benefits, in which respondents took away all the vignette family's income, were deleted at the suggestion of Duncan and Ponza (1986) and Smith (1986). Apparently these respondents (n = 127) misunderstood the task.

*Differences in means between family categories not significant at .05 level.
**N of respondents per vignette.

1985). Whites clearly prefer family "sources of care" for their elderly kin, while nonwhites prefer nonfamily "sources of care" (Sanders & Seelbach 1981). Black elderly tend to receive more income maintenance from the formal support system than white elderly, and it has been suggested that the black family serves as a complement, rather than a substitute, for the formal support system of the state (Mindel & Wright 1982; Mindel, Wright & Starrett 1986). Indeed, blacks have been found to be generally more supportive of social welfare than nonblacks (Cook 1979). Because blacks typically have fewer economic resources to assist needy kin, they traditionally have relied more on the state. We may, therefore, expect blacks to hold different norms for the balance of state and family responsibility. On the one hand, a strong family system may mean greater expectations for kin helping kin. On the other hand, blacks may be more accepting of state support regardless of family efforts.

As table 12–2 shows, men tend to give lower benefits, on average, than women. The differences between men and women respondents, however, are not statistically significant at the .05 level for any family circumstance among the young family or old woman vignettes. Furthermore, in assigning benefit levels, neither men nor women draw statistically significant distinctions based on the family circumstances detailed in the vignettes. For example, men do not give young families different benefits if the parents do or do not help. The overall impression is that both sexes are equally blind to family responsibility implications when it comes to giving out public assistance. Old women and young families are neither rewarded nor punished for how the middle generation carries out familial obligations.

Table 12–2 shows that black respondents tend to give significantly higher mean benefits than nonblacks. In two circumstances—when parents refuse to help and when the daughter won't ask—young families get significantly higher levels of public assistance from blacks than nonblacks. For the old woman vignettes, blacks give significantly higher mean benefits than nonblacks to women with sons, married children, and children who are or are not financially well off. In assigning benefit levels, however, neither blacks nor nonblacks make benefit levels conditional on family help. Again, the young and old are neither rewarded nor punished for the middle generation's helping patterns.

The consistent allocation of higher benefits by black respondents may indicate a realistic assessment of their need to turn to government income maintenance programs to supplement family assistance. Neither racial group adheres to a normative belief that certain intergenerational family circumstances merit greater or lesser benefits. As seen for men and women, blacks and nonblacks are blind to family circumstances in their benefit decisions. In short, public assistance is an entitlement rather than a substitute for or complement to intergenerational financial support.

Research Findings: Consensus

All norms imply consensus, because they are "acknowledged rules recognized as binding by the members of society in question" (Rossi & Berk 1985, 333). Any evidence of normative beliefs regarding family assistance, therefore, should be characterized by consensus, which is measured by the dispersion in assigned benefits for each vignette category. Higher standard deviations indicate either disagreement about what is appropriate or a lack of crystallized opinion about the matter altogether—that is, a nonattitude (Converse 1964; Smith 1984).

In general, men demonstrate more agreement on benefit allocations than women, as evidenced by lower standard deviations in table 12–2. When it comes to young families, men show significantly greater agreement than women when the parents help, when the parents could help but the daughter won't ask, and when the parents could help but refuse. Men also

Table 12–2
Benefits to Family Categories, by Respondent's Sex and Race

Young Family	Male			Female			Black			Nonblack		
	X̄	S.D.	N	X̄	S.D.	N	X̄	S.D.	N	X̄	S.D.	N
Parents help	$267.67	114.76*	135	271.68	133.70*	176	$306.36	135.88	37	264.40	123.15	285
Parents can't help	271.77	140.13	140	279.68	141.44	186	314.19	147.43	31	270.79	139.11	280
Parents could help, but daughter won't ask	259.69	122.74*	134	278.36	147.50*	179	323.37**	166.52**	33	263.93**	132.50**	277
Parents could help, but they refuse	265.97	127.52*	132	284.48	156.08*	181	323.84**	160.96	33	269.50**	141.03	283
Old Woman	X̄	S.D.	N	X̄	S.D.	N	X̄	S.D.	N	X̄	S.D.	N
No children	$253.20	144.30	56	260.55	154.92	79	$293.69	195.91	11	252.75	143.12	125
Son	237.89	137.75*	248	251.88	155.77*	324	287.02**	203.32**	68	239.47**	136.96**	519
Daughter	247.96	143.03	236	242.29	136.55	330	271.18	162.22**	60	241.22	135.70**	509
Married	238.44	142.62	236	242.86	138.13	326	276.60**	181.85**	69	235.67	131.83**	499
Single	246.69	138.30	248	251.01	153.85	328	282.98	189.85**	59	244.66	140.20**	529
Well off	235.78	136.14	245	244.29	144.30	311	277.70**	180.47**	54	235.54**	133.83**	515
Not well off	249.85	144.27	239	249.51	148.29	343	281.52**	190.19**	74	244.98**	138.53**	513

*Significant difference at .05 level between men and women

**Significant difference at .05 level between blacks and nonblacks

indicate significantly greater consensus than women about a son's responsibility to his aging mother.

In all cases, nonblacks show greater agreement than blacks. This is particularly evident for the old woman vignettes, where all family circumstances except "no children" register significantly higher levels of agreement for nonblacks than for blacks. For young families, however, nonblacks show significantly more agreement than blacks only when the daughter won't ask for help.

Men achieve greater agreement than women and nonblacks more than blacks. More relevant to our discussion of the responsibilities of the middle generation is the degree of consensus *within* each respondent subgroup about the various vignette categories. Men have significantly greater agreement about appropriate benefit levels when parents do help their daughter than when they cannot help. Similarly, women are in significantly greater agreement when parents help than when they refuse to help a needy daughter. Women also express significantly more consensus on a daughter's role toward her aging mother than on that of a son. Men and women sustain high consensus for daughters who receive financial assistance from their parents, regardless of any differences in mean benefits.

Categories indicating family ability to help out financially (such as having no children versus having a son or daughter, or having a child who is financially well off versus one who is not) fail to yield significant differences in consensus for any respondent subgroups. Blacks fail to show any significant differences in agreement between family categories. Nonblacks, however, agree significantly more about how much to give when parents help their daughter than when they cannot help or when they refuse to do so.

With the exception of blacks, all respondent subgroups are in greater agreement about appropriate benefit levels when parents give money to their needy daughter. This is not to say that respondents believe that these daughters should be given less public assistance (implying the state as a supplement to family assistance) or should be given more public assistance (suggesting the state as a complement to family assistance). Rather, the stimulus of parents' helping out provokes consensus among respondents about how much public assistance a needy daughter should or should not receive. This does not necessarily mean normative consensus, but rather greater clarity about the circumstances of intergenerational relations. Presumably, parents' helping is an unambiguous stimuli to which respondents can respond in a uniform way. Other vignette characteristics may lend themselves to differing interpretations and, hence, to different responses. For example, if the parent could help but the daughter won't ask, it may mean that she is either admirably self-reliant or utterly alienated from kin.

Conclusions and Implications

In general, Americans see state income maintenance efforts as an entitle-ment for the needy, whether young or old. Financial assistance by the middle generation has no effect on amount of state income maintenance payments the public thinks impoverished persons are entitled to receive. Respondents simply ignore family economic support patterns altogether, a finding that supports our hypothesis that public assistance has come to be seen as something to which the needy are entitled regardless of kin's ability and willingness to help.

Blacks and, to a lesser extent, women, tend to grant higher amounts of public assistance, not because they have fewer expectations of family assist-ance, but because they are generally inclined to support government aid in times of need. The question then becomes: are they also more certain about how much money the needy deserve? Our findings suggest the answer to be no, because blacks and women have significantly *less* agreement about benefit levels than nonblacks and men. All in all, respondents show mini-mal differences in consensus is response to different family characteristics. Only when the parents are said to help their daughter financially is there significantly more certainty about amounts. This may imply more norma-tive consensus about the appropriate benefits, given helping parents, or it may mean that this category is simply less ambiguous than other vignette categories. Furthermore, respondents do not punish or reward the daughter for receiving family assistance, but simply show less dispersion in their decisions to give out public assistance.

In the minds of Americans, expectations about intergenerational obliga-tions are not linked with judgments about social welfare benefits. Whether the middle generation helps out does not factor into decisions about the level of financial assistance the state should provide to needy members of the younger or older generation. From the perspective of political dialogue, this suggests there is no receptive constituency for social welfare reforms founded on appeals to intergenerational economic obligations.

On the one hand, Americans are not inclined to reward the needy with additional social welfare benefits just because their families have pitched in to help. Thus, there is little reason to expect that Americans will be particu-larly drawn to programs that offer incentives to encourage families to help. Americans may see intergenerational assistance as something kin should provide, because it is the right thing to do, not because of special induce-ments. On the other hand, Americans do not believe public assistance should be withheld from the needy when their families will not help out. Thus, there is no reservoir of support for family responsibility legislation that would tie state assistance to family support. Americans, it seems, assign responsibility for the support of the needy directly to the state and refuse to tie social welfare benefits to the performance of intergenerational helping networks.

These findings point to the need to refocus studies of the relation between intergenerational helping patterns and public efforts. While Americans accept the notion of financial assistance from the state, other kinds of support are still viewed as the province of the family. For example, family members are preferred over formal service-providers when it comes to financial management, food shopping, and confidences (Brody, Davis & Johnsen 1979). How and why are some intergenerational family support functions so readily surrendered? Why do other functions continue to be viewed as rightly the responsibility of kin?

Recent applications of transaction cost perspectives to intergenerational family life may offer a useful theoretical framework for pursuing these research questions (Treas in press). This approach suggests individuals will rely on the carefully cultivated loyalties and personalized social controls of the family when the quality and quantity of what is exchanged are difficult to measure. As this perspective would imply, monetary support, which can be measured unambiguously in dollars, need not come from kin. On the other hand, the quality of personal advice is much more difficult to gauge. Thus, kin, whose trustworthiness can be established, may continue to be preferred over professional counselors as confidants. The American public has little or no ambivalence about the rightful place of family and state in the support of younger and older generations. More fruitful analyses may center on other family functions undergoing renegotiation between state and family (such as long-term care) or on other nations that are only now institutionalizing public assistance programs.

References

Aldous, J. 1987. New views on the family life of the elderly and the near-elderly. *Journal of Marriage and the Family, 49,* 227–234.

Atchley, R. C. 1982. Retirement as a social institution. *Annual Review of Sociology, 8,* 263–287.

Baerwaldt, N. A., & Morgan, J. N. 1973. Trends in interfamily transfers. In L. Mandell, G. Katona, J. N. Morgan, & J. Schmiedeskamp (eds.), *Surveys of consumers, 1971–72* (205–232). University of Michigan: Institute for Social Research.

Belsky, J., & Rovine, M. 1984. Social network contact, family support, and the transition to parenthood. *Journal of Marriage and the Family, 46,* 455–462.

Brody, E.; Davis, L.; & Johnsen, P. 1979, November. *Formal and informal service providers: Preferences of three generations of women.* Paper presented at the meeting of the Gerontological Society of America, Washington, D.C.

Brody, E. M. 1981. "Women in the middle" and family help to older people. *The Gerontologist, 21,* 471–480.

Caldwell, J. C. 1982. *Theory of fertility decline.* New York: Academic Press.

Cantor, M. H. 1979. The informal support system of New York's inner city elderly: Is ethnicity a factor? In D. E. Gelfand & A. J. Kutzik (eds.), *Ethnicity and aging* (153–174). New York: Springer.

———. 1983. Strain among caregivers: A study of experience in the United States. *The Gerontologist, 23,* 587–604.

Cherlin, A. J., & Furstenberg, F. F. 1986. *The new American grandparent.* New York: Basic Books.

Cicirelli, V. G. 1981. *Helping elderly parents: The role of adult children.* Boston: Auburn House.

Converse, P. 1964. The nature of belief systems in mass publics. In D. E. Apter (ed.), *Ideology and discontent* (206–261). Glencoe: Free Press.

Cook, F. L. 1979. *Who should be helped? Public support for social services.* Beverly Hills: Sage Publications.

Daniels, N. D. 1988. *Am I my parent's keeper?* Oxford: Oxford University Press.

Davis, J. A., & Smith, T. W. 1986. *General Social Surveys, 1972–1986: Cumulative codebook.* Chicago: National Opinion Research Center.

Duncan, G. J., & Groskind, F. 1987. *Some methodological aspects of responses to the 1986 GSS welfare entitlement vignettes.* Unpublished manuscript, University of Michigan, Survey Research Center.

Haber, C. 1978. Mandatory retirement in nineteenth-century America: The conceptual basis for a new work cycle. *Journal of Social History, 12,* 77–96.

Hanson, S. L.; Sauer, W. J.; & Seelbach, W. C. 1983. Racial and cohort variations in filial responsibility norms. *The Gerontologist, 23,* 626–631.

Harris, L., & Associates. 1975. *The myth and reality of aging in America.* Washington D.C.: National Council on Aging.

Hays, W. C., & Mindel, C. H. 1973. Extended kinship relations in black and white families. *Journal of Marriage and the Family, 35,* 51–57.

Hill, R. 1972. *The strength of black families.* New York: Emerson-Hall.

Hofferth, S. L. 1984. Kin networks, race, and family structure. *Journal of Marriage and the Family, 46,* 791–806.

———. 1985. Children's life course: Family structure and living arrangements in cohort perspective. In G. H. Elder (ed.), *Life course dynamics* (75–112). Ithaca: Cornell University Press.

Horowitz, A. 1985. Sons and daughters as caregivers to older parents: Differences on role performance and consequences. *The Gerontologist, 25,* 612–617.

Kingson, E. R.; Hirshorn, B. A.; & Cornman, J. M. 1986. *Ties that bind, the interdependence of generations.* Washington D.C.: Seven Locks Press.

Linsk, N. L.; Keigher, S. M.; & Osterbusch, S. E. 1988. States' policies regarding paid family cargiving. *The Gerontologist, 28,* 204–212.

McAdoo, H. P. 1980. Black mothers and the extended family support network. In L. Rodgers-Rose (ed.), *The black woman* (125–144). Beverly Hills: Sage Publications.

Mindel, C. H., & Wright, R. 1982. The use of social services by black and white elderly: The role of social support systems. *Journal of Gerontological Social Work, 4,* 107–125.

Mindel, C. H.; Wright, R.; & Starrett, P. 1986. Informal and formal social and health service use by black and white elderly: A comparative cost approach. *The Gerontologist, 26,* 279–285.

Parsons, T., & Bales, R. F. 1955. *Family socialization and interaction process.* Glencoe: Free Press.

Rossi, P. H., & Berk, R. A. 1985. Varieties of normative consensus. *American Sociological Review, 50,* 333–347.

Sanders, L. T., & Seelbach, W. C. 1981. Variations in preferred care alternatives of the elderly: Family versus nonfamily sources. *Family Relations, 30,* 447–451.

Schorr, A. L. 1980. ". . . *thy father and thy mother . . .*"; *A second look at filial responsibility and family policy* (SSA Publication No. 13-11953). Washington, D.C.: U.S. Government Printing Office.

Seelbach, W. C. 1978. Correlates of aged parent's filial responsibility expectations and realizations. *The Family Coordinator, 27,* 341–350.

Smith, T. W. 1987. *A study of nonresponse and negative values on the factorial vignettes on welfare* (GSS Technical Report no. 69). Chicago: National Opinion Research Center.

———. 1984. Nonattitudes: A review and evaluation. In C. F. Turner & E. Martin (eds.), *Surveying subjective phenomena* (Vol. 2, 215–255). New York: Russell Sage Foundation.

Stack, C. 1974. *All our kin: Strategies for survival in the black community.* New York: Harper & Row.

Stoller, E. P. 1982. Sources of support for the elderly during illness. *Health and Social Work*, 7, 111–122.

———. 1983. Parent caregiving by adult children. *Journal of Marriage and the Family*, 45, 851–865.

Taylor, R. J. 1986. Receipt of support from family among black Americans: Demographic and familial differences. *Journal of Marriage and the Family*, 48, 67–77.

Thornton, A., & Fricke, T. E. 1987. Social change and the family: Comparative perspectives from the West, China, and South Asia. *Sociological Forum*, 2, 746–779.

Treas, J. In press. Money in the bank: Transaction costs and privatized marriage. *American Sociological Review*.

Part 3
Caregiving and Care-Receiving

13

Why Daughters Care: Perspectives of Mothers and Daughters in a Caregiving Situation

Alexis J. Walker
Clara C. Pratt
Hwa-Yong Shin
Laura L. Jones

Caregiving Motives

In 1965, Blenkner introduced the phrase *filial maturity* to the intergenerational literature. The widespread endorsement of filial maturity has been described in many different studies (Brody, Johnsen, Fulcomer & Lang 1983; Finley, Roberts & Banahan 1988; Hanson, Sauer & Seelbach 1983), but the motives underlying this endorsement have not been studied. A major question is the separate influences of obligatory and discretionary motives in undertaking filial responsibility.

Adams's 1968 study suggested that geographical proximity imposed, while geographical distance limited, intergenerational contact. Only at moderate distances could contact be fully discretionary. More recent data (Walker & Thompson 1983) have also shown that, at moderate distances, contact is positively related to intimacy between young adult women and their mothers. Although this relationship did not hold at near or far distances, nor for middle-aged women and their mothers (Walker & Thompson 1983), the distinction between obligatory and discretionary motives for contact is important to pursue because both obligatory and discretionary

This chapter is based on a paper presented at the 1988 annual meeting of the National Council on Family Relations in Philadelphia. Work on this project was supported by National Institute on Aging Grant #06766. We are grateful to Melanie Place, David Bird, Lois Mock, Sally Martin, and Louise Martell for assistance with coding and to Katherine Allen for her helpful comments on an earlier version of this paper. This chapter is in memory of Golda R. Hornstein.

motives have been endorsed by caregiving daughters (Walker, Shin, Jones & Pratt 1987).

Obligatory Motives

Circumstances such as the need for help on the part of an aging family member may engender obligatory motives for caregiving because this need imposes a responsibility on family members (Adams 1968; Blieszner & Mancini 1987; Callahan 1985; Leigh 1982; Matthews 1979; Nydegger 1983; Tobin & Kulys 1980). In addition, social patterns conspire to place women in the position of family caregiver (Finch & Groves 1983). Not only have women been socialized into nurturing roles (Graham 1983), their position in the labor market and the lack of palatable alternatives to family caregiving render their assistance essential (Abel 1986; Graham 1983; Hess & Waring 1978; Ungerson 1983; Walker 1983). Therefore, we expect obligation to be an important motivator for family caregiving.

Discretionary Motives

On the other hand, affection and interdependence built over the history of an intimate relationship may stimulate family members to ease the difficulties of their loved ones, thus underlying discretionary motives for caregiving (Callahan 1985; Cicirelli 1983; Finley et al. 1988; Leigh 1982; Marshall, Rosenthal & Synge 1983; Robinson & Thurnher 1979). Feelings of compassion and connectedness motivate women to give care (Graham 1983). These feelings may be especially important in mother-daughter relationships given the centrality of this bond to women's lives (Abel 1986). Further, Hess and Waring (1978) have argued that the obligation of filial responsibility has eroded and that discretionary motives now underlie the exchange of aid between generations. Therefore, we expect discretionary motives to be important incentives for family caregiving as well.

Mothers' and Daughters' Perceptions of Daughters' Motives

Data have shown that most mothers believe their daughters' motives for caregiving are discretionary, while most daughters report both obligatory and discretionary motives (Walker et al. 1987). These results suggested that mothers may find it less costly psychologically to presume discretionary caregiving motives.

Method

Sample

The sample included 173 mostly white elderly mother–adult daughter pairs from western Oregon who volunteered for a longitudinal study on mother-daughter relationships in adulthood. Daughters provided at least one of the following services for their mothers: transportation, housekeeping, meal preparation, laundry, personal care, and/or financial support. Mothers, aged sixty-five or older, lived within forty-five miles of their caregiving daughters, had no cognitive impairment, and were unmarried.

The median age of mothers was eighty-four. Most (88.4 percent) were widowed. Mothers' median education level was twelve years and median yearly income was $7,188. Mothers' estimates of how long their daughters had been assisting them ranged from zero months to forty-eight years with a median of 4.50 years. A majority (65.9 percent) lived alone while one-fifth (20.8 percent) lived with their daughters.

The median age of daughters was fifty-three. Nearly half (49.1 percent) were in their first marriage, although one-fifth (20.2 percent) were divorced. Daughters' median education level was fourteen years and median yearly family income was $28,000. Just over half (50.5 percent) were employed outside the home. Daughters' estimates of how long they had been providing care to their mothers ranged from zero months to fifty-one years with a median of five years.

Procedures

Data were collected in face-to-face interviews using structured question-naires. Separate interviews were conducted with mothers and daughters, primarily in the respondents' homes. Mothers and daughters were asked their perceptions of daughters' motives in caregiving, using both quantitative and qualitative measures. Demographic data also were collected. Although other information also was gathered, only data regarding caregiving motives and demographic characteristics are reported here. Interview length varied from twenty to 165 minutes for mothers ($m = 48$) and from thirty-five to 175 minutes for daughters ($m = 72$).

Measurement

Perceived Motives for Caregiving. Mothers and daughters were asked to what extent they believed daughters were assisting their mothers because they felt obligated to do so. Possible answers ranged from totally out of obligation (1) to not at all obligated (4). Both were also asked to what

Table 13–1
Obligatory and Discretionary Motives for Caregiving

Category	Example
Discretionary	
Relationship attitude	I love her.
	Because she loves me.
Personality trait	I enjoy helping people in general.
	She's a kind person.
Future implications	I would like to keep my mother's place.
Daughter's wishes for mother's future	She wants to protect me.
	I want to see her comfortable and happy.
Situational	She likes living here.
Obligatory	
Cycle to life	I brought her up; now I'm on the other side.
	I know she raised and cared for me.
Moral beliefs	You honor your parents.
	I feel it is my duty.
Coercion	I'm legally obligated.
	Because of my mother's opinion about nursing homes.
Socialization	She was raised to respect her parents.
	We have a family tradition of caregiving.
Daughter's negative attitudes toward nursing homes	I didn't want her to go to a nursing home.
Relationship obligation	You do for your parents because they are your parents.
	She is my mother.
Situational	There is no one else.
	She is closest geographically.

extent they believed daughters were assisting their mothers because they wanted to do so. Response categories ranged from totally because they wanted to (1) to did not want to at all (4).

Daughters who reported any degree of obligation were then asked an open-ended question: "Why do you feel obligated to help your mother?" Similarly, daughters who reported that to any degree they wanted to care for their mothers were asked: "Why do you want to help your mother?" The pattern was repeated for mothers although questions were reworded as appropriate.

Responses were coded by individuals knowledgeable about filial responsibility, including some project interviewers. Categories emerged from coders' discussion of the literature and consideration of recalled responses. Examples of responses in each category appear in table 13–1. Five categories of discretionary reasons for caregiving were identified: (a) Relationship Attitude, (b) Personality Trait, (c) Future Implications, (d) Daughter's Wishes for Mother, and (e) Situational/Discretionary. Seven categories of obligatory reasons were identified: (a) Cycle to Life Expectations, (b) Moral Beliefs, (c) Coercion, (d) Socialization, (e) Daughter's Negative Attitudes toward Nursing Homes, (f) Relationship Obligation, and (g) Situational/ Obligatory.

Because respondents could give more than one reason for caregiving, there was a total of 751 responses. Eight individuals independently coded 122 responses with 100 percent agreement. An additional forty-four responses achieved 75 percent agreement; sixty-two other items received less than 75 percent agreement. These sixty-two items were discussed and then independently categorized by the authors with 100 percent agreement. As most of the remaining items were synonyms, two coders independently coded the next 467 responses at 100 percent agreement. An additional fifty-six items coded by the authors were placed in the "other" category at 100 percent agreement. Items coded "other" did not respond to the question or provided insufficient information for coding (for example, a person just does these things; I wouldn't know). In preparing this chapter, these fifty-six responses were omitted. In addition, a number of responses came from additional pairs in which the mothers were not dependent on the daughters. As these women were not included in the present sample, their responses were omitted. Thus, the final number of 595 responses was drawn from pairs in which the mother had some degree of dependence on the daughter.

Results

More than two-thirds (69.4 percent) of the daughters reported some degree of obligation in caring for their mothers, while less than one-third (31.0 percent) of the mothers reported that their daughters had obligatory motives. Thus, daughters were significantly more likely than mothers to believe that caregiving was motivated at least in part by feelings of obligation ($X^2(1, N = 346) = 55.04, p < .001$).

When asked to elaborate on the obligatory and/or discretionary motives behind their caregiving, 60.6 percent of the daughters' total responses and 39.3 percent of the mothers' total responses reflected obligatory motives. Daughters were significantly more likely to give obligatory reasons than were mothers ($X^2(1, N = 595) = 24.45, p < .001$).

Obligatory Motives

Among the daughters who said they were, to some degree, obligated to provide care, the vast majority (91.0 percent) gave only obligatory reasons for caregiving when asked to elaborate. Relationship Obligation was the reason most frequently mentioned by daughters (31.4 percent), followed by Moral Beliefs (26.4 percent), Cycle to Life Expectations (22.3 percent),

Table 13–2
Percentage of Obligatory and Discretionary Motives for Daughters and Mothers

Motive type	Daughters obligated[a] to provide care		Daughters wanted[a] to provide care	
	D (n = 121)	M (n = 52)	D (n = 161)	M (n = 163)
Obligatory				
N	135	44	80	51
Relationship obligation	31.4 (38)	34.6 (18)	29.8 (48)*	17.8 (29)
Moral beliefs	26.4 (32)	15.4 (8)	10.0 (16)	6.1 (10)
Cycle to life	23.3 (27)*	3.8 (2)	3.7 (6)	1.8 (3)
Situational	17.4 (21)	19.2 (10)	3.1 (5)	2.5 (4)
Socialization	11.6 (14)	9.6 (5)	1.2 (2)	2.5 (4)
Anti-nursing home	1.7 (2)	——	1.2 (2)	0.6 (1)
Coercion	0.8 (1)	1.9 (1)	0.6 (1)	——
Discretionary				
N	11	14	128	132
Relationship attitude	6.6 (8)	13.5 (7)	54.7 (88)	51.5 (84)
Personality	0.8 (1)*	7.7 (4)	14.9 (24)*	24.5 (40)
Wishes for Mother	1.7 (2)	3.8 (2)	5.6 (9)	1.8 (3)
Situational	——	——	3.7 (6)	3.1 (5)
Implications for future	——	1.9 (1)	0.6 (1)	——
Total N of both motive types	146	58	208	183

Note: Respondents could state multiple motives.

[a]Women responding either somewhat, mostly, or totally obligated; somewhat, totally, or mostly desire to help.

Situational Obligation (17.4 percent), Socialization (11.6 percent), and Personality (0.8 percent). Except for Personality, these reasons are obligatory. (See table 13–2.)

Nearly three-quarters (72.0 percent) of the mothers who reported that their daughters were assisting them, at least in part, because of obligation reported only obligatory reasons. As with daughters, Relationship Obligation was most frequently mentioned by mothers (34.6 percent), followed by Situational Obligation (19.2 percent), Moral Beliefs (15.4 percent), Relationship Attitude (13.5 percent), Socialization (9.6 percent), Personality (7.7 percent), and Cycle to Life Expectations (3.8 percent). Note that Relationship Attitude and Personality are actually discretionary reasons for caregiving. (Table 13–2.)

Significantly more of the daughters' than mothers' reasons were classified as Cycle to Life Expectations ($X^2(1, N = 173) = 8.9, p < .003$), while significantly more of the mothers' than daughters' reasons were classified as Personality ($X^2(1, N = 173) = 6.1, p < .02$).

Discretionary Motives

More than 90 percent of the daughters and mothers reported that daughters were motivated to give care, at least in part, by discretion. Yet, just over half (54.7 percent) of the daughters who reported discretionary motives gave only discretionary reasons for caregiving in response to the open-ended question. The most commonly given discretionary reason was Relationship Attitude (54.7 percent), followed by Relationship Obligation (29.8 percent), Personality (14.9 percent), and Moral Beliefs (10.0 percent). Note that both Relationship Obligation and Moral Beliefs are actually obligatory reasons.

When asked to elaborate, most (73.0 percent) of the mothers who reported discretionary motives for daughters' caregiving also gave discretionary reasons for their caregiving. As with daughters, Relationship Attitude was the most common reason (51.5 percent), followed by Personality (24.5 percent), Relationship Obligation (17.8 percent), and Moral Beliefs (6.1 percent). As was true for some daughters, some mothers gave obligatory reasons, that is, Relationship Obligation and Moral Beliefs.

Daughters gave significantly more Relationship Obligation reasons than mothers ($X^2(1, N = 324) = 6.4, p < .05$), while mothers gave significantly more Personality reasons than daughters ($X^2(1, N = 324) = p < .03$).

Discussion

Striking among the findings of this inquiry is the number and diversity of motives given for caregiving. Further, there is a substantial mixture of obligatory and discretionary motives. It is clear that caregiving is motivated by complex interactions of feelings of duty and desire, particularly for daughters.

The complexity of interactions among obligatory and discretionary motives is apparent in the daughters' responses. Most daughters said there was some degree of obligation and discretion in their caregiving. When daughters who said their caregiving was motivated by obligation were asked to elaborate on these motives, most of their responses reflected obligatory motives. When daughters who said their caregiving was motivated out of desire were asked to elaborate on these motives, however, over one-third of their responses reflected obligatory motives. Daughters may have internalized obligatory motives to such an extent that they no longer separate these obligations from desire. Callahan (1985) has written that there may not be any incompatibility between a sense of duty felt by children and feelings of affection. The compatibility between obligatory and discretionary motives for caregiving has been supported here.

When elaborating on why daughters wanted to give care, the most commonly stated motive was Relationship Attitude, primarily, feelings of love and affection. More than half of all mothers and daughters said love or some other positive Relationship Attitude was the motive. These responses emphasize the emotional bond between two individuals as the most common motive for caregiving. Relationship Attitude was much less often given as a motive for obligatory caregiving. Clearly, caring and affection are discretionary motives for caregiving. Love and intimacy, according to Callahan (1985), are important foundations of the moral obligation between parents and their adult children. Cicirelli (1983) has reported that feelings of attachment influence a commitment to provide help in the future. And Finley et al. (1988) found affection to be strongly associated with filial responsibility for women, although affection was not always important in this regard. The findings here demonstrate that women do give care out of feelings of compassion and connectedness (Graham 1983). These feelings, as well as a socialized set of values and a relationship history (Hess & Waring 1978) contribute to caregiving motivated by discretion.

The second most frequently stated motive for caregiving was Relationship Obligation. Unlike Relationship Attitude, which focuses on the unique bond between two individuals, Relationship Obligation focuses on the duty that exists between daughters and mothers, regardless of their affection for one another. Thus, "I care for her because she is my mother," reflects Relationship Obligation. Mothers and especially daughters gave Relationship Obligation reasons as the most common motive for feelings of obligation to give care. Horowitz and Shindelman (1983) wrote that affection is not necessary to give care and Troll (1986) wrote that feelings of obligation or duty may motivate help giving. Similarly, Jarrett (1985) and Nydegger (1983) argued that obligation is given insufficient attention in the study of kin relations. The present findings demonstrate that reasons other than affection are important in family caregiving.

Moral beliefs including both religious beliefs and beliefs about the "right thing to do," were important motives for caregiving for 25 percent of the daughters and 15 percent of the mothers who believed that there was some degree of obligation in the daughters' caregiving. Moral beliefs were less frequently reported as reasons for desiring to give care.

Cycle to Life Expectations motives, more often given by daughters than mothers, included the perception that daughters were "paying back" their mothers for earlier care that the daughters had received and feelings of being on the "other side" of caregiving. These motives are seen in statements such as "She feels that I brought her up; now I am on the other side of the relationship," and "I want to pay her back for raising me." For nearly 25 percent of the daughters, such feelings were important motives behind the sense of obligation to provide care to their mothers. Callahan's (1985) idea that gratitude is one foundation of the moral ties between adult children and their parents is supported here. Still, Cycle to Life Expectations were much less frequent than has been predicted (Brody 1985). Fewer than 4 percent of the mothers' reasons and just over one-fifth of the daughters' reasons were classified in this way.

Situational Obligation was reported by almost one-fifth of both mothers and daughters. Situational reasons included geographic proximity and lack of other alternatives including available and/or willing siblings. Thus, not having any other choice was important for a significant minority of women.

Socialization reasons were reported by about one-tenth of both mothers and daughters. These women believed daughters were providing care because it was a family tradition or because they had been "reared" to.

Mothers were more likely than daughters to perceive that daughters wanted to provide care because of their "Personality." Discretionary reasons, more commonly given by mothers than daughters, may be less psychologically costly for mothers. Mothers who say "My daughter cares for me because that's the type of person she is," may not see themselves as demanding help or as being a burden to their daughters.

It should be noted that several classes of motives were rarely mentioned by mothers or daughters. Among these were Negative Attitudes toward Nursing Homes, Daughters' Wishes for Mother's Future, Coercion, or the wish to "gain something" financially from caregiving (Future Implications). Thus, while these motives have been noted in the literature as reasons for caregiving, they do not appear to be salient to most daughters and mothers when they discuss their actual reasons for caregiving. Situational Discretionary reasons (such as, "She likes living here") were also rare.

Implications

The multiple reasons for providing assistance offered by caregiving daughters and their care-receiving mothers—as well as the great variety of reasons—suggest that we should look anew at the concept of filial responsibility. The findings reported here assert that there is no simple notion of filial maturity. Instead, adult child caregivers accept the responsibility of providing help to an elderly parent in need, but they do so for a variety of reasons. Indeed, many of them report feelings of both desire and obligation to provide care. Similarly, their care-receiving mothers are aware of multiple motives, although motives of an obligatory nature are less salient to these older women.

The distinction among reasons may be crucial to the potential impact of caregiving on the parent-adult child relationship. Indeed, data have shown (Walker et al. 1987) that women who report that daughters provide care primarily for obligatory reasons report less intimacy in their intergenerational relationship than women who report that daughters provide care primarily for discretionary reasons. It is also possible that motives for caregiving may change over the history of assistance provision. One daughter in this study reported that she could not stop caregiving for her mother now because, "She wouldn't understand." This daughter is coerced into caregiving by the expectations she created in providing help to her mother at an earlier time. What may once have been an easy and desired task can become an oppressive and obligatory one.

Still, this study showed that coercive motives for caregiving are rare. Obligatory motives, however, are common. Both Nydegger (1983) and Jarrett (1985) recognized the obligatory nature of kin ties and lamented the rarity with which obligation appears in the research literature. Our findings suggest that researchers on family caregiving would be well-served by focusing on the obligations family members feel toward each other. In fact, Relationship Obligation was the second most frequently given reason for caregiving in this study. That some motives anticipated in the literature— Negative Attitudes toward Nursing Homes, Daughters' Wishes for Mother, Coercion, and Future Implications—were noticeably rare was surprising. The voluntary nature of the sample may be responsible, in part, for their absence. It is also possible, however, that researchers have overestimated the importance of these motives. More detailed research on filial responsibility will help clarify this issue. From a policy perspective, however, that few caregivers report a motivation to "gain something" may cause us to question the usefulness of financial incentives to provide care. What may be needed instead are adequate support services.

Obviously, additional investigation is needed. Rather than focusing exclusively on the extent to which individuals endorse notions of filial responsibility, as is characteristic of the caregiving literature, researchers must decompose filial responsibility into its underlying motives. The inquiry must be broadened to include both the obligatory and the discretionary aspects that underlie filial responsibility.

Philip Brickman (1987) has argued that commitment to a course of action, such as caregiving, contains positive and negative elements. When positive elements (such as the close, affectionate relationship shared by the caregiver and care-receiver) are dominant, the activity seems intrinsically motivated. This characterizes discretionary caregiving. When negative elements (such as the difficulties of reconciling demands from a parent with demands from other aspects of one's life) are dominant, however, the activity feels like work. That individuals persist despite the weight of the sacrifices necessitated is evidence that the call of duty or obligation is evident. What individuals feel—intrinsic motivation or the call of duty— depends on which aspects are salient, the positive or the negative, although people usually are aware that elements of both are also present (Brickman, Janoff-Bulman & Rabinowitz 1987).

The results of this study support Brickman's (1987) model and call into question the assumption that obligatory and discretionary motives for caregiving occupy opposite ends of a continuum. They also suggest that caregiving motives, in accordance with Brickman's model (Brickman, Dunkel-Schetter & Abbey 1987), are neither simple nor unchanging. More detailed and careful exploration of caregiving motives—positive, negative, and the connection between the two—will contribute to a more realistic and dynamic picture of the caregiving role. Further, it will point us toward a fuller understanding of parent-child relationships in later life.

References

Abel, E. K. 1986. Adult daughters and care for the elderly. *Feminist Studies, 12,* 479–497.

Adams, B. N. 1968. *Kinship in an urban setting.* Chicago: Markham Publishing.

Blenkner, M. 1965. Social work and family relationships in later life with some thoughts on filial maturity. In E. Shanas & G. Streib (eds.), *Social structure and the family: Generational relationships* (46–59). Englewood Cliffs, N.J.: Prentice-Hall.

Blieszner, R., & Mancini, J. A. 1987. Enduring ties: Older adults' parental role and responsibilities. *Family Relations, 36,* 176–180.

Brickman, P. 1987. Commitment. In C. B. Wortman & R. Sorrentino (eds.), *Commitment, conflict, and caring* (1–18). Englewood Cliffs, N.J.: Prentice-Hall.

Brickman, P., Dunkel-Schetter, C., & Abbey, A. 1987. The development of commitment. In C. B. Wortman & R. Sorrentino (eds.), *Commitment, conflict, and caring* (145–221). Englewood Cliffs, N.J.: Prentice-Hall.

Brickman, P., Janoff-Bulman, R., & Rabinowitz, V. C. 1987. Meaning and value. In C. B. Wortman & R. Sorrentino (eds.), *Commitment, conflict, and caring* (59–105). Englewood Cliffs, N.J.: Prentice-Hall.

Brody, E. M. 1985. Parent care as a normative family stress. *The Gerontologist, 25,* 19–29.

Brody, E. M.; Johnsen, P. T.; Fulcomer, M. C.; & Lang, A. M. 1983. Women's changing roles and help to elderly parents: Attitudes of three generations of women. *Journal of Gerontology, 38,* 597–607.

Callahan, D. 1985. What do adult children owe elderly parents? *The Hasting Center Report, 15*(2), 32–37.

Cicirelli, V. G. 1983. Adult children's attachment and helping behavior to elderly parents: A path model. *Journal of Marriage and the Family, 45,* 815–825.

Finch, J., & Groves, D. 1983. Introduction. In J. Finch & D. Groves (eds.), *A labour of love: Women, work, and caring* (1–10). London: Routledge & Kegan Paul.

Finley, N. J.; Roberts, M. D.; & Banahan, B. F.; III. 1988. Motivators and inhibitors of attitudes of filial obligation toward aging parents. *The Gerontologist, 28,* 73–78.

Graham, H. 1983. Caring: A labour of love. In J. Finch & D. Groves (eds.), *A labour of love: Women, work, and caring* (13–30). London: Routledge & Kegan Paul.

Hanson, S. L.; Sauer, W. J.; & Seelbach, W. C. 1983. Racial and cohort variations in filial responsibility norms. *The Gerontologist, 23,* 626–631.

Hess, B. B., & Waring, J. H. 1978. Parent and child in later life: Rethinking the relationship. In R. M. Lerner & G. B. Spanier (eds.), *Child influences on marital and family interaction* (241–273). New York: Academic.

Horowitz, A., & Shindelman, L. W. 1983. Reciprocity and affection: Past influences on current caregiving. *Journal of Gerontological Social Work, 5*(3), 5–20.

Jarrett, W. H. 1985. Caregiving within kinship systems: Is affection really necessary? *The Gerontologist, 25,* 5–10.

Leigh, G. K. 1982. Kinship interaction over the family life span. *Journal of Marriage and the Family, 44,* 197–208.

Marshall, V. W.; Rosenthal, C. J.; & Synge, J. 1983. Concerns about parental health. In E. W. Markson (ed.), *Older women* (253–273). Lexington, Mass: D. C. Heath.

Matthews, S. H. 1979. *The social world of old women.* Beverly Hills: Sage Publications.

Nydegger, C. 1983. Family ties of the aged: A cross-cultural perspective. *The Gerontologist, 23,* 26–32.

Robinson, B., & Thurnher, M. 1979. Taking care of aged parents: A family cycle transition. *The Gerontologist, 19,* 586–593.

Tobin, S. S., & Kulys, R. 1980. The family and services. In C. Eisdorfer (ed.), *Annual review of gerontology and geriatrics* (Vol. 1, 370–399). New York: Springer.

Troll, L. E. 1986. Introduction: Parent-adult child relations. In L. E. Troll (ed.), *Family issues in current gerontology* (75–83). New York: Springer.

Ungerson, C. 1983. Why do women care? In J. Finch and D. Groves (eds.), *A labour of love: Women, work, and caring* (31–49). London: Routledge & Kegan Paul.

Walker, A. 1983. Care for the elderly people: A conflict between women and the state. In J. Finch and D. Groves (eds.) *A labour of love: Women, work, and caring* (106–128). London: Routledge & Kegan Paul.

Walker, A. J.; Shin, H.; Jones, L. L.; & Pratt, C. C. 1987, November. *Mothers' and daughters' reasons for daughters' caregiving.* Paper presented at the meeting of the National Council on Family Relations, Atlanta, Ga.

Walker, A. J., & Thompson, L. 1983. Intimacy and intergenerational aid and contact among mothers and daughters. *Journal of Marriage and the Family, 43,* 841–849.

14

Parent Care by Sons and Daughters

Rhonda J. V. Montgomery
Yoshinoro Kamo

T he predominance of the family as the primary source of care for impaired elders has been consistently documented by researchers over the past decade (Cantor 1983; McAuley & Arling 1984; Stone, Cafferata & Sangl 1987). The extensive literature that has emerged has provided detailed descriptions of the assistance family members give to elders and the impact of this caregiving on family members and their lifestyles (Horowitz 1985a; Select Committee on Aging 1987).

While there is general consensus that most caregivers are spouses or adult children of the impaired elders, early studies of caregiving tended to treat caregivers as a homogeneous population. More recent studies have given attention to differences between spouses and children in their caregiving experiences, as well as to differences between husbands and wives (Fitting, Rabins, Lucas & Eastman 1986; George & Gwyther 1986; Zarit, Todd & Zarit 1986). Much less attention has been given to differences between sons and daughters.

To a large degree, the dearth of information about differences between sons and daughters probably stems from the fact that cross-sectional studies of caregivers have consistently found that daughters predominate as primary care providers. It has been estimated that 80 percent of children who care for parents are daughters and 20 percent are sons. The predominance of daughters as caregivers has resulted in research efforts and findings that have been primarily restricted to daughters. This trend appears to be a result of both the methodological difficulties involved with the study of sons as caregivers and of the apparent belief that sons' minority status among caregivers makes their activities and experience less important from the perspective of policy development.

This research was supported in part by the Health Care Financing Administration, Contract No. 95-C98281.

There are, however, some indications that sons do play a caregiving role in many families and that this role is quite different from that assumed by daughters. Based on findings from a sample of 131 adult children, Horowitz (1985b) concluded that sons who are the primary caregivers for their parents engage in fewer hands-on caregiving tasks and find the caregiving experience to be less stressful. Similar findings have been reported by Stoller (1983) and Matthews and Rosner (1988), who found sons spent fewer hours performing helping tasks for parents and engaged in fewer routine helping tasks that required personal care and household chores than did daughters. Horowitz reported that even when the extent of caregiving (that is, the amount of time spent doing caregiving tasks) was controlled, the relationship between sex and the experience of caregiving stress remained. As Horowitz notes, this finding is consistent with other studies that report this persistent relationship between sex and caregiving stress (Cantor 1983; Johnson 1983; Robinson & Thurnher 1979). This finding would suggest that when sons assume the role of primary caregiver they not only do so in a different manner, but they experience the role differently than do daughters.

This chapter reports findings from a recent study of caregivers that further delineate differences and similarities between sons and daughters in the ways in which they engage in caregiving and the way they experience their role. Additionally, the chapter explores plausible reasons for the differences and makes suggestions for future research.

Study Design

The data reported here were collected in 1984 and 1985 as part of an ongoing research project that used an experimental design to assess the impact of alternative support services for families caring for impaired elders (Montgomery & Borgatta 1987). The family units consisted of an elderly impaired person and at least one family member who was providing assistance to the elder, residing within King County, Washington. All family members lived within a one hour's driving distance of the noninstitutionalized elder. Families were assigned to one of five treatment groups or a control group after an initial interview. Members of the treatment groups were eligible to receive one or more support services, which included respite care, a seminar series, support groups, and family counseling. Of the 541 families in the study, 347 had an adult-child as a caregiver and these units were used for the analyses presented here.

Data were collected through structured interviews conducted with the adult child and the parent in their homes. Approximately 50 percent of the parents were too impaired to complete the interview and data for them were collected from the caregivers.

Measures

Caregiving Activities. The extent and length of caregiving activities were measured with an inventory that asked the amount of time a caregiver spent per week doing each of twenty-two tasks. Four scores for different types of tasks were constructed based upon findings of factor analyses. Items included in the score for personal care tasks are changing bed linens and assisting the elder with dressing, bathing, toilet, and hair care. Transportation tasks include providing transportation, accompanying the elder, taking the elder to friends and appointments, and shopping. Eating tasks consist of: preparing meals for the elder, cleaning the table after the meal, and shopping. Financial tasks include help with filling out forms, banking tasks, writing checks, and other legal matters. Four parallel scores were created to represent the length of time caregivers had engaged in each type of task. These scores represent the average number of months the caregiver had done each of the four types of tasks.

Caregiver Burden. Consistent with earlier work of the authors (Montgomery, Gonyea & Hooyman 1985), a distinction was made in this study between objective and subjective burden. Objective burden was defined as the extent of disruptions or changes in various tangible aspects of the caregiver's life and household caused by caring for the elderly person. Subjective burden was defined as the extent of perceived change in psychological aspects of stress caused by caregiving.

Caregivers were asked whether various aspects of their lives had changed during the past year as a result of caregiving. A caregiver's subjective burden score is an additive score of: stress in the relationship; whether the caregiver feels manipulated by the care receiver; nervousness and depression; and overly demanding care-receivers. A caregiver's objective burden score is the sum of the caregiver's scores for the time he or she has alone, time available for recreation and vacation, time for own work, and time for friends and relatives.

Love and Obligation. Based upon factor analysis of a twelve-item scale, two attitude scores were constructed to reflect caregivers' affection toward their parent and their sense of obligation to care for their parent. The affection scale consists of the caregiver's closeness, love, affection, liking, devotion, and attachment to the care-receiver. The obligation score was the sum of the caregiver's perception of duty to care for the elder and reported obligation to help the elder.

The elder's and caregiver's health rating was measured by the question: "Considering your age and sex, how would you rate your own health during the past year? Would you rate it as: 5. Perfect, couldn't be better; 4.

Very good; 3. Good, average for most persons; 2. Fair, not too good; or 1. Not good at all." This single-item question was found to be consistently related to several other measures of health, including an activities of daily living scale (ADL) for the elderly.

Other demographic variables such as marital status, employment, and income were measured with several response categories for each question. For the regression analysis, marital status and employment status were dichotomized (0 = Not married, 1 = Married; 0 = Not employed, 1 = Employed).

Findings

Caregiver Characteristics

The sample of adult children included sixty-four (19 percent) sons or sons-in-law and 273 (81 percent) daughters or daughters-in-law. With minor exceptions, the demographic characteristics of sons and daughters were very similar. The median ages for sons and daughters were fifty-one and fifty-five respectively. Approximately 60 percent of both groups were married. Sons who were single (37 percent) tended to be the "never married" (23 percent), while non-married daughters (41 percent) included more divorced (18 percent) or widowed persons (10 percent) than the "never married" (10 percent). The majority of adult children rated their health to be good, very good, or perfect; only a small number of sons (7.8 percent) and daughters (12.1 percent) rated their health as fair or not at all good.

As would be expected for this cohort of persons, a larger proportion of sons (58 percent) were employed full-time than were daughters (34 percent). However, it should be noted that more than half of daughters worked either full-time or part-time. Sons reported higher household incomes than did daughters, with the median income being $25,000 for sons and $21,900 for daughters. The majority of elders (64 percent) lived in the same household as the caregiver; this pattern was true for both sons and daughters.

Activities Reported by Sons and Daughters.

The amount of time that caregivers spent in each of the four types of tasks is reported in table 14–1. Consistent with previous studies, daughters reported spending more time in all types of caregiving tasks than did sons, except for assisting with financial and business matters, where the amount of time was almost equal. On average, daughters spent slightly more (7.1) hours helping elders with transportation than did sons (5.2). Of special note are the dramatic differences in time spent by daughters versus sons in meal preparation (12.2 versus 7.4 hours) and personal care tasks (6.4 versus 2.0 hours). The data reveal a pattern that suggests that, as an elder's need for assistance grows from a need for help with business matters and transportation to help with household chores and personal care tasks, daughters are more likely to assume or retain the role of caregiver than are sons.

Further evidence of this trend is found in the comparisons between sons and daughters of the length of time that they had provided assistance with the various types of tasks. As shown in table 14–1, there appears to be an established pattern for caregivers of progressively assuming more intense and time consuming tasks as their caregiving career is extended. On the average, sons have engaged in tasks related to financial management longer (forty-two months) than any other type of task. Both sons and daughters have engaged in activities to assist with transportation for longer periods of time (thirty-five and forty months respectively) than they have assisted with eating tasks (twenty-eight and thirty-five months) or personal care tasks (seven and sixteen months). Yet, even within this progression from less intensive to more intensive help, daughters have performed most of the tasks for a longer period of time, particularly the most demanding tasks of the personal care.

Caregiver Burden

Perhaps the most interesting finding about sons' and daughters' caregiving experience is the lack of difference in their levels of subjective and objective burden. Despite the substantially greater amounts of time spent by daughters in caregiving activities, sons and daughters report equal levels of burden. Two observations about this finding are important. First, it is consistent with the literature that reports little or no relationship between the tasks performed by caregivers and their level of burden (Zarit 1980). Second, it is inconsistent with findings that report males to be less burdened than females (Horowitz 1985b; Johnson 1983; Noelker & Paulschock 1982; Robinson & Thurnher 1979).

The fact that sons in this sample engaged in fewer and less intense caregiving tasks than did the daughters but reported similar levels of objective and subjective burden prompted further analyses of data to determine whether there were differences in the factors that promote or buffer burden. It was reasoned that knowledge of differences in predictors of burden might provide some insight into the differences in patterns of helping behaviors.

Guided by a theoretical framework detailed in previous work (Montgomery, Stull & Borgatta 1985), four sets of variables were identified and investigated as plausible factors influencing the level of burden. The varia-

Table 14–1
Gender Differences for Caregiver's Attitudes and Activities

	Means		T-Value
	Sons	Daughters	(pooled variance)
Objective burden	14.56	15.50	1.77
Subjective burden	10.27	10.95	1.66
Affection	4.44	3.96	.97
Obligation	4.81	4.61	.89
Transportation tasks	5.21	7.08	2.20*
Personal care tasks	1.98	6.41	3.38*
Eating tasks	7.38	12.24	3.63*
Financial tasks	3.00	2.68	.58
Months spent/Transportation tasks	35.20	39.72	.76
Months spent/Personal care tasks	6.93	16.50	2.60*
Months spent/Eating tasks	28.24	34.92	1.29
Months spent/Financial tasks	42.74	38.12	.74

*$p < .05$

bles included: caregiver characteristics, elder characteristics, caregiver activities, and attitudes of the caregiver toward the elder. Additionally, objective burden, or the felt infringement on tangible aspects of one's life space, was introduced as an independent variable affecting subjective burden. Parallel analyses were conducted for sons and daughters.

The small size of the sample of sons necessitated a reduction in the number of independent variables for the regression analysis. Variables that did not have a zero-order correlation with subjective burden were eliminated along with those variables that failed to add to the explained variance.

Table 14–2 reports findings from two sets of multiple regression analyses. The data reveal a number of similarities in the pattern of predictors of subjective burden for sons and daughters. For both groups the level of subjective burden is influenced by the caregiver's health, the level of affection, and the level of objective burden. Caregivers with poorer health are more burdened by the caregiving tasks even when other variables, including the amount and the length of the caregiving tasks and the objective burden, are controlled for. This relationship is, however, stronger for sons than for daughters. Caregivers who report greater affection felt less burdened but the level of felt obligation was not related to burden. Finally, lower levels of objective burden were associated with lower levels of subjective burden and this association appears stronger for sons.

Table 14–2
Regression Analysis for Caregiver's Subjective Burden Score

	Daughters			Sons		
	r	b	beta	r	b	beta
Employment	.151*	.142	.117*	.092	-.078	.061
Marital status	.078	.252	.088	-.076	-.476	-.141
Caregiver health	-.157*	-.362	-.113*	-.363*	-.969	-.382*
Number of children	-.168*	-.522	-.125*	-.003	-.257	-.085
Elder health	-.072	-.285	-.105	-.100	-.083	-.040
Affection	-.230*	-.159	-.199*	-.168*	-.175	-.340*
Obligation	.073	-.094	-.050	.035	.286	.217
Transportation tasks	.246*	.080	.159*	.301*	-.035	-.071
Personal Care Tasks	-.047	-.041	-.135*	-.163	-.117	-.176
Months Spent/Trans.	.012	.126	.087	.050	-.007	.006
Months Spent/Per.	-.176*	-.240	-.086	-.023	.302	.093
Objective burden	.383*	.272	.345*	.396*	.344	.518*

Note: Magnitudes of unstandardized regression coefficient (b) for Months spent on transportation and Months spent on personal care were multiplied by 100.

The sample size for daughters = 264. The sample size for sons = 61.

*p < .05

Despite these similarities between the two analyses, there are several differences reported in table 14–2 that are of interest. First, employment is a significant predictor of burden for daughters but not for sons. Employed daughters report greater burden than nonemployed daughters. Second, the number of dependent children is negatively associated with subjective burden for daughters but not for sons. That is, daughters with children report less subjective burden. Finally, the number of hours spent by daughters in transportative tasks is positively related to the level of subjective burden, while the relationship is negative and nonsignificant for sons. In fact, for sons, when all the control variables are entered into the regression model, neither the extent of care nor the length of time performing tasks are predictors of subjective burden.

Discussion

Several aspects of the findings are of interest because they reveal distinct patterns of caregiving for sons and daughters and because they provide some insight into the bases for these differences. Moreover, the results of the study raise additional questions that can guide future research concerned with parent-child relations.

Prevalance of Sons as Caregivers

One observation that emerges from the data concerns the incidence of sons as caregivers. Although it is widely accepted that most children who provide care are daughters, the analyses presented here might be used to question this fact. Certainly, the data support the notion that sons perform fewer hours of services and tend to engage in less intensive tasks for shorter periods of time. These patterns do not, however, support a conclusion that fewer sons than daughters provide care.

To the contrary, the data show that sons assist parents when their parents' needs are limited to finances and transportation. However, when the parents' need for help progresses to more intense tasks such as daily household chores or personal care, sons abdicate the role. This pattern of brief, less intensive caregiving by sons may have caused researchers, in the past, to conclude that sons are less likely to help parents rather than to more accurately conclude that sons are less likely to continue to help *throughout* the length of their parents' dependency period. One consequence of this temporally constricted caregiving cycle for sons is that, when samples are drawn for studies such as this, sons are often underrepresented because they have already abdicated their caregiver role. This argument parallels the logic used by Kastenbaum and Candy (1973) when they challenged the fact that only 4 percent of the population is institutionalized. It may well be that at any one time only 20 percent of adult children who are caregivers are sons but the actual percentage of sons who engage in caregiving *at some point* in time may be considerably larger. To test this hypothesis it would be necessary to start with a sample of adult children and ask about their caregiving careers rather than the more common practice of sampling impaired elders.

Differences in Style

While the findings challenge the prevailing belief about the sparse prevalence of sons as caregivers, the results also provide support for the notion that the caregiver role is distinctly different for sons than it is for daughters. On the average, daughters engage in more care and more intense care for a longer period of time than do sons. Yet sons report levels of burden associated with their caregiver role similar to that of daughters. Descriptive studies such as the one reported here are just the first step toward understanding this crucial difference between parent-son and parent-daughter relationships in families where the elder has become dependent. The critical question for scientists and policy makers interested in the welfare of impaired older adults may not be *how* these two relationships differ but, rather, *why* they differ.

Many reasons have been speculatively advanced by researchers (Brody 1985; Horowitz 1985b; Stoller 1983) to account for the tendency of sons to engage in fewer and less intense tasks. Among the reasons most commonly advanced are: (1) Sons are more likely to have employment responsibilities that compete for their time; (2) Sons feel less obligation to care for parents; and (3) Caregiving is women's work that requires skills and socialization traditionally defined as a part of woman's role.

Although the data reported here do not allow for a definitive resolution as to the reasons why sons provide less assistance than daughters but appear equally burdened, there are a number of clues that can be gleaned to support some factors more than others and to guide the development of future studies that could more directly address this issue.

From a common-sense perspective it would seem reasonable to assume that the greater prevalence of employment of sons than of daughters could account for the smaller number of hours spent by sons assisting parents. However, findings from previous research and additional analyses conducted on this data set do not support this conclusion. In her study of parental caregiving, Stoller (1983, 851) found that "being employed significantly decreased the hours of assistance provided by sons but did not have a significant impact on the hours of assistance provided by daughters." Similarly, Matthews and Rosner (1988) concluded that a job puts constraints on *when* assistance was given by daughters but it did not decrease the likelihood of routine involvement of children. Analysis of the data set presented here that were conducted only for the employed children also call into question the notion that employment can account for differences between sons and daughters. Only 21 percent of the employed sons in the sample reported spending one hour or more a week doing personal care tasks, while 64 percent of the employed daughters performed at least one hour of personal care a week. This result is consistent with the finding that employment affected subjective burden for daughters but not for sons. It is clear that employment causes sons to reduce caregiving activities preventing stress or burden but employment simply adds responsibilities for daughters. Together these findings suggest that employment *per se* does not account for differences between sons and daughters in the amount or type of caregiving. It appears that daughters persist in their more intensive activities regardless of their employment status. This conclusion prompts speculation on yet another plausible explanation for the differences between sons and daughters in their caregiving patterns. Perhaps daughters persist in their caregiving activities despite outside responsibilities because they have greater affection or obligation toward their parents. That is, sons will assist when it is convenient while daughters will assist despite personal costs because of their greater sense of devotion or obligation. Such a notion would be supported if lower levels of obligation and/or affection toward parents were to be found for sons than for daughters. As reported earlier, none of these differences in attitudes existed between sons and daughters in this sample. Hence, there is little support for the notion of greater obligation among daughters.

It is possible that sons and daughters do not differ in the level of felt obligation but, rather, in their view of the appropriate means of meeting their felt obligation. Archbold (1983) notes that caregiving can be done in different ways: it can involve hands-on care or it can involve care management. The differences between sons and daughters in style of caregiving are explicitly discussed by Matthews and Rosner. Daughters are more likely to assume a routine caregiving style while sons are more likely to assume a "backup," "circumscribed," or "sporadic style." It is interesting that Matthews and Rosner not only report this difference in styles but also an acceptance of this difference as nonproblematic by the daughters in their study. Hence, there appears to be a belief system held equally by sons and daughters that the style of caregiving that is appropriate for sons does not include personal care or routine tasks.

A son's sense of obligation to assist an elder does not extend to performance of personal service. Rather, their obligation to parent care is expected to be met through the purchase of services or through delegation of helping tasks to other family members. Perhaps this difference in perceived obligation reflects the rigid sex role attitudes that have been established and universally preserved through differential socialization of males and females. After the mid-nineteenth century, sex roles took the shape of the dichotomy of provider and housekeeper roles in the social milieu of adult life. Although little research has been done in the realm of caregiving tasks, much has been done and discussed in the realm of sexual division of labor in housework.

As a result of the separation between the work place and family caused by industrialization, men have assumed provider roles and women housekeeper roles (Lein 1979; Slocum & Nye 1976) Although recent female labor force participation has helped women cut into the provider role, the housekeeper role is rarely assumed by men. Many studies have found that people tend to endorse more egalitarian attitudes but do not behave accordingly (Araji 1977; Hiller & Philliber 1986; Slocum & Nye 1976). Moreover, both men and women are reluctant to give up traditionally prescribed roles of their own (Hiller and Philliber). Because the caregiving role is a part of the housekeeper role, it seems safe to assume that traditionally prescribed gender roles in caregiving tasks are also reproduced through socialization processes and are difficult to relinquish.

If sex role socialization were the only reason for differences between sons' and daughters' caregiving patterns, one would expect similar differences to be found between husbands and wives. This pattern was not found for the data set used here (Montgomery & Borgatta 1987), suggesting that still other reasons must underlie the observed differences.

Two plausible reasons that deserve consideration and further study are extensions of the sex role hypothesis. The first is a consideration of the proscriptions that may be placed on behavior as a result of sex role socialization and the second reason is tied to the likely consequences of sex role socialization in terms of differential resources available to sons and daughters. The socialization process not only prescribes behavior for certain groups but impedes or inhibits other behaviors and these behaviors can become defined as taboos. In the case of caregiving it may well be that sons are not only socialized to the provider role to the exclusion of the homemaker role but also may come to view certain types of personal care tasks as taboo. That is, hands-on care for a parent such as bathing, dressing, and toileting may be avoided not just because they are viewed as women's domain. They may also be avoided because they are viewed as inappropriate or taboo behaviors for a son because they border too closely on behaviors that break societal norms regarding incest. At this point such an interpretation is speculative at best but it would help to explain the observed patterns of behavior of sons and of husbands. Bodily contact between spouses would not be considered taboo despite sex role socialization and therefore we would expect more similarity in caregiving behaviors between husbands and wives than between sons and daughters.

Another plausible reason for differences in the caregiving patterns of sons and daughters that is tied to sex role socialization is the differential resources likely to be available to sons and daughters. It might be hypothesized that sons, because of their designated role as provider and their sisters' and wives' designated roles as housekeepers, have greater options for the purchase of services or the delegation of tasks than do daughters. That is, sons may assume the same level of responsibility as daughters to ensure care for their dependent parent but they may use their higher incomes to buy services or they may benefit from social norms that allow them to delegate care tasks to women in the family. In contrast, the daughters in this sample had lower household incomes and were less likely to be the primary source of the majority of their household income than were sons. Hence, they had fewer resources to purchase services. Similarly, daughters do not have the endorsement of social norms to delegate care to their brothers or husbands, since the homemaker role continues to be the property of women.

Apart from the fact that the daughters in the sample had lower household incomes, there are additional small pieces of evidence that can be gleaned from this study to support the notion that sons have greater resources for "buying out" of caregivings tasks. First, it could be argued that because of shared household income, husbands do not have greater resources than do wives and therefore are unable to purchase or delegate care tasks for wives. This reality could account for the lack of differences in the extent of care provided by husbands and wives even though the sex role hypothesis would suggest that such differences between husbands and wives should occur. Certainly there are numerous anecdotes within the literature describing spouses who take care of each other in a desperate situation where there is little option if any, available. In these "life boat" situations, gender role attitudes may not dominate the pattern of caregiving. Children as caregivers, however, usually have a leeway of not caring for their parent and, in this case, gender-role attitudes can play a more significant role in influencing behaviors.

The Common Experience of Burden

The analyses presented in this chapter provide one additional insight into the parent-child relations of families with a dependent elder and this stems from the finding that there was little difference between sons and daughters in the level of subjective burden despite the documented difference in the type and extent of care provided.

Clues to understanding this counterintuitive finding were gained from the results of the multiple regression analyses for subjective burden. Except for the level of the caregiver's health, none of the variables that were significantly related to subjective burden for sons were measures of the sons resources, the level of care given to the elder, or commitments to other persons. In fact, the findings are rather disappointing when objective burden is omitted from the analysis. All the other variables combined account for less than 10 percent of the variance in subjective burden and only caregiver health is a statistically significant predictor. These results suggest that the level of subjective burden for sons is not directly related to the effort expended nor to the resources available (such as other family members or uncommitted time). Instead, subjective burden appears to be better explained by attitudes of the son toward the parent (level of affection) and toward the situation (felt imposition on personal time).

In contrast, the level of subjective burden for daughters was found to be influenced by the type and amount of care provided, employment status, and the presence of children and a spouse. Together these findings suggest that daughters' sense of burden is influenced by the demands placed upon her as well as by her attitudes toward her parent and the situation. Daughters who are employed and married have greater responsibilities and greater demands placed upon them than do those who are unemployed and single.

While there is a positive relationship between marital status and burden for daughters, there is a negative relationship for sons. This may well reflect the fact, suggested earlier, that a husband is likely to create more demands on a wife who is caring for her parent while a wife is likely to reduce the task load of a husband who cares for his parent (Hartmann 1981; Matthews & Rosner 1988).

The negative correlation for daughters between number of dependent children and burden may reflect the availability of the children as a resource to assist the caregiver with tasks. In most cases, caregiving daughters are not in the early stages of childrearing but, instead, their dependent children are likely to be in their teens and viable sources of help.

One the most intriguing findings is the relationship between level of subjective burden and the number of hours spent doing transportation and personal care tasks. The positive relationship for daughters between burden and transportation tasks is more readily interpretable than is the negative relationship between burden and personal care tasks for daughters or the absence of any statistically significant associations for sons. It is consistent with a common-sense understanding that greater demands on a daughter's time to accompany or transport a parent would result in greater burden. The negative relationship between number of hours spent on personal care and burden may be explained by the routinization of such tasks. That is, the longer a daughter has been performing a task, the more efficient she is likely to have become. This efficiency is likely to result in lower burden.

Furthermore, personal care tasks such as bathing, grooming, and feeding are events that can be scheduled on a daily or weekly basis and, therefore, may be less likely to be perceived as stressful. This notion of routinization is supported by the negative relationship for daughters between the number of months that personal care tasks have been performed and the level of burden, although the relationship was not statistically significant.

To summarize, the level of subjective burden for daughters is a result of both attitudes and circumstances. Those daughters with fewer resources and more demands are likely to be more burdened. In contrast, the prediction of burden for sons is less clear. Perhaps, for sons who tend to restrict their direct care behaviors, the burden they experience is not associated with specific tasks but with the sense of responsibility they have for a dependent parent. This interpretation is in keeping with the earlier discussion that notes equal levels of obligation among sons and daughters but different perceptions of means to meeting that obligation.

Conclusion

This chapter has both questioned the prevailing belief that sons are less likely than daughters to assume responsibility for the care of their parents and supported the notion that the caregiving roles of sons and daughters are distinct in style. While it is true that sons are less likely to perform personal care and household tasks, it is not true that they feel less obligated to attend to the needs of their parents. Furthermore, there is evidence that sons may be equally likely as daughters to perform caregiving tasks for their parents, although the type of task and extent of care is considerably less. Sons appear to be more comfortable acting on their obligation through family members. That is, sons assume a manager role rather than a more direct helper role. It has been argued here that this difference in the perception of the way that care should be assured for parents is very much tied to sex role socialization rather than to employment patterns or to differences in felt obligation. However, the consequence of the traditional division of labor between men and women may contribute to observed patterns by giving sons more resources for purchase of services. Finally, it is important to note that despite differences in the extent of care that sons directly provide, they tend to experience equal levels of subjective burden. This finding, along with the analyses that indicate the level of burden of sons is almost exclusively a product of attitudes, would suggest that the burden of caregiving is not tied so much to the tasks performed but to the sense of responsibility. Because sons appear to experience an equal sense of responsibility, it is reasonable that they report equal levels of burden. Hence, in this last stage of parent-child relations we witness both similarities and differences between sons and daughters. Regardless of their sex, however, children do tend to assume the responsibility for care of their elderly parents and experience the stress that may accompany that responsibility.

References

Araji, S. K. 1977. Husbands' and wives' attitude-behavior congruence on family roles. *Journal of Marriage and the Family, 39,* 309–320.

Archbold, P. G. 1983. Impact of parent-caring on women. *Family Relations, 32,* 39–45.

Brody, E. 1985. Parent care as a normative family stress. *The Gerontologist, 25,* 19–29.

Cantor, M. H. 1983. Strain among caregivers: A study of experience in the United States. *The Gerontologist, 23,* 597–604.

Fitting, M.; Rabins, P.; Lucas, M.; & Eastman, J. 1986. Caregivers for dementia patients: A comparison of husbands and wives. *The Gerontologist, 26,* 248–259.

George, L. K., & Gwyther, L. P. 1986. Caregiver well-being: A multidimensional examination of family caregivers. *The Gerontologist, 26,* 253–259.

Hartmann, Heidi, I. 1981. The family as the locus of gender, class, and political struggle: The example of housework. *Signs, 6,* 366–394.

Hiller, D. A., & Philliber, W. J. 1986. The division of labor in contemporary marriage. *Social Problems, 33*(3), 191–201.

Horowitz, A. 1985a. Family caregiving to the frail elderly. *Annual Review of Gerontology and Geriatrics* (194–246). New York: Springer.

Horowitz, A. 1985b. Sons and daughters as caregivers to older parents: Differences in role performance and consequences. *The Gerontologist, 25,* 612–617.

Johnson, C. L. 1983. Dyadic family relations and social support. *The Gerontologist, 23,* 377–383.

Johnson, C. L. & Catalano, D. J. 1983. A longitudinal study of family supports to impaired elderly. *The Gerontologist, 23,* 612–618.

Kastenbaum, R. J. & Candy, S. E. 1973. The four-percent fallacy: A methodological and empirical critique of extended care facility population statistics. *International Journal of Aging and Human Development, 4,* 15–21.

Lein, L. 1979. Male participation in home life: Impact of social supports and breadwinner responsibility on the allocation of tasks. *Family Coordinator, 28,* 489–495.

McAuley, W. J. & Arling, G. 1984. Use of in-home care by very old people. *Journal of Health and Social Behavior, 25,* 54–64.

Matthews, S. H. & Rosner, T. T. 1988. Shared filial responsibility: The family as the primary caregiver. *Journal of Marriage and the Family, 50,* 185–195.

Montgomery, R. J. V.; Gonyea, J. G.; & Hooyman, N. R. 1985a. Caregiving and the experience of subjective and objective burden. *Family Relations, 34,* 1–8.

Montgomery, R. J. V.; Stull, D. E.; & Borgatta, E. F. 1985b. Measurement and the analysis of burden. *Research on Aging, 7*(1), 137–152.

Montgomery, R. J. V.; & Borgatta, E. F. 1987. *Effects of alternative family support strategies.* Final report to The Health Care Financing Administration, Dept. of Health and Human Services, Baltimore, Md.

Noelker, L. S., & Paulschock, S. W. 1982. *The effects on families of caring for impaired elderly in residence.* Final report submitted to the Administration on Aging. The Margarey Blenkner Research Center for Family Studies. The Benjamin Rose Institute, Cleveland, Ohio.

Robinson, B. & Thurnher, M. 1979. Taking care of parents: A family-cycle transition. *The Gerontologist, 19,* 586–593.

Select Committee on Aging, House of Representatives. 1987. *Exploding the myths: Caregiving in America.* A study by the Subcommittee on Human Services.

Slocum, W. L., & Nye, F. I. 1976. Provider and housekeeper roles. In F. Ivan Nye (ed.), *Role Structure and Analysis of the Family* (81–99). Beverly Hills: Sage Publications.

Stoller, E. P. 1983. Parent caregiving by adult children. *Journal of Marriage and the Family, 45,* 851–858.

Stone, R.; Cafferata, G. L.; & Sangl, J. 1987. Caregivers of the frail elderly: A national profile. *The Gerontologist, 27,* 617–626.

Zarit, S. H.; Todd, P. A.; & Zarit, J. 1986. Subjective burden of husbands and wives as caregivers: A longitudinal study. *Gerontologist, 26,* 260–266.

Zarit, S. H.; Reever, K. E.; & Bach-Peterson, J. 1980. Relatives of the impaired elderly: Correlates of feelings of burden. *The Gerontologist, 26,* 649–655.

15

Affection, Communication, and Commitment in Adult-Child Caregiving for Parents with Alzheimer's Disease

Rosemary Blieszner
Peggy A. Shifflett

T he norms of contemporary American society hold that adult children are to provide needed help to their aged parents (Blieszner & Mancini 1987; Brody, Johnsen & Fulcomer 1984; Seelbach 1984). Under ordinary circumstances, most elders enjoy fairly positive relationships with their adult children, characterized by frequent contact, affection, and open communication (Blieszner 1986). As long as older adults live independently and enjoy fairly good health, assistance from their children takes the form of emotional support, fellowship, advice, and occasional help with household tasks. When parents become frail and less independent, however, adult children often step in to give more direct aid with everyday tasks.

Taking care of sick elderly relatives is difficult under any circumstances (Cantor 1983; Montgomery, Gonyea & Hooyman 1985), but may be especially so when the parent suffers a dementing illness (Chenoweth & Spencer 1986; Pratt, Schmall, Wright & Clelland 1985). The most prevalent dementia is Alzheimer's disease (AD), in which degeneration in the cerebral cortex leads to memory loss and confusion in the preliminary stages, followed by increased mental deterioration, total helplessness, and death. The cognitive loss that accompanies this disease interferes with the patient's ability to maintain normal human relationships, yet family members continue to assume responsibility for most of the caregiving.

Commitment theory provides at least a partial explanation of offsprings' devotion to their parent with AD despite the many obstacles to

This research was funded by a Biomedical Research Support Grant from Virginia Polytechnic Institute and State University. The authors thank Phyllis Bridgeman and Laurie Shea for help with tape transcription and coding.

providing care and to maintaining a satisfying personal relationship. This theory encompasses internal and external factors that may account for consistency in behavior (Johnson 1972; 1978). As applied to close relationships, the internal construct, personal commitment, refers to the individual's long-term dedication to maintaining a relationship, and in this case, to caregiving. The external component, structural commitment, reflects events or conditions that constrain the individual to continue a line of action. These external sources of motivation can influence a partner to maintain a relationship or continue caregiving even when personal commitment is low. As Johnson (1982, 52–53) put it, "People stay in relationships for two major reasons: because they want to; and because they have to."

The purpose of this study was to examine the feelings of adult children about caring for their parents under the difficult and intensive circumstances of AD. We wished to explore the effects of this disease on aspects of the parent-child relationship such as affection, communication, and commitment, to better understand perceptions about the adult child role of those who meet this most demanding challenge.

Methodology

Research Technique

The research design consisted of four interviews beginning shortly after the patient was diagnosed as probably having AD (diagnostic certainty can be obtained only by brain autopsy) and continuing for eighteen months. We used an inductive, exploratory method including thorough, tape-recorded interviews with five adult children who were primary caregivers for AD patients. We identified the informants through an Alzheimer's Disease and Related Disorders Association support group in a small central Virginia city, population thirty-five thousand.

The interviews focused on five time periods as the disease progressed. The first interview covered the segment before any symptoms (T1) and that between the appearance of symptoms and the diagnosis of AD (T2). During the second interview we discussed the first four months after the diagnosis of AD (T3). The third (T4) and fourth (T5) interviews followed at six-month intervals.

We designed four interview schedules for data gathering. The first was retrospective and focused on T1 and T2. It included questions on demographic information for the caregiving adult children and the parent patients along with questions on patients' family roles, personality, early symptoms, and support by friends and relatives. Also, caregivers responded to the Miller Social Intimacy Scale (MSIS, described later) while reflecting on T1 and T2.

The other interview schedules focused on changes in patients' symptoms and behavior, caregivers' coping strategies, caregivers' feelings toward the patient, and the support patterns of social network members. The interview schedule for T4 also included questions concerning the caregivers' commitment to the parent with AD.

Instruments

Affection and Communication. We used the MSIS to measure adult children's feelings of affection toward and communication with their parent with AD. The MSIS contains seventeen items, six of which assess the frequency of intimate behaviors such as confiding and expressing affection. Respondents answer on a Likert scale ranging from 1 = very rarely to 10 = almost always. Also included are eleven items that measure the intensity of intimate feelings such as closeness, enjoying being with the person, and understanding each other. The response scale is 1 = not much to 10 = a great deal. The potential range of scores on the MSIS is seventeen to 170.

Commitment. We operationalized personal and structural commitment with six items each, reflecting the adult child's perceptions of the importance of each dimension in her or his decision to provide care to the Alzheimer's parent. The content of the items is indicated in the results section. Respondents answered on a scale from 1 = not at all important to 4 = very important. We assumed that the decision to provide care reflected, at least in part, the respondent's interest in maintaining a close relationship despite the parent's inability to participate in it as fully as in the past.

Findings

Respondents

Alice [pseudonym] is forty-seven years old and married with several teenage children. She completed post–high school training in a health care profession and enjoys excellent health. She works full-time and said at T1 that caring for her mother did not interfere with her work schedule. Alice's mother, seventy-one, had AD. She lived with another family in town who received payment for her room and board. She completed nine years of schooling and worked as a homemaker and part-time in a trade, but was unemployed at T1. Alice's mother, a widow, had been in excellent health, but died after the second interview.

Barbara is fifty-seven. She is married and her children are adults. Her health is excellent. Barbara completed high school and assists full-time in the family service-oriented business. She said caregiving interferes with work in the sense that sometimes she can't do anything in a day but look after her mother-in-law, the AD patient. Barbara's father-in-law is quite frail, so Barbara is responsible for their care. They live in their own home across town. The mother-in-law is seventy-five, completed high school, and has poor health. Besides homemaking, she worked part-time as a cashier in the family business, but is retired now.

Catherine is thirty-nine years old, a part-time clerical worker who completed high school. She is married and has several children. Her health is fair. So far, caregiving has not affected her work schedule. Catherine cares for her mother, who is sixty-eight years old. Her mother had eight years of schooling and worked as a homemaker. She is in poor health. Catherine and her husband recently sold their home and purchased a lot and two mobile homes to place on it—one for Catherine's family and one for her mother.

Dan is Alice's brother. He is forty-three and has a college education. Dan is divorced, has one child, and is in good health. He lived with his mother before she was placed in a room-and-board home. Dan pursues a management occupation full-time, and indicated that caregiving limited his work hours, forced him to turn down lucrative relocation offers, interfered with business travel, and was very disruptive to his career. As with Alice, Dan completed only two interview sessions because their mother died during the study.

Ellen is a thirty-seven-year-old administrative assistant who works full-time. She completed fourteen years of education, is married, and has one school-age child. Her health is excellent. At T1, she felt that caregiving did not affect her work. The AD patient is Ellen's mother, age seventy-two. She has a high school diploma and spent her adult years as a homemaker. She is still married and in excellent health. Ellen's parents live in a small apartment that Ellen and her husband recently constructed in the basement of their home.

Selection as Primary Caregiver

One factor that could affect the relationship between an adult child caregiver and a parent with AD is the reason that particular family member is providing care. Presumably, persons who choose the caregiving role have high levels of commitment and affection and cope better than those who perform the role involuntarily.

All participants except Ellen had siblings (and siblings-in-law, in Barbara's case). How did it happen that responsibility for taking care of the Alzheimer parent rested with this particular adult child? In the case of the sister-brother pair, Dan moved in with their mother following the breakup of his marriage, and thus was the primary caregiver for at least a year when her symptoms were increasing. Alice was involved in the planning for and decisions about their mother's care, and visited her regularly. Barbara felt she became the primary caregiver of her mother-in-law because her husband cared about his mother more than his siblings did. She sees herself as helping her husband, but in fact, she does more of the necessary work than he does. Catherine cares for her mother because none of her siblings is willing to be involved. Ellen assumed the caregiver role by default of being an only child, but it was not an atypical role for her. Her uncle, who had died of cancer, had lived with her near the end of his life, and Ellen also provided some care to her aunt, another victim of AD.

These five adult child caregivers gave their time and energy to their disabled parents because they felt love for them. Moreover, they appeared to have arrived at a stage of filial maturity that enabled them to relate to the parent in an adult-to-adult fashion. That is, despite the emotional strain and infringements on their own lifestyle, these persons were able to assess their parents' needs, evaluate plans of action, and follow a course of action they determined to be in their parents' best interests. The following sections explore the adult children's feelings and attitudes further.

Affection and Communication

The MSIS was the indicator of affection and communication between the adult children and their parents. The T1 scores represented the retrospective assessment of the respondents' feelings for the parent at the time before symptoms of Alzheimer's disease became apparent. Ranging from 105 (Barbara) to 143 (Ellen), these scores corresponded to the results that Miller and Lefcourt (1982) reported for college students rating relationships with the closest persons in their lives. Barbara is a daughter-in-law, not a daughter, so it is reasonable that her score is lowest.

Across the rest of the time periods under study, the MSIS scores declined gradually for Alice, Dan, and Ellen. Their T3 scores were 72, 81, and 82 respectively, and Ellen's T5 score was 78. Barbara reported a sharp drop in her feelings of affection between the early stages of the disease and the more recent periods (T3 = 25, T5 = 17). She explained that her mother-in-law's disruptive behavior and verbal abuse were very difficult for her, and she felt her father-in-law interfered with the help she was trying to give him and his wife.

In contrast, Catherine's responses to the MSIS items reflected a gradual increase in feelings of affection and closeness as her mother's condition deteriorated (T1 = 114, T3 = 124, T5 = 139). She found her mother's smile, hug, or "I love you" rewarding despite the difficulties involved in caregiving and lack of help from other relatives. She appreciated the fact that her mother had been good to her through the years.

Commitment

Results for the commitment items revealed that respondents' reasons for maintaining the relationship with the Alzheimer's patient were based more on personal than on structural commitment (means = 2.9 and 2.3 out of 4.0 respectively). Analysis of individual items showed that a positive attitude toward the relationship, as expressed by feelings of love ($M = 3.4$), a sense of personal dedication ($M = 3.1$), and wanting to repay past kindnesses ($M = 3.0$) were the aspects of personal commitment deemed most important by the respondents. Moral obligation, assessed in terms of believing that there was an unspoken contract requiring caregiving ($M = 2.9$) and living up to religious or ethical principles ($M = 2.8$), and definition of themselves in terms of the adult child caregiver role ($M = 2.4$) were less important aspects of personal commitment.

Social pressure as evidenced by wanting to live up to family tradition or obligation ($M = 2.8$) received the highest endorsement for the structural commitment items. Other aspects were termination procedures related to the inability to pay someone else to provide care ($M = 2.6$), lack of available alternatives to the relationship with the AD parent ($M = 2.5$), termination procedures related to the difficulty of making alternate care arrangements ($M = 2.3$), past investments of time, energy, and emotion in the relationship ($M = 2.3$), and social pressure in the form of criticism from others if the adult child did not provide care ($M = 1.4$).

The qualitative data yielded further understanding of the reasons why respondents retained feelings of commitment despite deterioration of the patient's personality and mental capabilities. The aspect of personal commitment reflecting one's attitude toward the relationship—affection, repaying past kindnesses, and personal dedication toward the patient—is exemplified by Catherine's comment:

> Well, that's part of it, right. Because when I was growing up she was a real good mother to me. And I could never mistreat her.

Personal commitment also involves a sense of moral obligation to the relationship partner. In response to the item concerning an unspoken contract to care for her mother, Catherine stated:

> Yes, I think even though she don't even know me any more, somewhere in the back of her mind, she knows I would do anythng for her. Because she has always, always said, "Catherine will do anything for me" even after she got sick. She'll look at me and smile and she'll say, "I just love you, you'd do anything for me."

These examples illustrate the strength of the personal aspects of commitment in the Alzheimer's caregiving role.

In contrast, structural commitment focuses on external constraints for continuing care. We found both endorsement and rejection of termination procedures related to finances and alternative arrangements as reasons for the caregiver continuing his or her role. For instance, Barbara rated the difficulty of making other arrangements for her mother-in-law's care as the most important of the structural reasons that motivate her. On the other hand, Catherine and Ellen, though acknowledging that they had no money to purchase alternative care, said this was not a major reason for their continuing to care for the Alzheimer's parent. Catherine said,

> Well, no, I can't afford to pay anyone to take care of her, but that's not the reason that I want to help with Mom. If I could afford it I would hire someone to come here in my house and take care of her. But the reason I take care of her is because I love her.

Similarly, she had not found the difficulty in making alternative arrangements to be a significant part of her continuity of care:

> That's not important. You know, you can always make some kind of arrangement if you really want to.

Another aspect of structural commitment is that people may continue caring for the Alzheimer's patient because of irretrievable investments they have made in the relationship, in the past and during the more immediate stressful period. Catherine and Ellen felt this reason influenced their caregiving but Barbara believed it did not:

> That's true. That's important. I've put a lot of time into taking care of her, helping with her, and I would never want to give up on her until she draws her last breath. I would never want to give up on her. [Catherine] I don't know, because I would gladly give it up if someone would take over . . . I don't want to sound like I don't care but yet, you know, if someone would do something with her, I would be more than happy. [Barbara]

We also explored structural commitment in the form of social pressure brought to bear by family caregiving traditions and others who might be critical if the caregiver did not provide care. Barbara rated this reason as somewhat important, but Catherine and Ellen said it was not important. According to Catherine,

> Oh, no. It's not that I'm obligated to take care of her or help with her. I do it because I love her and I know she would do the same for me. I'm not worried about what they say. None of them does anything anyway. But like I say, I do it because she's my mother and she would do it for me.

A final aspect of structural commitment is whether there are available alternatives to the relationship in question. Only Catherine, whose MSIS score increased over the course of the study, rated this reason as important in her decision to care for her mother.

Perceived Changes in the Parent-Child Relationship

Intimacy tended to decline in these parent-child relationships, yet personal commitment remained high. What changes did the adult child caregivers observe in their relationship with their parents as the AD symptoms emerged and the disease progressed? How were these changes related to affection, communication, and commitment?

Alice's discussion of changes focused on loss of "a normal mother-daughter relationship," as she put it. She expressed frustration that she no longer knew what her mother thought or felt and couldn't communicate with her any more.

> We don't get along or not get along. It's almost like she's one of my other patients now. The relationship is there, but it's not there.

Consequently, Alice visited her mother less often, giving lack of communication as the main reason.

Barbara had gotten along well with her mother-in-law before the symptoms of AD began. Now,

> I just can't be close to her like I used to be. If ever I'm in close contact with her, it looks like she will get to arguing with me, so I almost have to avoid her . . . it bothers me and it works on my nerves . . . it makes me feel sad.

Barbara had been going out of her way to fix special meals, bring flowers, and take care of the housework to help and please her mother-in-law, but the patient's inability to appreciate these efforts and her argumentative behavior caused Barbara intense frustration. She wished she could still be close to her mother-in-law, especially at this time when she was so sick.

Catherine noted that her relationship with her mother was no longer based on reciprocal interaction:

> As a daughter, I guess it's sort of a one-sided relationship. I know she, in her own way, loves me. But I understand if she can't love me as a daughter and I [still] love her as a mother.

Catherine also focused on communication problems:

> Since she's become sick she can't express her feelings to me or she can't tell me her problems or things that bother her.

Catherine found her mother's inability to express her needs quite frustrating.

Like the other adult children in the study, Dan said he still loves his mother but mentioned similar feelings of sadness about the paradox of her being the same person and yet being completely different in her responses and communication patterns now. He expressed anger about this change: "It just seems so unfair."

> Dan recounted ambivalent feelings about contacts with his mother: [There is] still that quandary of not knowing what I should do or what she wants and what is best for her. To take her out and do the little things [I] like to do that will make me feel better for doing them and seeing her enjoy those, this is wonderful a couple times, and [then] the next time . . . you go and see that she is so agitated and so hyped and you know your presence is really compounding that [so] you leave and you feel bad about leaving, and you're so damn glad to get out of there. Lot of guilt, 'cause you don't know what you should do in the sense that there's no two-way communication and you can't gauge response or receptivity or what's really needed. You're only second-guessing yourself, and that's not very rewarding.

These were new and problematic feelings that Dan had not experienced previously in his relationship with his mother.

Ellen, an only child, had enjoyed spending a lot of time with her mother, shopping together, visiting, and so on. She missed not only these shared activities, but also the good friend she had had in her mother:

> The relationship is dying. It's like losing or falling out of love with someone. Love is dying because she's no longer the same person.

Ellen said that she began to withdraw from her mother after the symptoms of AD became evident. At the time, her mother was critical and hurt and did not understand this reaction. As she adjusted to her mother's condition, Ellen was more accepting of the limitations associated with AD. Reflecting on the one-sided nature of her relationship with her mother, she said,

> . . . it's fine because I know she's done so much for me in the past. And I also know that she would do [things for me] now if she could. And I don't feel bad about that.

Discussion and Implications

Although most adult children do not provide direct care and continuous supervision to their aged parents, a significant minority do. More will assume this role as elderly people live longer in a frail condition. Most of the studies of family members providing care to Alzheimer's disease (AD) patients or other dependent aged persons have focused on objective burdens (constraints on time, activities, and finances) and subjective burdens (attitudes and feelings) associated with such caregiving. This study complements research on normal parent-child relations in adulthood and old age, extends previous investigations of caregivers by examining reasons why adult children assume the caregiving role and how that role affects the parent-child relationship, and points to important issues for future research and for applied gerontology.

Affection and Communication

As illustrated in the results for affection and communication, the problems adult children experienced when a parent had AD were not restricted to infringements on time and money or increased responsibilities. One of the major issues that they faced was loss of a significant relationship, even though the parent was still alive. Over the course of the eighteen months of the study, affection declined in all but one case. The adult children found that important aspects of close relationships, such as support, understanding, and shared activities, were missing. Each of the respondents cited the parent's loss of the capacity to communicate meaningfully as one of the most frustrating conditions of AD. Not only did this mean that the adult children could no longer discuss important ideas and feelings, it also hampered their attempts to provide appropriate care to the AD parents.

Clearly affection and communication are significant dimensions of any close relationship, but little research on affection and communication between adult children and their aged parents exists. More researchers should investigate these variables in both normal and problematic late life parent-child relations. Identification of typical and effective interaction patterns in normal relationships may provide useful insights for interventions when circumstances become problematic, as in the case of very frail elderly parents.

Commitment

One of the propositions of commitment theory is that the depth of a person's commitment to a given relationship influences the degree of personal and social disruption one experiences at the loss of that relationship (Johnson 1982). People typically expect parent-child relationships, friendships, and marriages to endure indefinitely, and express high levels of commitment to such relationships. On the other hand, most do not expect long-term continuity or emotional closeness with co-workers, neighbors, and others in the community, and consequently display relatively lower levels of commitment to relationships with these persons. Loss of these more distant relationships, then, rarely results in personal or social trauma, but loss of relationships characterized by high commitment does.

The adult children of AD parents in this study reported high levels of commitment for the time before the symptoms of the disease emerged. They expressed sadness, grief, and frustration about their parents' loss of the ability to communicate, share mutually enjoyable activities, and carry out other aspects of a close relationship as the disease progressed. These feelings correspond to the predictions of commitment theory. But despite the undesirable changes in the relationship, the respondents retained commitment to caring for their demented parents. Personal, internal sources of motivation were more important aspects of this commitment than external constraints against ending caregiving. The respondents were less concerned about the expectations of others or the difficulties in terminating caregiving than they were about expressing their love and appreciation for what the parents had provided them in the past. These reactions do not follow the pattern usually predicted for relationship decline, in which decreasing affection reduces personal commitment and leads to dissolution of structural commitments (Johnson 1982).

We propose that relationship changes associated with AD do not lead to theoretical consequences of relationship decline because existing models, based on dating and marriage, presume that the partners have some degree of choice in the process (Blieszner & Shifflett, in press). This is not the case when a disease, rather than personal preference, is the cause of the decline. Use of personal and structural commitment constructs in examinations of normal parent-child relations might prove fruitful for clarifying feelings and reasons for continued association under ordinary circumstances as well as problematic ones in this type of nonromantic relationship.

Interventions

Finally, the results of this study have important implications for family gerontology practitioners. They suggest that interventions aimed at reinforcing and supporting caregiver's feelings of personal commitment to patients may be more acceptable to caregivers and more successful in alleviating their feelings of burden than those dealing with external constraints. On the other hand, caregivers who are motivated by a long tradition of family caregiving may respond to encouragement to turn to another family member for respite from the situation, whereas caregivers who are less influenced by feelings that family members are morally obligated to help each other may avoid this option. Likewise, different approaches would be needed for caregivers who may be willing but cannot afford to hire outside helpers and those who feel morally obligated to fulfill a spoken or unspoken contract to provide care personally. Thus practitioners may be well-advised to ascertain caregivers' feelings about and motivations for providing care before attempting to suggest coping strategies.

References

Blieszner, R. 1986. Trends in family gerontology research. *Family Relations, 35,* 555–562.

Blieszner, R., & Mancini, J. A. 1987. Enduring ties: Older adults' parental role and responsibilities. *Family Relations, 36,* 176–180.

Blieszner, R., & Shifflett, P. A. In press. The effects of Alzheimer's disease on close relationships between patients and caregivers.

Brody, E. M.; Johnsen, P. T.; & Fulcomer, M. C. 1984. What should adult children do for elderly parents? Opinions and preferences of three generations of women. *Journal of Gerontology, 39,* 736–746.

Cantor, M. H. 1983. Strain among caregivers: A study of experience in the United States. *The Gerontologist, 23,* 597–604.

Chenoweth, B., & Spencer, B. 1986. Dementia: The experience of family caregivers. *The Gerontologist, 26,* 267–272.

Johnson, M. P. 1972. Commitment: A conceptual structure and empirical application. *The Sociological Quarterly, 14,* 395–406.

————. 1978, October. *Personal and structural commitment: Sources of consistency in the development of relationships.* Paper presented at the Theory Development and Methodology Workshop, Annual Meeting of the National Council on Family Relations, Philadelphia.

————. 1982. Social and cognitive features of the dissolution of commitment to relationships. In S. Duck (ed.), *Personal relationships 4: Dissolving personal relationships* (51–73). London: Academic.

Miller, R. S., & Lefcourt, H. M. 1982. The assessment of social intimacy. *Journal of Personality Assessment, 46,* 514–518.

Montgomery, R. J. V.; Gonyea, J. G.; & Hooyman, N. R. 1985. Caregiving and the experience of subjective and objective burden. *Family Relations, 34,* 19–26.

Pratt, C.; Schmall, V. L.; Wright, S.; & Clelland, M. 1985. Burden and coping strategies of caregivers to Alzheimer's patients. *Family Relations, 34,* 27–33.

Seelbach, W. C. 1984. Filial responsibility and the care of aging family members. In W. H. Quinn & G. A. Hughston (eds.), *Independent aging: Family and social system perspectives* (72–109). Rockville, Md.: Aspen.

16

Toward a Theory of Family Caregiving: Dependencies, Responsibility, and Use of Services

Timothy H. Brubaker
Ellie Brubaker

Family caregiving of older persons has received a great deal of attention from gerontologists and family studies scholars in the past decade. This research has provided substantial evidence that the care provided by families is extraordinary (Brody 1981; Cicirelli 1983, 1981; Horowitz 1985a; Seelbach 1984, 1978; Shanas 1979; Stolar, Hill & Tomblin 1986) and, in many instances, reciprocal (Thomas 1988; Wenger 1987). Given the evidence that family caregiving is frequent, it is important to note that caregivers, the assistance they provide, the family situations in which they are involved, as well as the services they use, are heterogeneous.

The fact of heterogeneity in families' responses to older members' needs for care results in a variety of formal policies, programs and services for caregiving. Some services match the needs of families, yet those families may not use the services. Other services are not employed because they do not meet family needs. While family heterogeneity has generated many types of services, lack of use often prevents those services from carrying out their intended purpose. A theory of family caregiving, in relation to use of services, is needed.

Within this chapter, a theory is developed about family caregiving and the use of services. The crucial concepts in understanding the use of services include: the types of dependencies experienced by recipients of family care; perceptions of responsibility for provision of services; and individual and family ethos. Family caregiving literature is reviewed, a model is presented and its use in working with caregiving families is illustrated through a case example.

Literature Review

Families are unique in their responses to the need for caregiving for their older members. As noted before, families respond idiosyncratically to *who provides care*, the *type of care provided*, the *situations in which they are involved* and the *services they use*. Family response to caregiving needs is influenced by, and influences, family ethos, types of recipient dependencies and perceptions concerning responsibility of services.

Caregiver Heterogeneity

Most individuals who provide care to family members are women (Brody 1981; Cantor 1983; Steinmetz & Amsden 1983; Stone, Caferata & Sangl 1987). However, family caregiving is not the exculsive responsibility of women. Men have been found to provide family caregiving as well (Horowitz 1985b; Miller 1987; Patterson 1987; Stoller 1983). Many family caregivers are daughters, although some are daughters-in-laws, husbands, nieces, or nephews.

For example, two families may have an older member living with them who has Alzheimer's disease. In each family, someone must be with the older member throughout the day. In one family a nephew and his wife provide primary care to an older aunt. Because they work and have young children, they have agreed to use adult day care services for the aunt. The nephew is comfortable with the day care program and feels he is providing good care for his aunt. In the other family, a daughter and her husband provide care to an elderly mother. The daughter has quit her job to stay at home with her mother. Although several adult day care programs and long-term care programs are available, the daughter has chosen not to use them. She has told her husband that she would feel guilty having someone else carry out what she perceives as her responsibility.

Heterogeneity of Assistance

The care provided by family members differs according to the kind of assistance given and the manner in which specific tasks are carried out. Some caregivers provide total care to an older family member, while others provide assistance with one or two daily activities (such as, transportation, telephones calls). Further, there are differences in caregiver affection toward the care-receiver (Jarrett 1985), caregiver effectiveness (Noelker & Townsend 1987; Townsend & Noelker 1987), range of caregiving activities (Cantor 1983; George & Gwyther 1986) and caregiver needs and use of services (Bass & Noelker 1987).

Variance in Family Situations

Another important characteristic of caregiving is that family situations differ greatly in structure and number of generations (Noelker & Wallace 1985). For example, in some families, a wife is caring for a frail, elderly husband without support from adult children. In other families, the wife who cares for her frail husband receives assistance from the couples' children and other family members. Still, in other families, the caregiver may be an adult daughter who may or may not be married, who may or may not have dependent children, and who may or not be working. Also, the caregiving families may include two, three, four or possibly five generations. There is little doubt that family caregivers of the elderly represent a heterogeneous structure and a varying number of generations.

Variation in Use of Formal Services

The use of formal services is a fourth factor that reveals considerable variation between families. Some families provide assistance to their dependent elderly members without the use of extrafamilial services. Others give the primary care and use services from public and/or private organizations. Still other families provide care that supplements the assistance given by outside public and/or private organizations. The variance in the use of services may not be related to the need for support, because research has suggested that families provide support without assistance even though the situation creates a great deal of stress (Springer & Brubaker 1984).

These variances in family responses to caregiving influence use of services. What factors are related to the use of assistance by families who provide care to a dependent older person? A theory of family caregiving and use of services could facilitate the development and targeting of services to best meet the needs of family caregivers and their elderly recipients.

Theory of Family Caregiving and Use of Services

Why are services used differently even though families may have similar needs? Why do some families provide extraordinary care at great cost to themselves, without the assistance of services that have been developed to assist them? This theory suggests that individual families define the caregiving situation differently and, consequently, use available services differently or not at all. For example, Montgomery (1984) reported that caregivers who need assistance often do not identify themselves as in need of services. Also, Lebowitz (1985, 457) noted, "families do not seek institutionalization of elderly persons to avoid giving care, but they do so only when the financial, emotional, and physical strains of caregiving and the continuing decline of the elderly person combine to exceed their capacity to provide care."

The theory is based on several assumptions. One, *families respond differently to different types of dependency.* Moore (1987) noted that there are varying thresholds of care that influence families caregiving activities. Others (Brubaker 1987; Litwak & Figueria 1968; Sussman 1977) have suggested that families are equipped to deal with some types of needs and bureaucracies are equipped to deal with other needs. Consequently, the family and bureaucratic organizations can cooperately provide services to meet the needs of older people. The crucial issue is the type of dependency and how families perceive their ability to deal with his type of dependency.

A second assumption is that *families hold different views on who should provide assistance.* For some types of dependency, the family considers itself responsible. For others, the responsibility may be assigned outside the family. This issue does not solely rest on the shoulders of individuals and families. This is a social policy issue. As Borgatta and Montgomery (1987, 19) examined family responsibility and aging social policy, they posited the following questions: "Should individuals be held responsible for the care of relatives based upon their status as spouse or child?" and "Should an individual's right to public dependency be determined by the presence or absence of a spouse or relative?" As the debate concerning responsibility continues at the social policy level, older people and their families make their own assessments of responsibility to meet their own daily needs.

A third assumption is that *each family develops a family ethos.* The family ethos defines the family's view of dependencies and who should help with these dependencies. Individuals and families may tend to seek assistance from family, public, or private organizations as a result of their beliefs about the use of services.

Figure 16–1 presents the relationships between the types of dependencies, assessment of responsibility to provide services, individual and family ethos, and the use of services. The relationship between use of services and type of dependency experienced by the older family member is mediated by the family's perception of who should provide assistance. Both use of services and perception of responsibility are influenced by individual and family ethos. Each factor is discussed in detail later. Practitioners working with family caregivers and their families may use this model to understand the likelihood that services will be used.

Types of Dependencies

More than twenty years ago, Blenkner (1965) discussed several types of dependency and, with slight modification, these types are relevant to the current caregiver situation (see Brubaker 1987). The needs of dependent older persons can be categorized into three areas. Some older persons have needs in one area and others' needs represent multiple areas. The three areas are financial, physical, and socioemotional.

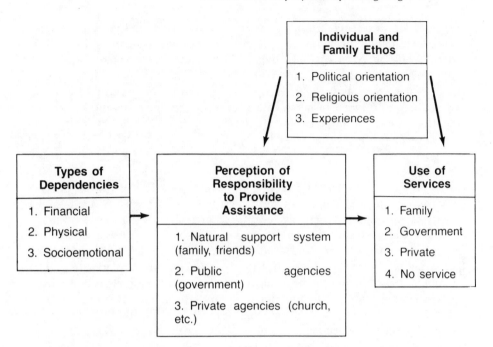

Figure 16–1. Model of Relationships between Type of Dependency, Responsibility to Provide Assistance, Individual and Family Ethos, and Use of Services

Financial. The need for the financial resources to meet the costs of day-to-day living is realized by older persons. Blenkner (1965) suggested that financial dependency results from the shift from a productive participant in the workforce to an economic consumer. The amount needed depends on the lifestyle to which the older person is accustomed. Pensions, annuities, social security, personal savings, and other financial support programs have been developed to provide resources for older persons. The management and use of these resources are a part of financial dependency concerns of older persons. Some older persons may have accumulated a sizable amount of financial security, while others have very little to meet their daily needs. Many older people rely on economic transfers (from one generation to another) to meet their financial needs (Kreps 1977).

Older persons may receive support from various sources to meet their financial needs. Income for 1984 indicated that families headed by a person sixty-five years old or older had the following distribution of income sources (U. S. Senate Special Committee on Aging 1986): social security or railroad retirement (32 percent), SSI or public assistance (1 percent), other pensions (15 percent), earnings (28 percent), and assets (24 percent). These data suggest that older persons are financially dependent on a variety of sources for the costs of daily living. The amount of income is another indicator of the financial dependency of older people. According to the U. S. Senate Special Committee on Aging (1986), 29 percent of people sixty-five and older are at or near the poverty level. Although most families exceed the poverty level, a sizable percentage appears to have a low enough income to be considered financially dependent as defined by the government.

Physical. As an individual ages, the normal process of aging affects physical capabilities. Muscle strength decreases, as does sensory acuity and, for many older persons, energy levels decrease. Blenkner (1965, 27) noted that physical dependency increases in later life as ". . .ordinary chores of living—personal self-care and grooming, keeping up one's living quarters, preparing and securing food, transporting oneself from place to place, shopping, participating in social functions, etc.—become increasingly difficult, strenuous, and eventually impossible to perform entirely without aid." Although most older people experience an increase in health difficulties, the issue of physical dependency is most acute in the seventy-five-and-older group of elders.

Socioemotional. The third type of dependency refers to the social support a person receives from interacting with other people. The amount of social contact may vary. "Whatever the interaction patterns of older people, it is clear that social contacts are important to older people. Contacts with family and friends are valued by older people" (Brubaker 1987, 14). One study (Blust & Scheidt 1988) found that caregivers and care-receivers assessed respect, warmth, and affection as the primary types of filial support. As individuals age, the need for social interaction may be impeded by the ability of the older person to initiate the interaction. Some older people are dependent on whoever visits or contacts them. Others continue to develop a network of interaction throughout their lives.

The Dependency Continuum. For each of the three types of dependency, there is a continuum of dependence and independence (Springer & Brubaker 1984). An older person's level of dependence may differ for each type of dependency. For example, a person may be financially independent (relying solely on assets and private pensions), physically dependent (limited mobility caused by arthritis), and socially independent (continues to interact with a network of family and friends). Consequently, the caregiving needs may differ depending on the degree to which the dependency end of the continuum is emphasized in each dependency area.

Responsibility to Provide Assistance

If older persons and their families decide help is needed, the primary question is: whose responsibility is it to provide assistance? The older person's needs can be met with the assistance of family members and friends or help can be solicited from sources external to the natural support system. Public (government) programs and private agencies (such as, church, service agencies funded by nongovernmental funds) are options from which to choose. As the older person decides on who will be approached for assistance, assessmet of the amount of responsibility for the specific need is important. For example, if an older person needs additional family support to meet daily expenses, he or she may not consider his or her children as responsible to provide it. In short, family members are not a financial resource because they are not considered responsible. If this older person decides to seek financial assistance, it is unlikely that he or she will seek the assistance from family members. However, if the older person is lonely and needs socioemotional support, he or she may consider family members as the responsible group and turn to them for assistance.

Individual and Family Ethos

The relationship between the types of dependency and the assessment of responsibility to provide assistance is mediated by the individual and family ethos. Ethos refers to the political and religious orientations of the individuals within the family. It also includes family members' experiences with services. Some families' political orientation encourages self-reliance and a reluctance to use governmental support. These families are unlikely to seek assistance from government programs.

Religious orientation may also be important. Some religious groups seek to meet the needs of their membership. For example, Hostetler (1980, 170) noted that the Amish maintain economic subsistence ". . . without government aid of any kind." It is unlikely that an older Amish person will turn to the government to deal with a financial dependency. Rather, he or she will turn to the family or church, which is the focus of their community. Similarly, if an older Amish person is physically dependent, family members will help. The religious orientation encourages the Amish to look within the family for assistance. "For the Amish, the need to provide assistance to dependent elderly is seen as a way to honor their parents. Their family life and religious values coincide to provide support to elderly family members" (Brubaker & Michael 1987, 115).

Experiences the family caregiver has had with the use of services may affect the decision. Some family caregivers have used services and have had a negative experience. They may be reluctant to use additional services even though they may need them.

Case Study

The following case example exemplifies the use of the theory of family caregiving and use by a human service practitioner. Although the service provider may have had several families use and benefit from a service, this does not necessarily encourage other families with whom she works to try the service to meet their own needs.

Mrs. Jonson, an adult service worker at the county department of human services received a call from a Mrs. Liven, concerning Mrs. Liven's mother. Mrs. Liven requested information about services available for older adults in their area.

Mrs. Jonson told Mrs. Liven that a number of services were available for elderly individuals, but that she would need more information about Mrs. Liven and her mother to help them determine the services that would best fit their needs. A meeting was set between Mrs. Jonson, Mrs. Liven, and Mrs. Liven's mother, Mrs. Craig.

At the meeting Mrs. Liven and Mrs. Craig said Mrs. Craig lived alone in her own home in the community. She lived several blocks away from Mrs. Liven and her family. Since a stroke a year ago, Mrs. Craig had been unable to perform some household tasks, such as heavy cleaning and grocery shopping. In addition, Mrs. Craig had occasionally forgotten to turn off her oven after cooking dinner. Mrs. Liven had been doing the grocery shopping and cleaning, but said she frequently felt overwhelmed and unable to carry out her job requirements, meet the needs of her own children, and care for her mother as well.

Mrs. Jonson discussed the various services that could lighten Mrs. Liven's load and meet the needs of Mrs. Craig. Mrs. Jonson suggested that a home health agency could provide a homemaker to do the housekeeping. Mrs. Liven responded positively, but Mrs. Craig said she could not pay for a homemaker aide to clean for her and was emphatic that she would not accept charity and have "welfare" pay for a stranger to clean her house. Mrs. Craig said, "My husband and I made it through the Depression without outside help and I'm not about to start taking charity now. This is our family's responsibility and no one else's."

Rather than trying to talk Mrs. Craig into accepting a service with which she was uncomfortable, Mrs. Jonson discussed with both women the family situation and their beliefs and values.

She learned that Mrs. Liven had two teenage daughters who spent time with their grandmother on a regular basis. Mrs. Craig wistfully said she wished they could shop and clean for her and agreed to ask them if they would be willing to take turns doing that.

Mrs. Jonson then explained the local meals-on-wheels program. This program could provide Mrs. Craig with a hot meal on a daily basis, eliminating the need for her to use her oven. Because the program charged recipients a dollar a day, Mrs. Craig felt she was paying her share and willingly agreed to participate in the meals-on-wheels program.

Mrs. Craig and her family were eager for her to remain in her own home. However, Mrs. Craig was not willing to sacrifice her principles to accomplish this. While some clients do not perceive receiving social services as conflicting with their value system, religion, or general world view, others do. The social service worker would have accomplished little had she attempted to talk Mrs. Craig into receiving services she did not want. By gaining information about Mrs. Craig's specific needs, her beliefs, and the family's resources, the social worker was able to help Mrs. Craig and her daughter meet their needs in a manner congruent with their family ethos and their perceptions of how services should be provided and used.

Conclusion

Within this chapter, a theory of family caregiving and use of services was developed. Family caregiving varies from family to family. In some families, an older member experiences a need and families use a formal service structured to meet that need. In other families, the same need may result in a refusal to use that same service. The dilemma this poses for social policy makers and service providers was discussed.

The theory of family caregiving and use of services directs attention to the types of dependencies experienced by elderly recipients of family care. The relationship between the type of dependency and use of services is mediated by the perceptions of responsibility to provide assistance. Individual and family ethos influences the family's perception of responsibility to provide assistance as well as the use of services.

The relationships presented in this model of family caregiving provide directions for future research. For example, the relationship between perceptions of responsibility for assistance, use of services, and family ethos needs additional attention. To what extent is family ethos an influencing factor in the family caregiving experience? To what degree does the perception of responsibility to provide services mediate the relationship between the types of dependency and use of services? Practitioners, family caregivers, and their families can use this information to facilitate service use in a dynamic situation.

References

Bass, D. M., & Noelker, L. S. 1987. Influence of family caregivers on elder's use of in-home services: An expanded conceptual framework. *Journal of Health and Social Behavior, 28,* 184–196.

Blenkner, M. 1965. The normal dependencies of aging. In R. A. Kalish (ed.), *The dependencies of old people* (27–37). Ann Arbor, Mich.: Institute of Gerontology. The University of Michigan—Wayne State University.

Blust, E. P. N., & Scheidt, R. 1988. Perceptions of filial responsibility by elderly Filipino widows and their primary caregivers. *International Journal of Aging and Human Development, 26,* 91–106.

Borgatta, E. F., & Montgomery, R. J. V. 1987. Aging policy and societal values. In E. F. Borgatta & R. J. V. Montgomery (eds.), *Critical issues in aging policy* (7–27). Newbury Park, Calif.: Sage Publications.

Brody, E. M. 1981. Women in the middle and family help to older people. *The Gerontologist, 25,* 19–29.

Brubaker, T. H. 1987. The long-term care triad: The elderly, their families, and bureaucracies. In T. H. Brubaker (ed.), *Aging, health, and family: Long-term care* (12–22). Newbury Park, Calif.: Sage Publications.

Brubaker, T. H., & Brubaker, E. 1981. Adult children and elderly parent household. *Alternative Lifestyles, 4,* 242–256.

Brubaker, T. H., & Michael, C. M. 1987. Amish families in later life. In D. E. Gelfand & C. M. Barresi (eds.), *Ethnic dimensions of aging* (106–117). New York: Springer.

Cantor, M. 1983. Strain among caregivers: A study of experiences in the United States. *The Gerontologist, 23,* 23–34.

Cicirelli, V. G. 1981. *Helping elderly parents: The role of adult children.* Boston: Auburn House.

———. 1983. Adult children and their elderly parents. In T. H. Brubaker (ed.), *Family relationships in later life* (31–46). Beverly Hills, Calif.: Sage Publications.

George, L. K., & Gwyther, L. P. 1986. Caregiving well-being: A multidimensional examination of family caregivers of demented adults. *The Gerontologist, 26,* 253–259.

Horowitz, A. 1985a. Family caregiving to the frail elderly. In C. Eisdorfer (ed.), *Annual review of gerontology and geriatrics*, (Vol. 5, 194–246). New York: Springer.

———. 1985b. Sons and daughters as caregivers to older parents: Differences in role performance and consequences. *The Gerontologist, 25*, 612–617.

Hostetler, J. A. 1980. *Amish society* (3d ed.). Baltimore: Johns Hopkins University Press.

Jarrett, W. H. 1985. Caregiving within kinship systems: Is affection really necessary? *The Gerontologist, 25*, 5–10.

Kreps, J. M. 1977. Intergenerational transfers and the bureaucracy. In E. Shanas & M. B. Sussman (eds.), *Family, bureaucracy, and the family* (21–34). Durham, N.C.: Duke University Press.

Lebowitz, B.D. 1985. Family caregiving in old age. *Hospital and Community Psychiatry, 36*, 457–458.

Litwak, E., & Figueria, J. 1968. Technological innovation and theoretical functions of primary groups and bureaucratic structures. *American Journal of Sociology, 73*, 468–481.

Miller, B. 1987. Gender and control among spouses of the cognitively impaired: A research note. *The Gerontologist, 27*, 447–453.

Montgomery, R. J. V. 1984. Services for families of the aged: Which ones will work best? *Aging, 347*, 16–21.

Moore, S. T. 1987. The capacity to care: A family focused approach to social work practice with the disabled elderly. *Journal of Gerontological Social Work, 10*, 79–97.

Noelker, L. S., & Townsend, A. L. 1987. Perceived caregiving effectiveness: The impact of parental impairment, community resources, and caregiver characteristics. In T. H. Brubaker (ed.), *Aging, health and family: Long-term care* (58–79). Newbury Park, Calif.: Sage Publications.

Noelker, L. S., & Wallace, R. W. 1985. Organization of family care for impaired elderly. *Journal of Family Issues, 6*, 23–44.

Patterson, S. L. 1987. Older rural natural helpers: Gender and site differences in the helping process. *The Gerontologist, 27*, 639–644.

Seelbach, W. C. 1978. Correlates of aged parents' filial responsibility, expectations and relations. *The Family Coordinator, 27*, 341–350.

———. 1984. Filial responsibility and the care of aging family members. In W. H. Quinn & G. A. Hughston (eds.), *Independent aging* (92–105). Rockville, Md.: Aspen Publications.

Shanas, E. 1979. Social myth as hypothesis: The case of the family relations of old people. *The Gerontologist, 19*, 3–9.

Springer, D., & Brubaker, T. H. 1984. *Family caregivers and dependent elderly.* Beverly Hills, Calif.: Sage Publications.

Steinmetz, S. K., & Amsden, D. J. 1983. Dependent elders, family stress, and abuse. In T. H. Brubaker (ed.), *Family relationships in later life* (173–192). Beverly Hills, Calif.: Sage Publications.

Stolar, E.; Hill, M. A.; & Tomblin, A. 1986. Family disengagement—myth or reality: A follow-up study after geriatric assessment. *Canadian Journal on Aging, 5*, 113–124.

Stoller, E. P. 1983. Parental caregiving by adult children. *Journal of Marriage and the Family, 45,* 851–858.

Stone, R.; Cafferata, G. L.; & Sangl, J. 1987. Caregivers of the frail elderly: A national profile. *The Gerontologist, 27,* 616–626.

Sussman, M. B. 1977. Family, bureaucracy, and the elderly individual: An organizational/linkage perspective. In E. Shanas & M. B. Sussman (eds.), *Family, bureaucracy, and the elderly* (2–20). Durham, N.C.: Duke University Press.

Thomas, J. L. 1988. Predictors of satisfaction with children's help for younger and older elderly parents. *Journal of Gerontology, 43,* S9–S14.

Townsend, A. L., & Noelker, L. S. 1987. The impact of family relationships on perceived caregiving effectiveness. In T. H. Brubaker (ed.), *Aging, health, and family: Long-term care* (80–99). Newbury Park, Calif.: Sage Publications.

U.S. Senate Special Committee on Aging. 1986. *Developments in Aging: 1985* (Vol. 3). Washington, D.C.: United States Government Printing Office.

Wenger, C. 1987. Dependence, interdependence, and reciprocity after eighty. *Journal of Aging Studies, 1,* 355–377.

17

Contextual and Relational Morality: Intergenerational Responsibility in Later Life

Linda Thompson

Aside from a passing reference to debt and duty, most family scholars study intergenerational responsibility as though it were not a moral matter. This may be because scholars believe the bonds between parents and children in current North American culture are personal relations founded on love rather than formal relations founded on obligation (Nydegger 1983). Scholars may believe that thinking about parents and children as a moral matter denies the personal and emotional nature of family bonds (Blustein 1982). The fault lies in how we think about morality. Prevailing thought on morality developed in economic, political, and public spheres; it is impersonal, general, abstract, and untainted by emotion or circumstance (Benhabib 1987; Tronto 1987). No wonder it makes sensitive scholars cringe when applied to something as personal, private, and fraught with emotion as families. Rather than ignore the moral content of family life, we need to develop moral theory that applies to personal and private life, or, better yet, theory that transcends the false barrier between private and public life (Tronto 1987).

In this chapter, I begin the task of conceptualizing intergenerational responsibility as contextual and relational morality. I borrow these conceptual components from feminist discussions of morality (Gilligan 1982; Kittay & Meyers 1987; Noddings 1984; Tronto 1987) and from others who criticize prevailing moral thought (Haan 1983; Haan, Aerts & Cooper 1985; Sampson 1983). There are glimmers of this perspective in the work of family scholars who study intergenerational relationships, and I want to turn these glimmers into guiding lights.

Intergenerational responsibility is defined as follows: Responsibility is the activity of receiving and responding to another. Each generation should be sensitive to the suffering, desires, and needs of the other generation. Family members strive to meet everyone's needs, prevent harm, and take positive action to protect and promote each other's welfare.

Responsibility does not mean family members must be servile or self-sacrificing to be sensitive to the needs of others. Striving to meet everyone's needs includes both one's own and other's needs. Indeed, the moral dilemma of intergenerational responsibility is the accommodation of the needs of both aged parent and adult child. I adapted this definition of responsibility from the work of several authors: Bernard (1981) wrote of the love and/or duty ethic; Bellah and his colleagues (1985) referred to commitment; Ferguson (1980) discussed compassion; Gilligan (1982) and Noddings (1984) described care; and Schorr (1980) and Seelbach (1984) considered filial responsibility.

Previous thought on intergenerational responsibility in later life has focused exclusively on the responsibility of adult children to their aging parents rather than mutual responsibility. Most researchers have concerned themselves with the *substance* of and the *motivation* for filial responsibility. Concerning the substantive nature of responsibility, the purpose of much research is to discover what kinds of attention, assistance, and affection make up filial responsibility. The research question is: What do aged parents need and expect from their children, and what are adult children committed to do for their aged parents? Concerning motivation for filial responsibility, researchers have grappled with affection and obligation as reasons for response to parental desires and needs. The research question is: What grounds do aged parents have for their expectations for filial response, and what compels children to respond to their parents? Answers to these questions depend on the people involved and their circumstances, but scholars rarely consider context. And, although aged parents and their adult children are implicated in these questions, scholars rarely consider both generations or the nature of their relations.

A conceptualization that is contextual and relational reforms questions of substance and motivation and forms new research questions. To give life to the conceptualization, I quote a conversation from Vivian Gornick's memoir of her relationship with her mother, *Fierce Attachments* (1987, 42–45). In this conversation, Gornick captures the complexity of intergenerational responsibility. Vivian and her mother are sitting in a Greek coffee shop in Manhattan:

> "I was talking to Bella this morning," my mother says, . . . shaking her head from side to side. "People are so cruel! I don't understand it. She has a son, a doctor, you should pardon me, he is so mean to her. I just don't understand. What would it hurt him, he'd invite his mother out for a Sunday to the country?" . . . "Okay, okay, so what did he do now?" "It isn't what he did now, it's what he does always. She was talking to her grandchild this morning and the kid told her they had a lot of people over yesterday afternoon, what a nice time they all had eating on the porch.

You can imagine how Bella felt. She hasn't been invited there in months. Neither the son nor his wife have any feeling for her."

"Ma, how that son managed to survive having Bella for a mother, much less made it through medical school, is something for Ripley, and you know it."

"She's his mother."

"Oh, God."

"Don't 'oh, God' me. That's right. She's his mother. Plain and simple. She went without so that he could have."

"Have what? Her madness? Her anxiety?"

"Have life. Plain and simple. She gave him his life."

"That was all a long time ago, Ma. He can't remember that far back."

"It's uncivilized he shouldn't remember!"

"Be that as it may. It cannot make him want to ask her to sit down with his friends on a lovely Saturday afternoon in early Spring."

"He should do it whether he wants to or not. Don't look at me like that. I know what I'm talking about. . . . Say what you will, children don't love their parents as they did when I was young."

"Ma, do you really believe that?"

"I certainly do! My mother died in my sister's arms, with all her children around her. How will I die, will you please tell me? They probably won't find me for a week. Days pass. I don't hear from you. Your brother I see three times a year. The neighbors? Who? Who's there to check on me? Manhattan is not the Bronx, you know."

"Exactly. That's what this is all about. Manhattan is not the Bronx. Your mother didn't die in her daughter's arms because your sister loved her more than we love you. Your sister hated your mother, and you know it. She was there because it was her duty to be there, and because she lived around the corner all her married life. It had nothing to do with love. It wasn't a better life, it was an immigrant life, a working-class life, a life from another century."

"Call it what you want," she replies angrily, "it was a more human way to live. . . . all I can say is, if he wasn't her son Bella would never lay eyes on him again."

"That makes two of them, doesn't it? He certainly wouldn't lay eyes on her again if she wasn't his mother, would he?"

My mother gazes steadily at me across the table. "So what are you saying, my brilliant daughter?"

"I'm saying that nowadays love has to be earned. Even by mothers and sons."

Her mouth falls open and her eyes deepen with pity. What I have just said is so retarded she may not recover the power of speech. Then, shaking her head back and forth, she says, "I'll tell you like the kid told me, "Lady, you've got the whole thing upside down.""

Contextual Morality

Contextual morality involves the immediate context and the broader, sociohistorical context. Rather than search for absolute, abstract, universal rules about what is right and wrong, contextual morality attends to the everyday experience of particular people in particular circumstances in a particular society at a particular historical moment (Benhabib 1987; Gilligan 1982; Noddings 1984; Tronto 1987).

Immediate Context

To understand Bella and her son's responsibility to each other, we need to know that Bella made sacrifices for her son but, also, often made life miserable for him. We need to know that her son was having friends over on the afternoon that Bella felt left out. That is, to understand intergenerational responsibility, we must consider the history of the relationship and also the responsibilities and relationships each person has outside of the intergenerational tie. Matthews and Rosner's (1988) work offers a glimmer of the contextual nature of filial responsibility. They considered family histories of favoritism and alliance as well as adult children's competing commitments to wage work, husbands and wives, and their own children. Matthews and Rosner also considered another particular of the immediate context—siblings as alternate sources of assistance.

The purpose of much previous research on filial responsibility is to find out how strongly aged parents and adult children endorse simple ethical rules: For example, should children live with or close to their parents, care for sick parents, or provide financial support to their parents? Schorr (1980) pointed out that people often endorse filial responsibility if it is offered to them in such simple, abstract ethical terms. If people are provided with a context, however, their answers change. It makes a difference whether people are speaking for themselves rather than in general, whether other sources of aid are available, and whether the adult child's rights or other responsibilities are considered. Schorr reported that endorsement of filial responsibility wanes as contextual detail is added to the deliberations. Brody and her colleagues (1983) also reported that endorsement of filial duty wanes and generational differences in endorsement fade when items include the particulars of a situation. Researchers should allow parents and children to provide the context for their responsibility or, if researchers provide hypothetical circumstances, the invented context should be rich in necessary detail (Gilligan 1982). Otherwise, we will never know how the immediate context shapes intergenerational responsibility. What particulars of a situation encourage or discourage parents and children to respond to each other's needs and desires?

Responsibility—all morality—is an inevitable and incessant part of everyday life (Haan et al. 1985). For Bella, responsiveness would be her son's inviting her to dinner on a Saturday afternoon as a way of letting her know he cares. If we want to understand the immediate context of intergenerational responsibility, we should study ordinary life day by day, not just dramatic circumstances in which the elderly parent is decrepit, destitute, thoroughly dependent, or dying (Blieszner & Mancini 1987).

When researchers attend to the mundane aspects of filial responsibility, the results too often are a chronicle of helping behaviors. There are many forms of responsiveness to the needs and desires of another, aside from provision of services. For example, Matthews and Rosner (1988) reported a monitoring component to filial responsibility. As Vivian's mother puts it, "Who's there to check on me?" Adult children watch over their aged parents; they are ready to respond, although often find it in their parents' best interest to do nothing. *Not* taking action, *not* providing services, may be the most caring, responsible course (Gubrium 1988; Matthews & Rosner 1988; Noddings 1984). No act is invariably the right way to express responsibility and moral goodness (Blustein 1982; Gubrium 1988; Noddings 1984). Services themselves are often less important than what they express; that is, the other's desire to protect and promote our well-being (Blustein 1982; Noddings 1984). In contextual morality, we cannot assume that any specific behavior or service betokens responsibility, whether it is visiting, living together, or helping out with housework. It all depends on the particulars of the people involved and of the immediate situation.

Contextual morality can also shed new light on the obligation and affection imbroglio. Part of what people find alienating and hurtful about responsiveness founded on duty and obligation is that it feels as though the other person is treating you as some "generalized other" according to some fixed rule rather than as an individual with particular needs and desires (Benhabib 1987; Noddings 1984). We associate responsiveness founded on duty and obligation with routine, rule-bound behavior (weekly visits and so on) or with institutionalized norms ("she's his mother, plain and simple"). In both cases, it may be the impersonal nature of responsiveness, not duty and obligation themselves, that offend the recipient. Duty and obligation mean that adult children are compelled to respond to their parents' needs, in part, because their parents responded over many years to the needs and desires of the children (Blustein 1982). Children can respond to the special needs of their aged parents in a personal way and still be motivated by duty and obligation. Responsibility must be studied in context to know exactly what it is about duty and obligation that rankles both generations. Scholars may have contributed to giving duty and obligation a bad name by linking these motives with general, universal rules that apply across people and circumstances.

Broader Sociohistorical Context

Most renditions of morality, even contextual morality, ignore the broader context (Haan et al. 1985; Sampson 1983; Tronto 1987). A full understanding of morality requires recognition that public and private are entangled, that the personal is political. The broader context—cultural myths and metaphors, historical change, economic conditions, ethnic traditions, race and class diversity, and government policies and services—sustains and shapes intergenerational responsibility in families. The dilemmas faced by Vivian and her mother, by Bella and her son, are not simply personal problems of their own making.

Historical Change. Vivian's mother was the youngest of eighteen children, eight of whom lived to adulthood, but she has only Vivian and a son to count on. Fewer children, longevity, and wage-working women have all changed the nature of intergenerational ties in later life (Treas 1977). Scholars have not fully analyzed, however, how these historical changes are experienced by aged parents and their adult children.

The nature of filial responsibility changed as government took over health care, practical support, and economic sustenance of the elderly. Interdependence between generations shifted from economic to emotional, and aged parents' coercive power over adult children dwindled along with their economic control (Nydegger 1983). Nydegger speculated that guilt induction may be one of the few control mechanisms left to aged parents in our culture. When disinheritance is not much of a threat, God and public opinion hold little sway, and filial support laws are ignored, Vivian's mother has little choice but to resort to guilt to ensure Vivian's responsiveness (Nydegger 1983). All this historical change creates cohort differences between aged parents and their adult children. Generations come of age in different times, so they view intergenerational responsibility differently (Seelbach 1984). When Vivian's mother describes how her own mother died in her sister's arms, Vivian tells her that she is thinking of "a life from another century." Vivian's mother was a Russian immigrant who spent her girlhood in a cold-water flat with ten other people, including a boarder. Families stayed close together to survive. Although Vivian also came of age in a New York tenement, she had a room of her own, and she did not have the turn-of-the-century, immigrant struggle that her mother had. History comes between Vivian and her mother as they try to figure out their responsibilities to one another.

Following Nydegger's (1983) example, we should pay more attention to the sociohistorical context of intergenerational ties. We should consider how historical change and cohort differences shape the personal dilemmas of aged parents and their adult children. Allen and Pickett's (1987) study of lifelong single women is a rare and rich example of historical analysis of filial responsibility. The women they studied were the same birth cohort as Vivian's mother. Similar to Vivian's mother, they were raised in working-class, financially insecure, immigrant families. Many were youngest daughters. The women were raised to value a familistic ideology from the past; they were committed to family cohesion, survival, and caregiving. Coming of age during the Depression, these daughters responded to their parents' need for nurturant or economic support by sacrificing or delaying their own desires for marriage. Intergenerational responsibility was shaped by historical circumstance, social class, family composition, and gender.

Cultural Myths, Metaphors, and Contradictions. Americans distort history and create myth. Vivian's mother speaks longingly about a time and place when children looked after and loved their parents. Although most people cherish this belief, it is a myth that evokes anger and hurt from aged parents and guilt and despair from children (Brody et al. 1983; Jarrett 1985; Nydegger 1983; Schorr 1980). Nydegger argued that there is no culture where old people are loved and revered simply for being old, and no historical time when children looked after and lived with their aged parents out of fondness alone. The source of disappointment for Vivian's mother is more than personal; we can trace it to a myth that pervades American people. There are many such cultural myths, methaphors, and contradictions that shape personal responsibility between aged parents and their children.

Responsibility is a suppressed ethic in American culture. People talk about their family ties in the language of economics, and freedom from interference, rather than responsibility, is the most deeply held moral ground (Bellah et al. 1985). Vivian says "love has to be earned" even by mothers and sons. Several scholars have traced these economic and individualistic understandings of self and relationship to liberal capitalism (Bellah et al. 1985; Sampson 1983; Wexler 1983). The individualism that dominates public life is reproduced in private life.

Consider the controversy about obligation and affection as motives for filial responsibility. Vivian's mother implies that Bella's son owes a debt to his mother because "she gave him his life." The notion of indebtedness enters into most discussions of obligation as the source of filial responsibility (Blustein 1982; Callahan 1985; English 1979; Schorr 1980; Seelbach 1984). Adult children "owe" their parents for nurturance, sacrifices, and life itself. The metaphor is the contract. Yankelovich (1981, 104) reported that 67 percent of his respondents believed that "children do not have any obligation to their parents regardless of what their parents did for them." The question is posed and answered in a contractual manner. Children can disregard the debt, however, because they did not consent to the contract: "I didn't ask to be born" (English 1979). Besides, children can never fully repay their parents (Seelbach 1984).

Many people, once they leave the idiom of contracts and debt, do not know how else to think about obligation, so they discount obligation and move on to affection. Vivian talks about responsibility based on choice and love. To her, if parents and children are not fond of each other, they should not have to spend time together and look after each other. Adult children respond to their parents' needs and desires because they love them. The metaphor is friendship, a voluntary association founded on affection (English 1979). Parent-child relationships are not by choice, however; neither parent nor child chooses the particular other. Also, many children do not like or love their parents (Jarrett 1985; Nydegger 1983).

The discourse on obligation and affection as motives for filial responsibility is individualistic; it reflects American culture. Both metaphors—contract and friendship—view parents and their adult children as "'free agents," and nether metaphor works very well when it comes to intergenerational responsibility. Although Vivian speaks in the metaphors of contract and friendship, her bond with her mother contradicts her imagery. Her relationship with her mother is "'not good" and is often filled with rage, hate, and exhaustion. But Vivian continues to live within a mile of her mother, visit, and endlessly walk the streets of New York with her mother. Bellah and his colleagues (1985) found that, although people speak of their most personal ties in the language of freedom and economics—the dominant American tongue—they also, hiddenly and hesitatingly, speak of responsibility and commitment. Responsibility is experienced but suppressed in our individualistic culture.

Some scholars try to break out of the free agency of contracts and friendship by considering an ethic based on need and interdependence. For example, Callahan (1985) offered dependence as the source of filial responsibility. Disgruntled by debt and affection, Callahan suggested that utter need, sheer dependence, makes moral claims on family members. Aware that their parents rely on them and that their welfare is entrusted to them, adult children feel compelled to respond. Faced with need and dependence, a morally responsible person feels, "I must do something" (Gilligan 1982; Noddings 1984).

Talk of need and dependency rankles Americans, however. Aged parents want to be independent; their greatest fear is to be a burden to their families, and children contain their involvement and interference in order to preserve parental independence (Brody, Johnsen & Fulcomer 1984; Matthews & Rosner 1988). Parental need and dependency becomes a failure and an imposition (Schorr 1980). Even Cicirelli (1981), who admits that perhaps we place too much emphasis on self-reliance, defines elderly dependent parents as those who can no longer satisfy their own needs or wants by themselves and require help and support from others. Who would want to be so independent? It is difficult for anyone in our culture—aged parents, adult children, and scholars—to talk about responsibility and an ethic based on mutual need and interdependence. What Vivian and her mother feel as personal anguish, confusion, and ambivalence, in part, can be traced to cultural contradictions (Wexler 1983).

Consider another cultural contradiction: Although most Americans believe it is all right for aged parents to accept practical and economic support from community sources, they continue to believe that social and emotional support should come from children (Brody et al. 1984). Americans believe that families, not communities, are responsible for older parents (Nydegger 1983; Seelbach 1984). But American kinship structure—with its emphasis on the marital bond and the next generation—places aged parents outside what Americans think of as their primary attachments and responsibility (Jarrett 1985; Nydegger 1983; Schorr 1980; Seelbach 1984). This cultural contradiction becomes a personal dilemma for families. We believe both that families are the only source of emotional sustenance and intimacy and that older parents must stand far back in line for familial love and care. Barrett and McIntosh (1982) analyzed the antisocial nature of families: By keeping love and closeness captive within families, we deny other sources of emotional sustenance—church, community, friends, and neighbors. As scholars, we can help people see the connection between their personal experience and the broader context of their lives. It is a way to create new possibilites for families.

Government Policies and Services. Callahan (1986) recognized that the ethical foundation of our policies on aging are, at best, vague. He questioned whether the pragmatic, economic, cost/benefit approach used by government enhances intergenerational responsibility. Government policies and services promote competition between generations for scarce resources; this competition is bound to become a personal issue between aged parents and adult children or between elderly and young (Callahan 1986; Pifer 1986). The myth of social security as earned income or insurance also undermines intergenerational responsibility. Social security is not a simple, individual contract but a complex ethical bond between generations based on need and interdependence (Wynne 1986). Government service agencies and policies provide a way of thinking about intergenerational responsibility. Scholars ought to study how bureaucrats and service providers help shape the moral dilemmas and experiences of families (Addelson 1987). Government appears to provide an individualistic, economic, and competitive model for family responsibility.

Government romanticizes family but insists on an individualistic approach to family policy and services. Government views itself as a substitute for family rather than as a companion source of support and services; the state provides only when families falter and cuts back on provision if family provision expands (Pascall 1987; Schorr 1980). Some policy analysts (Schorr 1980; Treas 1977) have suggested that government trust the judgment, interdependence, and responsibility of families and give subsidies directly to families. Evaluation of policies and services should attend to how such community supports modify family bonds in later life and responsibility between aged parents and adult children (Schorr 1980). For example, incomprehensible, disorganized community services create a new aspect of filial responsibility: Adult children must guide their aged parents through a daunting bureaucracy (Cicirelli 1981; Schorr 1980; Seelbach 1984).

There is an unnatural separation in the way family scholars tend to think about public and private life, community and family services, and material and emotional supports. Americans of all ages think it is all right for government and community to assume practical and economic responsibility for older people (Brody et al. 1984). Family scholars argue that if government provides instrumental support, families could devote themselves to emotional support (Seelbach 1984). Brody and her colleagues (1983) reported, however, that, although in their questioning they tried to offer family and community as contrasting sources of help, respondents did not always see things that way.

It is false to split public and private life by splitting practical from emotional and ethical matters. Community and government cannot, perhaps, provide love and affection, but they can provide respect and concern (Noddings 1984). The provision of practical services and money can be caring or uncaring, responsive or unresponsive, whether these provisions come from formal sources or families. On the one hand, we should not expect emotional responsiveness from families apart from practical responsiveness; in part, we show respect, concern, and love by cooking a meal, cleaning the house, and mowing the lawn (Cancian 1988). On the other hand, we should not accept practical services and money from public sources as simple material support; such provisions have subjective, emotional meaning. Home and institutional care of the elderly are not opposed (Jarrett 1985). Romanticizing families and home care of aged parents, and separating emotional and material support, are ways to avoid talking about public responsibility (Graham 1983; Pascall 1987). Families are caught between a culture that splits life in two and everyday experience that belies such a split. It is not a personal problem when aged parents prefer community provision of practical services so they will not become a burden on their families and, then, come to feel that no one, neither family or government, truly cares about them.

Cultural Diversity. To explain her aunt's deathbed vigil, Vivian cites social conditions that compelled American, working-class, immigrant family members to respond to each other's needs. Scholars have not attended much to diversity in morality by gender, race, class, and ethnicity (Tronto 1987). There is some evidence that people disadvantaged by race, class, and gender hold a stronger ethic of responsibility, generosity, mutual dependence, and cooperation (Cicirelli 1981; Harding 1987; Seelbach 1984; Tronto 1987). By necessity, Tronto (1987) based her conclusions about moral diversity on circumstantial evidence, although researchers have studied gender differences in morality directly. Seelbach summarized the spare research on group differences in filial responsibility by gender, class, and race. Rather than simply comparing diverse groups using gender, race, class, and ethnicity as a variable, we should consider how the immediate and broader contexts of disadvantaged people shape their moral activity. Seelbach, for example, speculated that family responsibility may be stronger among blacks because of economic necessity, religious values, and mutual protection from discrimination. For many groups disadvantaged by race or class, survival may depend on the responsiveness of others. We cannot assume that mutual aid, living together, or even deathbed vigils are founded on filial piety and love (Schorr 1980).

Tronto (1987) and Harding (1987) considered the connection between powerlessness, exploitation, and an ethic of responsibility. Several scholars have suggested that caregiving of aged parents by women is exploitation and takes a great burden off the public (Abel 1986; Jarrett 1985; Sommers & Shields 1987; Treas 1977). Schorr (1980) asked who will care for aged parents as wage-work opportunities for women expand. As part of considering the broader context of intergenerational responsibility, we should study diverse and disadvantaged families directly and in their own right.

Relational Morality

Intergenerational responsibility is relational. That is, it emerges from the relationship between parents and children, from their interdependence. Responsibility is not simply mulled over in the solitary minds of individual family members; it is something that is struggled over together to shape a shared understanding about what is right and wrong, good and bad. Responsibility is never fully resolved; it is episodic and changeable; it is an ongoing social accomplishment for parents and children. Relational morality means that the tension between self and other creates moral dilemmas; our moral selves evolve through our relations with others; morality is evident in how we treat each other day by day; and we construct morality through dialogue (Benhabib 1987; Ferguson 1980; Haan et al. 1985; Lyons 1983; McCarthy 1978; Noddings 1984).

Almost every scholar who reviews the morality literature calls for more—or any—research that goes beyond the individual and studies the interactional processes through which pairs negotiate common expectations and understandings (Austin & Tobiasen 1982; Deutsch 1985; Folger 1984; Lyons 1983; Reis 1984; Sampson 1983; Wexler 1983). Only Haan and her colleagues (1985) have done research on interactional morality; no one has done research on relational morality in families. Even Gilligan (1982), who has examined the individual's relational conception of self as part of responsibility, has not examined pattern and process between individuals. We must move beyond isolated, separate moral agents and begin to consider the moral connection and contingency between aged parents and their adult children.

Pattern

Vivian and her mother do not share an understanding about adult children's responsibility to their parents. Vivian talks about responsibility based on affection, love that is earned rather than compelled. Vivian's mother disagrees. She wants love but believes that Bella's son ought to be responsive to his mother whether he feels like it or not. What Vivian and her mother teach us is that, to understand intergenerational responsibility, we have to know the points of view of both parent and child, not just one person judging and acting alone.

People differ in their moral schemata—cognitive maps that help them settle whether or not something is right or wrong (Lyons 1983; Reis 1984). Reis (1984) noted that although partners may agree they desire fairness, it is unlikely they share the same view on what would be fair. Different personal schemata can result in misunderstanding between partners in close relationships (McClintock 1983). If partners do not have some common moral understanding, then everything is up in the air all the time and their relationship is subject to incessant quarreling or negotiation (Bellah et al. 1985). One important area of study, therefore, is the pattern between aged parents' and children's understandings of intergenerational responsibility.

To be responsible, aged parents and adult children strive to meet everyone's needs, prevent harm, and take positive action to promote each other's well-being. Comparing the views of adult children and their aged parents, Cicirelli (1981) found generational differences in perceptions of parental needs. Adult children underestimated their parents' needs for safety, contact with the outside world, and someone to deal with agencies and businesses. Adult children overestimated their parents' concerns about personal and home health care. It is hard for adult children and aged parents to respond to each other's needs if they do not accurately perceive those needs. Comparing both generations perceptions of need is part of studying the relational pattern of responsibility. Better yet, according to Cicirelli, would be to study communication and the interpersonal process of helping.

Process

It is through ongoing interaction and dialogue that we struggle with and shape intergenerational responsibility. Vivian and her mother only got to the point in their dialogue where each offers her own view. If they had moved beyond this phase of the dialogue, Vivian and her mother may have been able to comprehend and consider the legitimacy of each other's claims and needs and move toward a common understanding about what is right and good between parents and their children (Haan et al. 1985). Cicirelli (1981) speculated that aged parents and their children who spend time together are more likely to share their feelings, worries, and concerns. Such communication, he suggested, would enhance adult children's awareness and responsiveness to their parents' needs. In a rare instance of studying the social process of family responsibility, Gubrium (1988) found that Alzheimer's caregivers assign meaning to their own responsibility based on how they compare their own experience with the related experiences of others. I suggest that intergenerational responsibility as moral dialogue has four essential processes: attribution, disclosure, empathy, and cooperation.

Attribution. Attribution is part of making sense of responsibility. We observe each other's verbal and nonverbal behavior and make attributions about the other's needs, intentions, and character, as well as attributions about the nature of our relationship (Kelley 1979). We also make attributions about our own behavior. Vivian's mother makes attributions about Bella and her son based on his failure to invite his mother to dinner: He has no feeling for his mother; he is mean and cruel; he is not a good son. Studying attribution helps us understand how adult children and their parents interpret each other's behavior as need or responsiveness and how they get into trouble when their attributions conflict. So far, however, there has been little thought given to how attribution contributes to moral activity in family and close relationships.

Responsibility depends on need interpretation (Benhabib 1987). Cohen (1982) suggested that, to respond to need, one partner in a relationship must make two attributions about the other partner's need: Who is responsible for creating the need, and who is responsible for alleviating the need? If, for example, an adult child perceives the need as created by the parent's character, then the child is likely to let the parent fend for him or herself. If the child is willing to take some responsibility for the parent's need or attributes responsibility to something outside of the parent's doing, then the child is likely to respond to the parent's need.

Certain attributions may be necessary, therefore, before intergenerational partners act responsibly. We can infer from Cicirelli's (1981) findings that adult children are making misattributions about parental needs. On what parental behaviors are children basing their attribution of need? Whom do children see as creating the need—themselves, annoying or defective aspects of their parent's character, or careless community and government? And how do children come to believe they are the ones who should respond to the needs of their aged parents?

In studying attribution of responsibility and blame, researchers have found that partners make different attributions merely because one is the actor and the other is the observer. Actors are more likely to attribute blame for a moral lapse to situational and environmental conditions, while observers are more likely to attribute blame to personal character (Cohen 1982; Kelley 1979). Bella, feeling hurt and slighted, blames her son for his enduring insensitivity and lack of affection for her. Bella's son, the actor in this instance, is more likely to blame his insensitivity on situational demands: He has been busy, did not know how important the invitation was to his mother, and so on. We should study these attributional predispositions in the context of intergenerational responsibility.

Studying attribution of motivation would shed light on the affection and obligation imbroglio. There seems to be an aversion to being responsible out of obligation and duty, for both partners (Baron 1984). Adult children feel guilty and resentful if they respond to their parents out of duty rather than love (Jarrett 1985; Noddings 1984). Aged parents feel alienated, ignored, and hurt if they believe their children are responding out of duty alone. How do adult children come to attribute their responsiveness to fondness and/or duty? How do aged parents make attributions about their child's motivations? What are the processes involved?

Baron (1984) suggested that duty is repugnant only when the responsive person—the adult child, in this case—is sanctimonious, hostile, annoyed, self-pitying, or grudging. Baron pointed out that this is not responsible behavior anyway, if responsible behavior is doing something for the good of the other. What is important is concern for the other's well-being. It is important for both partners to believe that the responsive one has an abiding readiness to act on behalf of the one being responded to, regardless of whether the motivation is love or duty (Baron 1984; Jarrett 1985; Noddings 1984). We do not know how family members show and make attributions about concern for the other's well-being. We know, however, that family members are better at communicating hostility to one another than love, and that there is less distress for everyone if responsiveness is gracious and attributions are generous and forgiving (Gaelick, Bodenhausen & Wyer 1985; Noddings 1984; Utne and Kidd 1980). In her memoir, Vivian describes the "rough bullying style" her mother used to show tenderness and the scorn, ridicule, and criticism her mother used to convey need, grievance, and despair. Attribution is perilous under such conditions. Such everyday episodes also show the importance of considering emotion and feeling, as well as behavior and thought, when studying family responsibility (Haan et al. 1985; Noddings 1984; Seelbach 1984). Our experience of love, anger, hurt, and guilt may be how we make attributions.

Disclosure. Intergenerational responsibility requires comprehension of each other's needs. Moral activity in families is unique because members reveal and share parts of themselves that outsiders never comprehend (Callahan 1985). Cicirelli (1981) speculated that adult children may be making misattributions about parental need because parents are not communicating their feelings, worries, and concerns. Rather than ask for help in a straightforward way, aged parents may simply get angry, exaggerate complaints, pretend helplessness, or demand attention (Cicirelli 1981).

Noddings (1984) suggested that disclosure is essential to responsibility and caring. Moral activity is realized through dialogue. Unless the care-receiver reveals personal aspirations, accomplishments, thoughts, and needs, the caregiver cannot show concern and respond in beneficent ways (Noddings 1984). Noddings is not suggesting that we have to make blatant appeals for help, but rather that the care-receiver must disclose enough about the self so that the caregiver can respond in the best interests of the other. Without disclosure it is difficult for intergenerational partners to comprehend and respond to each other's needs. The claims and needs of both partners cannot be coordinated if they are not known; to be silent is a moral lapse (Haan et al. 1985).

There are many constraints to full and honest disclosure. Habermas (McCarthy 1978) observed that most people do know what they want, what is good for them, what they need, and why they do certain things; when asked, they feign certainty and make their best guess. Bellah and his colleagues (1985) also noted that such self-knowledge is shaky, although partners communicate with one another as though it were stable and sound. Dialogue is necessary to discover the truth of each partner's best interests. Some family members may assume others' interests and temper their own requests without even bothering with disclosure and dialogue. In this case, all concerned probably come up with less than they need and deserve (Rubin & Brown 1975).

Disclosures may also be tainted by defensive or ideological distortions (Haan et al. 1985; McCarthy 1978). Talk about family responsibility is often threatening. It calls into question our connection with each other and our sense of ourselves as moral. Disclosure may be distorted, trouble suppressed, to preserve family harmony and a pleasing opinion of the self. Aged parents who suppress their needs to preserve a sense of independence may be serving American ideology rather than personal good. And adult children and their parents who fail to disclose their own needs because they see no difference between pursuing their own good and selfishness are also confined by American ideology. While some silence themselves, others are silenced by others. One partner's anger, hostility, power, or pure pigheadedness may silence the other partner. No one has studied disclosure between aged parents and their adult children or as part of intergenerational responsibility.

Bellah and his coauthors (1985) reported that, for most of the people they spoke with, the clear expression of one's desires, needs, and feelings was their primary, if not only, moral responsibility in close relationships. As long as partners were honest with one another, they had fulfilled their moral responsibility to the other. Intergenerational responsibility cannot be accomplished without disclosure, because to be responsive to the needs of the other, each partner must know the needs of the other. The information provided by disclosure, however, does not necessarily lead to mutual beneficent response. Vivian portrays herself and her mother as highly disclosing. She describes conversations with her mother, however, in which her mother does not even seem to know that Vivian is there. Her mother tells Vivian about her needs, deprivation, and misery, but does not consider that Vivian may see the situation differently or that the litany of pain oppresses her daughter. There is more to responsibility than full and honest disclosure.

Empathy. Disclosure is telling. Empathy is looking, listening, and understanding. Intergenerational partners can disclose openly and honestly and still be self-righteous and self-absorbed—closed off from each other. Empathy takes partners beyond their own personal concerns and righteousness. Empathy is taking the standpoint of the other; it is receptivity and sensitivity (Benhabib 1987; Ferguson 1980; Lyons 1983; Noddings 1984).

At the very least, empathy is the accuracy with which partners send their own messages and receive the messages of the other; such accuracy is important to both communication and coordination of everyone's concerns (Gaelick et al. 1985; Knudson, Sommers, & Golding 1980; Noller 1984; Pruitt 1981). At the most, according to Ferguson (1980, 122), empathy is "a complex process of expression, imagination, reflection, and appreciation."

Cicirelli (1981) hinted that adult children may be insensitive to their parents' needs. They may deny or distort their parents' needs, or simply hold different notions about what is best for their parents (Cicirelli 1981). In the conversation between Vivian and her mother, there is little evidence of empathy. Each offers her standpoint but does not comprehend the reality of the other. Perhaps because Vivian is the author of the memoir, she appears more empathic than her mother. She tries to imagine the standpoint of her mother as a proud, poor imigrant woman, born at the turn of the century, and widowed young. Vivian does not portray her mother as sympathetic, however. She reports that her mother uses her own experiences and interpretations as universal and is not bothered by the notion that the world might look different from another's point of view. This is not an unusual thing to say about aged parents (Seelbach 1984). One generational partner must take the standpoint of the other generation to truly comprehend and respond to the other's needs. If empathy is not mutual, however, responsiveness can become a burden.

Most scholars who consider empathy in moral activity think of it as simply putting oneself in the other's place. Vivian's mother and The Golden Rule are examples of this approach. A partner who treats others the way she would like to be treated is considering the other but using the self as a standard. This is one way of putting oneself in the other's place, but the assumption is that the other is the same as the self. Several moral theorists have offered a different approach: Empathy requires entering into the situation of others to understand how others experience—see, think about, feel—the situation in their own terms (Benhabib 1987; Bologh 1984; Ferguson 1980; Lyons 1983; Noddings 1984; Sampson 1983). Partners acknowledge and accept their differences. For generations to be fully responsible, to promote each other's good and act on each other's behalf, they must have empathy for one another. Empathy does not mean that partners have to hold the same perspective or meaning; each partner can comprehend the other without sharing that view for the self. Responsibility can still be bothersome and burdensome, however, if there is conflict between the desires and needs of the two partners or if there is disagreement about what each thinks is best for the other (Noddings 1984). Family scholars should consider how adult children and their aged parents come to construe or misconstrue each other's needs and how they deal with conflict and difference.

Cooperation. Cooperation, sometimes called coordination, is a willingness to enter dialogue, change one's stance and self, and act on one's combined concerns for self, other, and relationship (Benhabib 1987; Haan et al. 1985; Kelley 1979; Pruitt 1981; Rubin & Brown 1975). Cooperation is an acceptance of interdependence and the mutuality of partners' fates. There is an emphasis on shared understandings and common solutions. Cooperation includes a willingness to change the self based on the connection with the other; personal claims and needs are open to revision. One's needs, desires, emotions, concerns, and best interests are legitimate topics of moral dispute. Cooperation means the other's welfare is considered and responded to right alongside one's own welfare. If intergenerational responsibility involves striving to meet everyone's needs, preventing harm, and taking positive action to promote each other's well-being, then cooperation is an essential process.

Scholars have not given much thought to cooperation between aged parents and their adult children. There has been some thought given to the waning coercive power of parents as their economic clout over grown children has weakened historically (Callahan 1985; Nydegger 1983; Schorr 1980; Treas 1977). But we have not yet studied the social processes, such as cooperation, or the control mechanisms that supposedly have replaced coercive power. The emphasis on filial responsibility rather than mutual intergenerational responsibility also undermines the study of cooperation. Within families and between generations as age groups, it is rare to have anyone attend to the elderly's responsibility for younger generations (Blieszner & Mancini 1987; Torres-Gil 1986). In light of the competition between generations for scarce resources at the level of age groups, we should give thought to the possibilities of cooperation.

Cooperation is a characteristic of the intergenerational pair. If even one partner is intransigent or individualistic, the process breaks down. If even one partner refuses to yield, clings to self-righteousness, considers only her own interests, or focuses on how to outdo the other, cooperation crumbles. Morality, including intergenerational responsiblity, cannot fully be realized in the face of an intransigent other (Bologh 1984; Ferguson 1980; Noddings 1984). Cicirelli (1981) hinted that some aged parents make it very difficult for their children to serve and care for them. Elderly parents can be uncompromising and impossible to please. This does little to sustain the responsible efforts of their children (Noddings 1984). Vivian's mother often refuses to listen, be consoled, change her views, reconsider her needs, or consider her effect on her daughter. Probably, adult children can be as intransigent as their parents. In her memoir, Vivian describes instances where she and her mother achieve common ground by attending to and acknowledging each other's needs. In these instances, they both feel pleased with themselves and with each other.

The essential processes of intergenerational responsibility accrue as we move from attribution, through disclosure and empathy, to cooperation. Attribution is risky without disclosure. Empathy is impossible unless both partners engage in full and open disclosure. Cooperation founders unless both partners comprehend the standpoint of the other. Finally, without cooperation, mutual responsibility cannot be realized.

Conclusion

In this chapter I offered the beginnings of a conceptualization of intergenerational responsibility that attends to context and relation. I attempted to take responsibility beyond the individual and restore its social meaning. I drew on literature far removed from intergenerational relationships because, for the most part, the contextual and relational nature of family ties in later life has been neglected. Because of the shortness of the chapter and the newness of the notions, my conceptualization is spare and, at times, unsatisfying. David Reiss (1981) wrote that a conceptualization is engaging if it resonates with readers in its plausibility, is sound in its essential structure, but is incomplete enough so that readers can contribute to its elaboration and correction. I know my conceptualization of intergenerational responsibility is incomplete enough to invite elaboration and correction. I hope it also captures the imagination of readers and researchers who will struggle with it as I have.

References

Abel, E. K. 1986. Adult daughters and care for the elderly. *Feminist Studies, 12,* 479–497.

Addelson, K. P. 1987. Moral passages. In E. F. Kittay & D. T. Meyers (eds.), *Women and moral theory* (87–110). Totowa, N.J.: Rowman & Littlefield.

Allen, K. R., & Pickett, R. S. 1987. Forgotten streams in the family life course: Utilization of qualitative retrospective interviews in the analysis of lifelong single women's family careers. *Journal of Marriage and the Family, 49,* 517–526.

Austin, W., & Tobiasen, J. 1982. Moral evaluation in intimate relationships. In J. Greenberg & R. L. Cohen (eds.), *Equity and justice in social behavior* (217–259). New York: Academic Press.

Baron, M. 1984. The alleged moral repugnance of acting from duty. *The Journal of Philosophy, 81,* 197–220.

Barrett, M., & McIntosh, M. 1982. *The anti-social family.* London: Verso.

Bellah, R. N.; Madsen, R.; Sullivan, W. M.; Swidler, A.; & Tipton, S. M. 1985. *Habits of the heart: Individual and commitment in American life.* Berkeley, Calif.: University of California Press.

Benhabib, S. 1987. The generalized and the concrete other: The Kohlberg-Gilligan controversy and moral theory. In E. F. Kittay & D. T. Meyers (eds.), *Women and moral theory* (154–177). Totowa, N.J.: Rowman & Littlefield.

Bernard, J. 1981. *The female world.* New York: Free Press.

Blieszner, R., & Mancini, J. A. 1987. Enduring ties: Older adults' parental role and responsibilities. *Family Relations, 36,* 176–180.

Bologh, R. W. 1984. Feminist social theorizing and moral reasoning: On difference and dialectic. In R. Collins (ed.), *Sociological theory 1984* (373–393). San Francisco: Jossey-Bass.

Blustein, J. 1982. *Parents and children: The ethics of the family.* New York: Oxford University Press.

Brody, E. M.; Johnsen, P. T.; Fulcomer, M. C.; & Lang, A. M. 1983. Women's changing roles and help to elderly parents: Attitudes of three generations of women. *Journal of Gerontology, 38,* 597–607.

Brody, E. M.; Johnsen, P. T.; & Fulcomer, M. C. 1984. What should adult children do for elderly parents? Opinions and preferences of three generations of women. *Journal of Gerontology, 39*, 736–746.

Callahan, D. 1985, April. What do children owe elderly parents? *The Hastings Center Report*, 32–37.

——. 1986. Health care in the aging society: A moral dilemma. In A. Pifer, & L. Bronte (eds.), *Our aging society: Paradox and promise* (319–339). New York: W. W. Norton.

Cancian, F. M. 1986. The feminization of love. *Signs, 11*, 692–708.

Cicirelli, V. G. 1981. *Helping elderly parents: The role of adult children*. Boston: Auburn House.

Cohen, R. L. 1982. Perceiving justice: An attributional perspective. In J. Greenberg & R. L. Cohen (eds.), *Equity and justice in social behavior* (119–160). New York: Academic Press.

Deutsch, M. 1985. *Distributive justice: A social-psychological perspective*. New Haven: Yale University Press.

English, J. 1979. What do grown children owe their parents? In O. O'Neill & W. Ruddick (eds.), *Having children: Philosophical and legal reflections on parenthood* (351–356). New York: Oxford University Press.

Ferguson, K. E. 1980. *Self, society, and womankind*. Westport, Conn.: Greenwood Press.

Folger R. 1984. Emerging issues in the social psychology of justice. In R. Folger (ed.), *The sense of justice: Social psychological perspectives* (3–24). New York: Plenum Press.

Gaelick, L.; Bodenhausen, G. V.; & Wyer, R. S., Jr. 1985. Emotional communication in close relationships. *Journal of Personality and Social Psychology, 49*, 1246–1265.

Gilligan, C. 1982. *In a different voice: Psychological theory and women's development*. Cambridge, Mass.: Harvard University Press.

Gornick, V. 1987. *Fierce attachments: A memoir*. New York: Farrar Straus Giroux.

Graham, H. 1983. Caring: A labour of love. In J. Finch & D. Groves (eds.), *A labour of love: Women, work, and caring* (13–30). London: Routledge & Kegan Paul.

Gubruim, J. F. 1988. Family responsibility and caregiving in the qualitative analysis of the Alzheimer's disease experience. *Journal of Marriage and the Family, 50*, 197–207.

Haan, N. 1983. An interactional morality of everyday life. In N. Haan, R. N. Bellah, P. Rabinow, & W. M. Sullivan (eds.), *Social science as moral inquiry* (218–250). New York: Columbia University Press.

Haan, N.; Aerts, E.; & Cooper, B.A.B. 1985. *On moral grounds: The search for practical morality*. New York: New York University Press.

Harding, S. 1987. The curious coincidence of feminine and African moralities: Challenges for feminist theory. In E. F. Kittay & D. T. Myers (eds.), *Women and moral theory* (296–315). Totowa, N.J.: Rowman & Littlefield.

Jarrett, W. H. 1985. Caregiving within kinship systems: Is affection really necessary? *The Gerontologist, 25*, 5–10.

Kelley, H. H. 1979. *Personal relationships: Their structures and processes*. Hillsdale, N.J.: Lawrence Erlbaum.

Kittay, E. F., & Meyers, D. T. (eds.). 1987. *Women and moral theory.* Totowa, N.J.: Rowman & Littlefield.

Knudson, R. M.; Sommers, A. A.; & Golding, S. L. 1980. Interpersonal perception and mode of resolution in marital conflict. *Journal of Personality and Social Psychology, 38,* 751–763.

Lyons, N. P. 1983. Two perspectives: On self, relationships, and morality. *Harvard Educational Review, 53,* 125–145.

Matthews, S. H., & Rosner, T. T. 1988. Shared filial responsibility: The family as the primary caregiver. *Journal of Marriage and the Family, 50,* 185–195.

McCarthy, T. 1978. *The critical theory of Jurgen Habermas.* Cambridge: Massachusetts Institute of Technology Press.

McClintock, E. 1983. Interaction. In H. H. Kelley, E. Berscheid, A. Christensen, J. H. Harvey, T. L. Huston, G. Levinger, E. McClintock, L. A. Peplau, & D. R. Peterson, *Close relationships* (68–109). New York: W. H. Freeman.

Noddings, N. 1984. *Caring: A feminine approach to ethics and moral education.* Berkeley, Calif.: University of California Press.

Noller, P. 1984. *Nonverbal communication and marital interaction.* New York: Pergamon Press.

Nydegger, C. N. 1983. Family ties of the aged in cross-cultural perspective. *The Gerontologist, 23,* 26–32.

Pascall, G. 1987. *Social policy: A feminist analysis.* London: Tavistock.

Pifer, A. 1986. The public policy response. In A. Pifer & L. Bronte (eds.), *Our aging society: Paradox and promise* (391–413). New York: W. W. Norton.

Pruitt, D. G. 1981. *Negotiation behavior.* New York: Academic Press.

Reis, H. T. 1984. The multidimensionality of justice. In R. Folger (ed.), *The sense of injustice: Social psychological perspectives* (25–61). New York: Plenum Press.

Reiss, D. 1981. *The family's construction of reality.* Cambridge, Mass.: Harvard University Press.

Rubin, J. Z., & Brown, B. R. 1975. *The social psychology of bargaining and negotiation.* New York: Academic Press.

Sampson, E. E. 1983. *Justice and the critique of pure psychology.* New York: Plenum Press.

Schorr, A. 1980. *". . . thy father and thy mother . . ." a second look at filial responsibility and family policy* (DHHS Publication No. 13–11953). Washington, D.C.: U.S. Government Printing Office.

Seelbach, W. C. 1984. Filial responsibility and the care of aging family members. In W. H. Quinn & G. A. Hughston (eds.), *Independent aging: Family and social systems perspectives* (92–105). Rockville, Md.: Aspen.

Sommers, T., & Shields, L. 1987. *Women taking care: The consequences of caregiving in today's society.* Gainesville, Fla.: Triad.

Torres-Gil, F. 1986. Hispanics: A special challenge. In A. Pifer & L. Bronte (eds.), *Our aging society: Paradox and promise* (219–241). New York: W. W. Norton.

Treas, J. 1977. Family support systems for the aged. *The Gerontologist, 17,* 486–491.

Tronto, J. C. 1987. Beyond gender difference to a theory of care. *Signs, 12,* 644–663.

Utne, M. K., & Kidd, R. 1980. Equity and attribution. In G. Mikula (ed.), *Justice and social interaction* (63–93). New York: Springer-Verlag.

Wexler, P. 1983. *Critical social psychology.* Boston: Routledge & Kegan Paul.

Wynne, E. A. 1986. Will the young support the old? In A. Pifer & L. Bronte (eds.), *Our aging society: Paradox and promise* (234–261). New York: W. W. Norton.

Yankelovich, D. 1981. *New rules: Searching for self-fulfillment in a world turned upside down.* New York: Random House.

Part 4
Current and Future Perspectives on Theory and Research

18
Aging Parents and Adult Children: New Views on Old Relationships

Jay A. Mancini
Mark J. Benson

S everal years ago older adults and their families were referred to as "pioneers." The idea of pioneers and the process of pioneering involve being the first of a kind and preparing the way for others. Because of the changing roles, expectations, rights, and obligations among older adults and their families, it is probably accurate to apply the pioneer term to aging parents and their adult children. Moreover, if recent and current cohorts of older people and their offspring are pioneers, then those who discuss and investigate older adults and their families are also pioneering. One question that remains, however, is when does the pioneering end? In the introductory chapter to this book a number of literature critiques were examined, and it was concluded that calls for theory development and new methodologies often went unheeded. If the pioneering work in this area has already occurred, it is now incumbent upon family gerontologists to *develop* this previously uncharted area. A question we now ask is now has the present volume advanced theory and research in family gerontology?

The Interweave of Parent-Child Relationship Dimensions

In this book are eighteen chapters. The first provided a summary of the field and an overview of the volume. This last chapter seeks to interweave the intervening sixteen chapters. This final chapter also will display the range of theory and future research that has been suggested by the various chapters. At present, though, we will paint the broad picture reflected by the chapters, and then note some of the detailed brushstrokes. The chapters are organized into three sections: Family structure and kin context, parent-child dynamics and interaction, and, caregiving and care-receiving. The sections are not mutually exclusive across the chapters, in that many chapters could have been placed into more than one section. We see this as positive and desirable because issues of family and aging are broad and multidimensional.

What characterizes these aging parent-adult child relationships? What ought to be considered when conducting research on these relationships, teaching about them, and actually working with families?

History

The chapters in this book suggest that we ought to recognize the enduring character of these relationships, and attend to their history and to their future. In this regard we need to be mindful of the vagaries that typify the relationship where all are mature adults but in which the relationship was originally quite different. We must be continually mindful of how early family experience finds its way into adult life. Part of that family process across generations involves the pivotal role of mental images that various family members have of one another in the transactions that occur between family members.

Context Events

Two important contexts that should be taken into account are gender and the role that in-laws play in these relationships. All too often in-law relationships have not been taken seriously by social scientists as significant avenues of support in the later years. Marital separation and divorce represent a twist in contemporary social life that should also be taken into account. In a more general sense, it has been shown that unanticipated life events are important players in the welfare of a family.

Family process and interaction change even as family structure changes. Family transactions occur within a context, or within an array of contexts. While it is attractive to examine individual dyads, we ought to recall the systemic nature of family life. A part of the context of a particular parent-child dyad is the other relationships that a parent has with other children (the siblings of any one child in the family). Family structure as a part of context cannot be ignored; we have already mentioned that multiple parent-child relationships are relevant, and more generally, overall family size is also a consideration. The importance of a single relationship within the context of other relationships must be considered because only then can we know what the parent-child relationship provides to an older person.

Relationship Qualities

Throughout this book we have been reminded of the variety of connections that occur in relationships. For example, the role of emotional security and sharing of the self-concept are important qualities of these relationships.

Connections may also be reflected in expectations of support for, and from, family members.

Norms, Motives, and Exchange

The context of the norms that help govern these expectations are noteworthy, and they may involve how attachment is viewed, as well as the sense of autonomy. We have already mentioned norms and the range of obligations. We add to that the idea of discretionary motives, the nature of burden, and the level of commitment found when children are faced with caring for a parent who is in frail health. A theme found in many of the chapters could be termed *beliefs* about the respective rights and obligations of parents and children. A principal reason older people and their families can be called pioneers is because of the changes in relationships involving moral matters. How a relationship is negotiated and functions over time may be because of what people think and feel is right and proper. One bottom-line issue that should be continually pursued involves what an older parent gains through the relationship with an adult child. These provisions may be influenced by the range of motives that are behind why people spend time together. In that regard, it should be noted that there are various ways of understanding how exchange between the generations occurs. Many of the chapters point to the necessity of examining why children do what they do regarding support for parents.

Government

We should focus not only on what adult children provide to aging parents (as well as what children owe their parents), but also on support from government. It has long been recognized that a principal role of today's family is to intervene between the state and older family members.

To summarize, the above discussion reflects the suggestions of the preceding chapters. They show the multidimensional nature of the aging parent-adult child relationship and demonstrate the complexity engendered by the relationship dynamics, by the many contexts that surround parents and their children, and by special events that families confront.

The Range of Theorizing

Theory development takes many forms; it may be entirely grounded in research, may reflect an encompassing grand theory, or may be seen as middle-range. This book reflects this range of theorizing.

While it is not the purpose of this chapter to discuss the philosophic nature of theory, we do want to note our basic definition of a theory. Briefly, it is a series of statements or propositions that indicate the conditions under which certain events occur (or under which certain attitudes are held). A theory must show the connections between concepts. If the connections are absent, then it is best to refer to the set of propositions as conceptualization. In family gerontology we have a mix of theory and concept; it is true of the contents of this book. All the chapters have touched on concept and theory in some fashion. Some reflect testing hypotheses derived from theory while others compare and contrast core concepts that provide alternative explanations of behavior. We will briefly summarize how each chapter has drawn upon theory.

In chapter 2 Kivett draws from the *anthropology of kinship system contexts* in focusing on the role that daughters-in-law and daughters play in *associational solidarity*. In describing this context, she discusses the *asymmetry principle* and employs *life span attachment theory* to explain protective and attachment behaviors in affinal relationships. After providing empirical information on her model of associational solidarity, she suggests that theories of *conflict, social exchange,* and *symbolic interaction* could be readily applied to her research questions. Johnson (chapter 3) also draws upon *kinship theory* in her discussion of the impact of divorce on the generations. She also discusses the utility of the *structural-functional approach* in studies of the impact of divorce. Her chapter places family breakdown and reorganization in a kinship context. Quinn (chapter 4) approaches family context from a processual-therapeutic perspective. Using the concepts of *scripts, transaction,* and *transition,* he notes that relationships are organized by mental processes, role images, and scripts. He also shows that the interactions of one dyad are related to the functioning of the entire network of social relations. Matthews and Sprey (chapter 5) discuss a *systems perspective* and the web of family relations, and note that one context of the interactions within a particular dyad is the other dyads in the family. They suggest that theories of the family in later life simultaneously consider systemic and dyadic family ties. Atkinson (chapter 6) provides several alternatives to conceptualizing relationships in terms of *solidarity: attachment, crescive bonds,* and *identity salience*. In the course of discussing these specific concepts she links them to the "grander" *social exchange* and *symbolic interaction* theories. Shehan and Dwyer (chapter 7) also discuss their research from a *social exchange* viewpoint. They discuss *valued resources, alternative resources, norms* that govern exchanges, and *fairness*. Of note are their remarks on the legitimization of dependence and the *power-dependence framework*. Lee and Shehan (chapter 8) also investigate the norms that help to govern adult relationships; they focus on the antecedents and consequences of the *filial responsibility expectations* of older parents. The discussion of their findings leads them to note that *social exchange* may be deficient in dealing with family norms. Glass and Dunham (chapter 9) argue for using theory that accounts for the *structural characteristics* of families. Toward this goal they discuss the varying perspectives of *stratification theorists, critical Marxists, family demographers, social psychologists, psychodynamic theorists, family systems theorists, social learning theorists,* and *socialization theorists.* Long and Mancini (chapter 10) access a framework that is particular to social support and which focuses on *relationship provisions.* Their chapter substantiates a number of relationship provisions already discussed in the literature, and develops several additional provisions relevant to older adults. Their data address the *fund of sociability* and *functional specificity of relationships* hypotheses. Cicirelli's chapter (chapter 11) describes the specifics of *attachment theory,* including *symbolic attachment* as well as *secure and insecure attachment.* As a preface to the discussion of attachment, *theories of equity and obligation* are outlined. Treas and Spence (chapter 12) contribute to the understanding of how parents and their mature children interrelate by discussing beliefs about what the middle generation owes its grown children and aging parents within the context of government programs. A *historical perspective* and the nature of *normative structures* are discussed in the course of showing the interplay between beliefs about family responsibility and government responsibility. Walker, Pratt, Shin, and Jones (chapter 13) also discuss the concept of *filial responsibility,* and derive their study from ideas of *obligatory and discretionary caregiving motives.* They discuss a number of dimensions of both general categories of motives (for example, Relationship Attitude, Personality Trait, and Situational aspects of discretionary motives, and Coercion, Socialization, and Moral Belief aspects of obligatory motives). Montgomery and Kamo (chapter 14) introduce gender into the issues of who cares for parents in need. Their comparison of sons and of daughters operates from a *sex-role hypothesis* and notes the roles of differential resources and common experiences of burden. Blieszner and Shifflett (chapter 15) present a study of Alzheimer's disease and discuss *commitment theory.* Within commitment theory the concepts of *affection and communication* are pivotal in understanding the strain of caregiving. Brubaker and Brubaker (chapter 16) provide a more general treatment of caregiving and care-receiving in a model that involves *types of dependency, perceptions of responsibility for provision of services, individual and family ethos,* and the *use of services.* Thompson (chapter 17) discusses intergenerational responsibility with regard to the concepts of *contextual and relational morality.* Key terms from this approach include the *immediate context* and *sociohistorical context* as well as *pattern, process, attribution, disclosure, empathy,* and *cooperation.*

We note that the major theories in family studies are discussed in these chapters and seem to reflect the field in general. Symbolic interaction, social exchange, feminist, systems, developmental, and structural-functional theories are used to address varying aspects of the aging parent-adult child relationship. Meanings, cost-benefits, moralities, levels of family interaction, the dimensions of time, and the functions of these relationships are given attention. The authors approach parents and children from macrosociological, microsociological, subjective, and objective perspectives. The demography and the social psychology of the aging family are presented, in effect moving toward an ecology of family relationships. In these chapters less has been said about feminist and developmental perspectives. With regard to the former it appears that in the family studies field generally, we are now just observing increased use of that approach. And in the case of the latter it may be that the approach has yet to regain its popularity from earlier years. Family gerontologists ought to consider use of the feminist and developmental approaches, because the one may be especially fruitful for understanding the nexus of gender and aging, and the other important in understanding how relationships ebb and flow over time. Other major theories are also meritorious. For example, symbolic interaction lends itself to an understanding of the meanings that parents and children attach to their relationship. Social exchange can be useful regarding the question of how the parent-child relationship compares with other close relationships, since it would be possible to examine the relative costs and rewards of the various relationships. Structural-functionalism enables the theorist-researcher to capture what older people gain from social relationships, and also would be useful in discussions of the impact of family change on various people in the family. This approach is important when we need to account for the role that structure plays in family transaction and interaction. A systems perspective has a great deal of utility because of its sensitivity to the many layers and multiple relationships in families.

This collection of chapters demonstrates the applicability of social science theories to parent-child relationships in adulthood. Perhaps it is no longer appropriate to lament the lack of theory in family gerontology. Perhaps we ought to be equally concerned with the number of conceptual lenses through which these relationships can be viewed. The argument concerning whether it is preferable to have many or few conceptual frameworks or theories is far beyond the scope of this book. Although myriad and diverse theories are not readily integrated into a whole understanding, one or two frameworks may fail to capture the intricacies of family life. We do know, however, that the chapters contained in this book demonstrate the many levels on which these relationships can be investigated. Moreover, we see the number of theoretical perspectives that are relevant for exploring these long-standing relationships. A logical step for social scientists who study the interface of aging and family life is the integration of concepts, conceptual frameworks, and theories.

Future Research

Each chapter in *Aging Parents and Adult Children* has discussed needs and directions for future investigations. In tables 18–1 and 18–2 we have summarized the many suggestions that have been presented. We have asked two questions about analyzing needs for future research: What dimensions of the parent-child relationship are discussed? In what contexts are these relationship dimensions discussed?

Relationship Dimensions

Table 18–1 summarizes the parent-child relationship dimensions and includes several categories: affective, cognitive, power and control, exchange, identification, dependency, perception of parents' expertise, protectiveness of other's feelings, relationship provisions, caregiving, morality, cooperation, attitude consensus, interpreting parental role norms, and personal commitment.

This summary of relationship dimensions provides a general roadmap for future research with specific routes elaborated within the individual chapters. As stated by Glass and Dunham (chapter 9), however, more refined measurement of the variables represented in table 18–1 is necessary to advance research. In addition, there are repeated calls for the need for theoretical models to integrate the various relationship dimensions (Atkinson, chapter 6; Lee & Shehan, chapter 8).

One direction for future research is to investigate the relationships across these variables. The following set of questions drawn from the chapters highlights questions about relationships across variables. Although the list is not exhaustive, it presents examples of fruitful questions.

What are the effects of power in parent-child relations on the decision-making of parents and children, and what are the consequences for autonomy (Shehan & Dwyer, chapter 7)? What is the association between secure/insecure attachment and psychological closeness or caregiving (Cicirelli, chapter 11)? What are the effects of attribution, disclosure, empathy, and cooperation on morality (Thompson, chapter 17)? Does interdependence function as a mediator between dependence and feeling comfortable with the negative feelings associated with dependence (Long & Mancini, chapter 10)?

Table 18–1
Dimensions of Parent-Child Relations Indicated as Research Needs

Relationship Dimension	Chapter
Affective	
Attachment, psychological closeness	6, 11
Emotional exchange, emotional health	2, 6, 7, 10
Acceptance, nurturance, support	7, 10
Empathy, disclosure	17
Cognitive	
Life or daily decisions	7
Attributions	17
Power and control	7
Exchange (instrumental, resource, emotional)	2, 7
Identification	
Crescive bonds	6
Identity salience	6
Children's identification with parents	7
Dependency	
Dependency (types, needs)	7, 10, 16
Legitimization of dependency	7
Independence, autonomy (needs)	7, 10
Parental reliance on child	10
Reciprocal dependency	7
Perception of parents' expertise	7
Protectiveness of other's feelings	10
Relationship provisions	10
Caregiving (quality, quantity, level, duration)	11, 12, 14, 16, 17
Morality (responsibility and perception)	16, 17
Cooperation	17
Attitude consensus	9
Interpreting parental role norms	10
Personal commitment	15

Note: Figures in the right-hand column represent chapter numbers in *Aging Parents and Adult Children*.

The Contexts of Parent-Child Relationships

In addition to understanding associations across aspects of parent-child relationships, understanding the contexts in which these associations occur is equally critical. The importance of context in future research is strongly endorsed throughout this book. Table 18–2 presents a list of the contexts as suggested by the various chapters.

    This summary of the contexts includes several categories: family type, ethnicity/religion, nonfamily networks, employment, sociocultural contexts,

Table 18–2
Contexts of Parent-Child Relations Suggested as Foci for Future Research

Contexts	Chapter
Family type	
Marital status, parent-child characteristics	10
Emerging family types, changing family	2
Normal versus problem families or circumstances	15
Ethnicity/religion	
Disadvantaged families, diversity in families	5, 17
Ethnicity	2
Religiosity and religious behavior	9
Nonfamily networks	
Alternative sources of valued resources	7
Family social systems (membership, participation)	5
Individual social systems	5
Employment	4, 11
Sociocultural contexts	
Broader sociocultural context and social meaning	17
Cultural contradictions, metaphors, myths	17
Cross-cultural comparisons	12
Societal changes (economics, values, family, policy)	2, 3, 11
Government and service provision	12, 17
Norms	
Commitment, equity, affection, communication	2, 11, 15
Family ethos on caregiving	16
Obligatory and discretionary	11, 13
Variation and averages in norms	5, 8
Physical proximity	4, 10
Role load	2
Health	2, 7
Economic and financial exchanges/resources	2, 7, 10
Time	
Changes and stability	2, 5, 9
Process in transactions over time	2, 5, 6, 10, 13
Family life cycle and adaptation to transitions	2, 3, 6, 7
History of the parent-child relationship	4, 5, 9, 10
Age	2, 7
Gender	10, 14
Unit of analysis (other dyads, triads, multiads)	2, 3, 4, 5, 6, 11, 17

Note: Figures in the right-hand column represent chapter numbers in *Aging Parents and Adult Children*.

cross-cultural comparisons, societal changes, government and service provision, norms, physical proximity, role load, health, economic and financial resources, time, age, gender, and unit of analysis. Each of these contexts may influence the relationship dimensions. The following are some examples of how the authors have linked relationship dimensions with context.

How is caregiving influenced by the child's marriage (Kivett, chapter 2), time (Long & Mancini, chapter 10; Walker, Pratt, Shin & Jones, chapter 13), norms (Cicirelli, chapter 11), family ethos (Brubaker & Brubaker, chapter 16), government policy (Treas & Spence, chapter 12), sibling relationships (Matthews & Sprey, chapter 5; Cicirelli, chapter 11), or gender (Long & Mancini, chapter 10; Montgomery & Kamo, chapter 14)? What are the effects of gender and perception of the parental role on relationship provisions (Long & Mancini, chapter 10)? How do time or history influence independence, protectiveness, relationship provisions, and parent-child affect (Glass & Dunham, chapter 9)? How do financial and health resources influence the legitimization of dependency in the young and the old (Shehan & Dwyer, chapter 7)? How do cultural myths, metaphors, and contradictions influence personal responsibility in families (Thompson, chapter 17)? What are the effects of employment, divorce, and remarriage on attachment in parent-child relationships (Cicirelli, chapter 11)?

These questions assume contexts as independent variables and relationship dimensions as the dependent variables. However, the reverse causal direction is equally plausible. For example, the amount of caregiving may influence whether an adult child can continue working or whether a child's marriage can withstand caregiving stressors. Although viewing relationship dimensions as causing particular contexts may be a fruitful approach to research, we suspect that because of the fledgling nature of our explorations in this area, most research will continue to treat context as predicting relationship dimensions.

New Views on Old Relationships

An important quality of the aging parent-adult child relationship is its enduring character. By the time a parent reaches retirement age the relationship has a history of between twenty-five and forty or more years. Over that time behaviors, expectations, and situations have changed dramatically. Norms for dependence, independence, and interdependence have also varied throughout the period. In some respects the enduring parent-child relationship is old. The relationship is experienced and developed, and has matured. However, the relationship also is young because of the normal fluidity of adult life and because it is not insulated from change. This change occurs in individual people and in collections of people. In this chapter we have used the terms relationship dimensions and contexts to describe what happens within and around these family relationships. Our goals for *Aging Parents and Adult Children* were to illuminate the application of social and behavioral science theories and to suggest the directions that future research might take. These are the new views on old relationships.

SUBJECT INDEX

AUTHOR INDEX

About the Contributors

MAXINE P. ATKINSON is an associate professor and associate head of the Department of Sociology, Anthropology, and Social Work at North Carolina State University. Her research focuses on changing marital structures, intergenerational relationships, and gender stratification. Recent publications are in *Journal of Gerontology, Journal of Marriage and the Family,* and *Criminology.*

MARK J. BENSON is an assistant professor in the Department of Family and Child Development at Virginia Polytechnic Institute and State University. His research centers on social cognition in families with particular focus on attributions among family members and intimate others.

ROSEMARY BLIESZNER is an associate professor in the Department of Family and Child Development, and associate director of the Center for Gerontology at Virginia Polytechnic Institute and State University. Her research focuses on family and friend relationships and life events in adulthood and old age, with an emphasis on the contributions of close relationships to psychological well-being. She is co-editor of *Older Adult Friendship: Structure and Process.*

ELLIE BRUBAKER is an associate professor in the Department of Sociology and Anthropology at Miami University, Oxford, Ohio. Her research has been published in a number of scholarly journals and she has contributed chapters to several books. Recently she wrote a book titled *Working with the Elderly: A Social Systems Approach* (1987).

TIMOTHY H. BRUBAKER is a professor of Family and Child Studies at Miami University, Oxford, Ohio. He is also director of the Family and Child Studies Center at that university. His books include *Aging, Health and Family: Long-Term Care* (1987), *Later Life Families* (1985), *Family Caregivers and Dependent Elderly* (1984), and *Family Relationships in*

Later Life (1983). Currently he is the editor of *Family Relations*, published by the National Council on Family Relations.

VICTOR G. CICIRELLI is a professor of Developmental and Aging Psychology in the Department of Psychological Sciences at Purdue University. He has published articles in a wide range of academic and professional journals and is the author of the book *Helping Elderly Parents: Role of Adult Children*.

CHARLOTTE DUNHAM is a research assistant at the Andrus Gerontology Center at the University of Southern California. She is currently finishing her doctoral thesis on the family determinants and consequences of youth's social activism.

JEFFREY W. DWYER is a postdoctoral fellow in the Center for Health Policy Research, University of Florida. Recent publications are on the relationship between life events and elderly drinking behavior, and on the importance of psychosocial information in training medical students to assess the medical problems of elderly patients. His current research focuses on caregiving of the functionally limited elderly.

JENNIFER GLASS is an assistant professor in the Department of Sociology at the University of Notre Dame. She is interested in the family as an active agent in social change over time. Her research has recently appeared in *Journal of Marriage and the Family, Gender and Society,* and *Social Science Research.*

COLLEEN L. JOHNSON is a professor of medical anthropology at the University of California, San Francisco. She has conducted research on the late-life family and social supports, and is the author of numerous works including the books *Growing up and Growing old in Italian American Families, The Nursing Home in American Society,* and *Ex-Familia: Grandparents, Parents and Children Adjust to Divorce.*

LAURA JONES is a doctoral candidate in the Department of Human Development and Family Studies at Oregon State University. Her research interests include intergenerational relationships and caregiving to elderly parents.

YOSHINORI KAMO is a doctoral candidate in the Department of Sociology, University of Washington-Seattle. His research interests include the division of household labor among married couples, caregiving tasks of the elderly by family members, cross-cultural aspects of family structure and interaction, and quantitative methodology. His research has appeared in *Journal of Marriage and the Family* and *Research on Aging*.

VIRA R. KIVETT is a professor in the Department of Child Development and Family Relations, University of North Carolina at Greensboro. She is the author of more than eighty publications in gerontology, many of which deal with family issues. She is the 1988 recipient of the Southern Gerontological Society's Distinguished Academic Gerontologist Award.

GARY R. LEE is a professor of sociology at the University of Florida. His research has concentrated on comparative family organization, intergenerational relations and psychological well-being among older persons, as well as related aspects of aging and the elderly.

JANIE K. LONG is a doctoral candidate in the Department of Family and Child Development at Virginia Polytechnic Institute and State University. She received her M.R.E. degree from Duke University. Her main area of concentration is in marriage and family therapy with a special interest of working in therapy with older adults and their families.

SARAH H. MATTHEWS is an associate professor of sociology at Case Western Reserve University. She is the author of two books, *The Social World of Old Women* and *Friendships through the Life Course*. Her recent articles and ongoing research on older families reflect her continued interest in understanding the significance of social relationships, both kith and kin.

RHONDA J.V. MONTGOMERY is director of the Institute of Gerontology and an associate professor of sociology at Wayne State University. She is interested in health service use among, and social policy for, the elderly. Her recent interests and work has focused on decision-making process concerning institutionalization, caregiving, and the impact of support interventions on families.

CLARA COLLETTE PRATT is a professor of Human Development and Family Studies at Oregon State University. She has been director of the university's multidisciplinary Program on Gerontology since 1978. Her primary area of research is family caregiving, including its ethical aspects and interactions between care recipients and care providers in decision-making. She is also active as a consultant to community programs on the development and evaluation of education and service programs for caregiving families.

WILLIAM H. QUINN is an associate professor and director of clinical training at the McPhaul Marriage and Family Therapy Clinic, Department of

Child and Family Development, University of Georgia. He has published in numerous journals and has edited a book titled *Independent Aging: Family and Social Systems Perspectives*. His research interests include families and transitions, client ethnographies of family therapy, and marital interaction.

CONSTANCE L. SHEHAN is an associate professor, Department of Sociology, and acting director, Women's Studies Program, at the University of Florida. Her research has focused on gender stratification as it operates in and through the work-family nexus. Recent examples of her work have appeared in *American Sociological Review*, *Journal of Marriage and the Family*, and *Journal of Family Issues*.

PEGGY A. SHIFFLETT is an associate professor in the Department of Sociology and Anthropology at Radford University. Her current research interests include social factors affecting participation of older persons in wellness programs. Her research has appeared in *The Gerontologist*, *Journal of Applied Gerontology*, and *Medical Care*.

HWA-YONG SHIN is a doctoral candidate in the Department of Human Development and Family Studies at Oregon State University. Her research interests include intergenerational relationships and cross-cultural perspectives on intergenerational relationships.

MICHELE SPENCE is a sociology graduate student at the University of Southern California. She holds an M.A. from the University of Texas at El Paso and has worked as a primary home care supervisor for the aged.

JETSE SPREY is a professor of sociology at Case Western Reserve University. He is a past editor of the *Journal of Marriage and the Family*, and has written extensively in the areas of family conflict and organization.

LINDA THOMPSON is a professor in the Department of Child and Family Studies at the University of Wisconsin-Madison. She has an abiding interest in the relationships between adult children and their parents. Her current focus is the moral content of close relationships and the integration of feminism and family studies. She is working on the biography of Jessie Bernard.

JUDITH TREAS is a professor and chair of the Sociology Department at the University of Southern California and Research Associate at the Andrus Gerontology Center. Author of numerous works on family aspects of aging, her most recent piece is "The Three Sociologies: Age, Aging, and Aged," appearing in *The Future of Sociology*, edited by Borgatta and Cook. She also serves as elected chair of the Section on Aging of the American Sociological Association and is a member of the Board of Overseers of the NORC General Social Survey.

ALEXIS WALKER is an associate professor of Human Development and Family Studies at Oregon State University. She is interested in intergenerational relationships, particularly those between mothers and daughters. Her work has appeared in *Journal of Marriage and the Family* and *Family Relations: Journal of Applied Family and Child Studies*.

About the Editor

JAY A. MANCINI is professor and chair of Family and Child Development at Virginia Polytechnic Institute and State University. He received his doctoral degree from the University of North Carolina at Greensboro. His most recent publications have appeared in *Journal of Marriage and the Family* and *Family Relations: Journal of Applied Family and Child Studies*. Ongoing research interests include time-use and the family, parent-child relationships in adulthood, contemporary family values, and the family and social change. He and his family live in Roanoke, Virginia.